good Enough
MOTHERS

Good Enough
MOTHERS

CHANGING
EXPECTATIONS
FOR OURSELVES

MELINDA M. MARSHALL

PETERSON'S

PRINCETON, NEW JERSEY

Permission to reprint excerpts from the following is gratefully acknowledged:

Backlash by Susan Faludi, copyright © 1991 by Susan Faludi. Reprinted by permission of Addison-Wesley Publishing Company, Inc.

The Hurried Child (pp. 37–38, 120–121, 124–127, 129) by David Elkind, copyright © 1981 by David Elkind. Reprinted by permission of Addison-Wesley Publishing Company, Inc.

A Lesser Life by Sylvia Ann Hewlett, copyright © 1986 by Sylvia Ann Hewlett. Reprinted by permission of William Morrow & Company, Inc.

Remaking Motherhood by Anita Shreve, copyright © 1987 by Anita Shreve. Reprinted by permission of Viking Penguin, a division of Penguin Books USA, Inc.

The Second Shift by Arlie Hochschild and Ann Machung, copyright © 1989 by Arlie Hochschild. Reprinted by permission of Viking Penguin, a division of Penguin Books USA, Inc.

Excerpts from "Mommy Myths" and "The Good Father" reprinted by permission of *Redbook,* copyright © 1993 by the Hearst Corporation. All rights reserved.

Library of Congress Cataloging-in-Publication Data

Marshall, Melinda M., 1961–
   Good enough mothers : changing expectations for ourselves /
   Melinda M. Marshall.
      p. cm.
   Includes index.
   ISBN 1-56079-433-X
   1. Mothers—Employment. 2. Expectation (Psychology) I. Title.
   HD6055.M28 1993   93-5838
   331.4'4—dc20   CIP

Text design by Virginia Pope

Composition by Peterson's

Printed in the United States of America

10 9 8 7 6 5 4 3 2 1

Originally published in hardcover by Peterson's in 1993.

For Moo and for Grandma

CONTENTS

PART THREE

Resolving Key Relationships: Arriving at Compromise

Acknowledgments

The ranks of boosters and believers in this project have swelled to the point where I can barely begin to thank them all, but at the very beginning there was Nancy Kalish, who listened to me try to articulate my feelings on working motherhood one day over a business lunch and convinced me I should put them down in writing and contact her agent, Ling Lucas. Then there was Carol Hupping, my editor, whose faith in me never flagged despite some of the frightful detours my writing took. And with Carol came the entire team at Peterson's, whose enthusiasm probably did more to shape the book than all their considerable editorial, graphic, and marketing talents combined.

At the beginning and with me to the bitter end were also, significantly, my family and friends, without whose help not one page of manuscript would have been written. I am indebted to Ken, my husband, on so many fronts: for being a sounding board when I needed to hear my thoughts, for offering editorial insight when I needed to be shown what I was doing, for providing the germ of an idea when I believed I had exhausted all my own; for networking interview candidates and bird-dogging apposite research; for cooking the meals, cleaning the floors, and taking care of the kids; and for never begrudging me his wholehearted support. I am grateful, similarly, to Celia Baldwin, Catherine Fredman, Judith Newman, Gretchen Seefried, and Madeline Wilson for sticking by me even when I was no fun to be around. And I owe more than can be quantified to my parents, who never asked any questions aside from "How can we help?"

My greatest debt, however, is to the women who gave their time, their opinions, and their innermost thoughts so that I might validate my thesis on what it means to be a good enough mother. All told, there were nearly 70 of them, full-time, working, and "retired" mothers who tolerated my inquiries as though we had known each other for years and who answered them with a candor normally reserved for psychotherapists and priests. My thanks, too, to Effie Alpert, Cathy Beinlich, Joanne Brady, Yvonne Kearney, Doris Mackenzie, Irene Meschter, Joanne Murphy, Regina Peasley, and all those cited above for helping me find these forthright and even inspirational women.

And last—but not at all least—my thanks to Angela Malcolm, whose devoted efforts on behalf of my children make me look like a better mother than I am.

Preface

Ihad but one goal in my endeavor to write this book: I wanted to find role models, women who not only grasped the concept of balance but had attained it and *maintained* it, against formidable odds. I didn't care who they were, or how representative they might be of certain ethnic, religious, socioeconomic, or generational populations. One and only one consideration determined whom I would interview and whom I would not: the age of the offspring. Mothers of young children (six and under) tend to confront the same hurdles, across all barriers of race, income, or age. I had initially thought to confine my inquiry to mothers of a certain generation, but quickly discovered generationally correct age brackets of 32 and older or 31 and younger (Boomers and Thirteeners, according to those who compile and compare statistics)[1] were of no use to me in my particular quest.

I am not a demographer, keen on charting society according to statistical samplings. I am not a sociologist, trained to see, in those samplings, historical trends. I am not a psychologist, analyzing trends for behavioral insights. Hence this book is not a study, a survey, or an attempt to ascertain who women really are these days. I am a mother, eager to listen to other mothers for any clues as to how they've managed to keep their personal demons at bay, and I am a journalist, which is to say I've been trained to convey what people actually say rather than what I think they mean to say. Had I a kitchen table large enough and this were 1956, I wouldn't have needed to write a book to hear from my peers. But it is 1993 as I write this, and my kaffeeklatsch is geographically scattered, critically short on time, and so accustomed to thinking and acting in a veritable vacuum of feedback that they have forgotten a community of like-minded women even exists.

That community, I can attest, is alive and well. I've tried to give voice in this book to its more articulate and empathetic representatives. It seems a sad fact of our modern lives that we let our friendships drift to the point where only a personal crisis motivates us to reel them back in; the sadder consequence is our isolation. We have no way of gauging how we're doing—or even what needs to be done. I know that I, like one architect and mother I spoke with, lost such essential contact with my friends that I began to believe I had nothing in common with them, that I alone grappled with the conflict endemic to being a working mother. I imagined them to have somehow reined in their insecurities, silenced their detractors, assuaged their guilt, and organized their lives along the tidy lines sketched by countless self-help books and magazine articles. Totally ridiculous, I realize. But I had to embark on a book to prove otherwise.

How did I find these role models? I networked—through professional organizations and play groups, professional contacts and support groups. I picked up names on line at the supermarket, in the backseat of cabs, and in the pediatrician's waiting room. I hit up former classmates, former colleagues, and former neighbors for recommendations in their neck of the woods. I recruited everybody who showed the slightest interest in the book to generate more names for me. And I never ended an interview without getting phone numbers of other women. It got so neither my husband nor I could go anywhere, do anything, or see anybody without soliciting another contact.

As my pile of index cards grew, two "handicaps" became apparent: I could not physically meet with everybody, lacking the time and money to fly all over the country, and I knew next to nothing about my interviewees beforehand. That meant cold-calling women and asking them to commit at least an hour of their precious work day or evening at home to discuss fairly intimate questions with a perfect stranger. A recipe for disaster, you would think.

On the contrary, the anonymous and nonvisual format of the telephone interview garnered more honest results. Women can be awfully threatened by each other. I'll never forget the long silences that greeted several of my questions when I attempted to interview four full-time mothers, all of them friends with each other, around a dining room table: For all their daily intimacy, none cared to volunteer information that might sound a jarring note to her peers. It turned out the less my interviewees and I knew of each other, the less we could judge one another prematurely on the basis of what we looked like and how we dressed and what kind of car we drove or house we lived in or office we occupied; and the more likely it was that we would never meet again, the more forthcoming my interviewees were in their answers. Indeed, on the phone I rarely had to press for details, as the medium ensured an almost confessionlike dialogue. ("Only women can get away with this kind of exchange," noted my husband.) One interviewee laughed when I apologized for taking so much of her time. "You're easier to talk to than my shrink," she explained, "and you're a whole lot cheaper!" Many women even allowed me to use their real names; those who requested a pseudonym I've indicated with an asterisk.

When it came to deciding whom to quote and whom to leave out, I made my selection with an eye to achieving as great a variety in backgrounds as possible, lest anyone erroneously conclude that there is some "formula"—a certain income, a certain ethnic or class background, a certain type of job—that guarantees happiness. *Good Enough Mothers* is predicated on the belief that there is *not* any one factor predisposing women to either fulfillment or exploitation. It is not a self-help book in the usual sense: Who you want to be and how you get there is entirely up to you. I've never believed in the concept that one size fits all, that there is one standard for all to emulate. My hope, in trotting out women who have inspired me, is not to suggest that the pool of answers is limited to their examples but rather to affirm the almost infinite ways in which women can attempt to find that ever-elusive peace of mind. Being "good enough," for all my ensuing attempts to describe its universal tenets, is different for every individual.

I owe the title of this book to pediatrician-turned-psychotherapist D. W. Winnicott, who coined the phrase twentysome years ago in his discussion of how an infant matures to gradually distinguish between illusion and reality. "The good-enough 'mother' (not necessarily the infant's own mother)," he writes, "is one who makes active adaptation to the infant's needs, an active adaptation that gradually lessens according to the infant's growing ability to account for failure of adaptation and to tolerate the results of frustration."[2] From this rather clinical definition I have taken considerable liberty to construct my own, but like Winnicott I am eager to underscore how forgiving the parameters of motherhood truly are. My role models share but one thing completely in common: They're no longer interested in being perfect.

"Except," admitted one compromiser, "I guess I'm now trying to be perfect at trying not to be perfect."

Melinda M. Marshall

A Question of Choice

In the course of my interviews for this book I spoke to a recently divorced mother of a kindergartner who pined for more time to simply "be" with her child. Whenever she picked up her daughter from school she felt a jealous stab looking at all the mothers arriving in their Volvos, wearing Lycra and makeup, their nails manicured, their unfurrowed brows suggesting plenty of sleep and time to read the newspaper. "They've got something I'd like," sighed this single mom. Then, unsure whether I wanted to hear more from her or more from the women in the Volvos, she asked, "Is this a book for women who *choose* to work or who *have* to work?"

Sixty-seven percent of all women working are mothers; 58 percent of the female work force have children at home under six years old.[1] While that means the majority of mothers are *not* at home, the statistics do not indicate how many of these women *must* work—for obvious reasons. We all interpret financial "necessity" differently: For some, it means working to keep a family off welfare; for others, it means enabling them to afford a new house or a second car. There's something heroic about a woman who puts bread on the table, something selfish about one who works to afford a nicer table. The former warrants our sympathy; the latter, our condemnation.

Or so women must think, because it was the rare individual I interviewed who didn't claim some sort of economic excuse for working for fear I would think her priorities skewed or I might automatically dismiss her as a "bad" mother. Those who admitted they worked by choice were consumed by guilt, not simply because they were putting their kids "unnecessarily" in surrogate care, but because they were so conscious of how other women judged them. "I'm in a wonderful position really," Jan Neiman*, a photographer and soon-to-be mother of two, explained to me, "in that I have the choice of working. But it makes me feel like I'm choosing *not* to be with my son. It'd be so much easier if I *had* to work instead of working because I need to feel productive and creative and because—I know this sounds like a rationalization—I'll be a better person for my child."

How sad, after 30 years of fighting for the freedom to make our own choices, to find that we're afraid to make any for fear of making the wrong one. What a shame that *women*—not men, or the old-boy corporate network—are still arguing about who has the "right" to be in the work force. What a pity that we continue to complicate already agonizing decisions with such an irrelevant quandary. Men accept work as a given, a nonchoice, and yet manage to exercise plenty of free will in structuring their personal goals and ambitions around this mandate. But women, despite overwhelming evidence that they're in the work force to stay, insist on tormenting themselves or antagonizing each other with "ideal" scenarios in which work plays no part, as though any kind of job outside the home were automatically a detraction from a mother's job within it. If we're working, for whatever reason, why can't *we* regard it as a given, so that we might channel any dissatisfaction we feel into improving our situation instead of flogging ourselves for not being home?

Consider how we shoulder the "burden" of being parents. Children are a challenge and even a complication, an irreversible reality, a responsibility we might have elected to pass up—but did not. We chose to have them, and no matter how

---

Women who requested a pseudonym are indicated with an asterisk.

tough it gets, we never for a moment actually wish we hadn't had them. Work, similarly, is a responsibility most adults assume, a burden at times, a complication, but also a challenge that, like children, requires enormous energy and that holds the potential for qualitative, as well as quantitative, rewards. Isn't this the only constructive perspective for women who have no choice but to work? And isn't it a more healthy attitude for women writhing with guilt because they choose to compound the challenges of motherhood with work they enjoy?

That we should even be deliberating such a question is a luxury, a luxury born of the massive wealth we as a country generated in the postwar twentieth century. Sociologist Kathleen Gerson points out in *Hard Choices: How Women Decide About Work, Career, and Motherhood* that for centuries staying home has been a privilege only the upper class could afford; the '50s were a historical aberration, the culmination of our zeal to emulate the leisured lifestyle of European women coupled with the advent of industrialization, which created a separate workplace in which wives and children could no longer labor, as they did on the farm, side by side with the men.

When postwar prosperity removed the need for most women to work, we thought we had reached the apogee of civilization. Child rearing consequently assumed sacred status; children might remain perfect creatures as long as they had mothers on hand to attend to their every emotional or physical need and fathers who worked to ensure that they never knew want. For perhaps the first time in history, children themselves were a luxury, a drain on family resources instead of an essential component of the family's survival strategy.

As the offspring of this uniquely privileged generation, as torchbearers of the Great Society, we grew up believing in a world where everybody might know material comfort, unlimited opportunity, and the full flowering of their self-potential—because that was our experience as children.

"We were spoiled rotten," contends Betsy Latham*, a mother of two who spent nine years at home trying to recreate this illusion of painless plenty for her children before sheer exhaustion and dissatisfaction with her marriage prompted her to wonder why. "No wonder most of us are so unhappy and feel we can't cope," she observes. "After you're waited on hand and foot, promised the world, and given every material advantage to buffer you from reality, adulthood is a rude shock. Suddenly you have to work all day just to live. I decided I didn't want to set my kids up for such disappointment."

When Betsy elected to return to work full time, she made her husband and two children pick up the slack at home; now even her six-year-old is responsible, one night a week, for helping to get dinner on the table. "I thought I was lucky to be able to stay home," she reflects. "I thought my kids were lucky to have the perfect mom. I feel I'm a better mother now, working, than I ever was as the family doormat. And I feel I have more choices, not fewer."

This is a book about choice for women who believe they don't have any. Our expectations about motherhood, not our financial circumstances, too often deny us a sense of the myriad options we may exercise, whoever we are. I believe *every* woman can either choose to feel good about herself, her marriage, her children, and yes, even her job, *or* elect to change what makes her desperately unhappy, recognizing and accepting the trade-offs such change inevitably entails. We should, as the feminists insist, be entitled to pursue what we want, whether it is the presidency of the United States or a quiet home life with our children. But let's remember that choice is as much a burden as a freedom in that we must choose not only what we want but also what we are willing to give up in order to get it. We needn't compromise our goals, but we most surely will have to make compromises to achieve them.

For Betsy Latham, motherhood used to mean being nothing

short of perfect: a wife any husband would find desirable, a daughter any parent would be proud of, a parent any child would adore, a friend to admire, a neighbor to envy. Short of being all things to all people, Betsy could not find in herself a person worthy of love or respect. But even if she had been able to sustain the illusion of being the perfect wife, mother, daughter, neighbor, and friend, it would not have netted her what she wanted: a loving and nurturing partner, capable and giving children, understanding and supportive parents, friends whom she could lean on and embrace. Only when going back to work forced her to lower her expectations did she begin to feel less straitjacketed; only when she couldn't possibly do it all did she wonder why she had ever tried.

If I sound somewhat biased in my support of working mothers, it is no doubt because I am one. Like Betsy Latham, I found *not* working put me at the mercy of expectations I couldn't possibly hope to fulfill. But for the sizable population of mothers for whom staying at home is a choice they will fight to keep, I'm hardly advocating dumping their kids in surrogate care and putting in eight hours at some office job.

I'm inclined to agree, in fact, with Amy Dacyczyn, author of *The Tightwad Gazette* and publisher of a newsletter with the same name, who believes that more women *could* stay home if only they were willing to contemplate a radical change in lifestyle— radical meaning moving to a cheaper part of the country, driving an older car, eating less meat, saying no to expensive fashion trends, and using less disposable merchandise. This choice, too, involves lowering certain expectations, but it may offer salvation to the millions of women in factory or clerical jobs who believe they have no choice but to work. Amy and her husband, Jim, managed to live in Leeds, Maine, on $30,000 a year for seven years, saving 23 percent of their income and spending 18 percent of it on things like new furniture, cars, and major appliances. She feeds her family of eight for $170 a month by economizing on clothing, gift giving, entertainment, and household items.[2] And she makes it work because to her, staying home to rear children is of paramount importance and worth any material sacrifice.

Hers are trade-offs many Americans would consider rather severe. But Amy chooses them—they are not imposed on her—in order to realize her goal of staying home. I choose not to live that way, but I acknowledge that the balance I have achieved between work and family roles comes at a cost, and every day I must weigh whether I live with that cost happily or guiltily, or whether some other lifestyle entails trade-offs I might accept more readily. It is always my choice: to change what I cannot tolerate, or tolerate what I cannot—or will not—change.

All women, single moms and heads of households included, have some choice; many of us have more choice than we think we do, and a privileged few have more choice than they know what to do with.

This book is for every one of us.

PART ONE

The Roots of Our Dissatisfaction: Uncompromising Role Models & Outrageous Expectations

CHAPTER ONE

Feminists & Antifeminists

American women, by all accounts, are in one hell of a bind. Without the economic advantages of our European counterparts—six-month paid maternity leave, job protection during and after pregnancy, and subsidized day care—and without society-wide acknowledgment that women require such compensatory measures in order to function, let alone compete, in the workplace, we cannot hope to excel at our job or career. But neither can we afford to drop out of the work force, given our tenuous foothold in a shrinking economy and the financial implications of a 50 percent divorce rate. As a result, our children, our relationships, our self-esteem, and our hopes of ever breaking free from this double bind are severely compromised.

Such is the rather hopeless scenario painted in exhaustive detail by Sylvia Ann Hewlett in *A Lesser Life: The Myth of Women's Liberation in America,* published in 1986 but clearly relevant in the 1990s. An economist of sterling academic credentials and the mother of four children, Hewlett understands with rare empathy the working mother's lose-lose situation: As a professor at Barnard during the height of the women's movement in the mid-'70s, she claims she was denied tenure by her ostensibly feminist peers for devoting her extra hours and energies to her toddler and nursing infant—for failing to give her job the number of hours her male colleagues, unburdened by responsibilities on the home front, could dedicate with relative ease. At the same time, she felt denied the support of nonworking mothers; La Leche League refused to help her secure the breast pump she needed in order to continue nursing her premature infant while trying to keep her job because, she says, the league disapproved of nursing mothers working. Hewlett cites her own experience as grounds for her thesis that working mothers, far from being "liberated," lack both the support they once enjoyed as domestics and the support they must be accorded in the workplace if they are ever to enjoy economic security.

"Way back in the 1950s," she observes, "a traditional division of labor gave women a substantial degree of financial security. Maybe many were stuck in bad marriages, but the man did go out every day and earn enough to support his family. In exchange the woman ran the home and brought up the children. With the sexual revolution and liberation this all changed. Divorce became common—in fact, it became three times more common—and women could no longer count on marriage to provide the economic necessities of life."[1]

As a result, Hewlett continues, "American women are locked into a no-win situation. They have lost the guarantees and protection of the past—marriage has broken down as a long-term and reliable source of financial security—and at the same time they have failed to improve their earning power as workers in the labor market, for the wage gap between men and women is as wide and as stubborn as it ever was."[2]

Without economic security, she argues, women will never enjoy freedom of choice. And, she concludes, "Neither the feminist movement nor the antifeminist movement has yet had much success in improving women's economic security."[3]

Myth or Reality?

Let's examine our own predicament for a moment. We will find, no doubt, that Hewlett has painted it correctly: There are few policies in effect, few "lifeboats" out there to buoy us through the economic fallout of divorce or the discriminatory dynamics of the workplace or the physical and emotional challenges associated with birthing and rearing our children. There isn't a working woman who hasn't encountered some form of harassment, glass ceiling, or old-boy network in her struggle to be rewarded on the basis of merit; there isn't a working mother who hasn't known, additionally, the burden of finding, affording, and retaining decent child care. There isn't a divorced or single mother who hasn't wondered, in the absence of a helpmate and father for her children, if maybe her life is unduly hard, uniquely disadvantaged.

Hence we can all readily sympathize with Hewlett, who lost a set of twins when, she believes, the stress of her job provoked preterm labor. Women are still in no position to do their best by either their employers or their families, given inadequate maternity leaves, unsatisfactory child care, zero job security, ex-husbands who default on child support, and a workplace generally hostile to those who give priority to their role at home. And yet women still can't afford to stay home: In the absence of family support policies, the birth of a child reduces the average woman's future earning capability by 19 percent.[4]

Much of *A Lesser Life* is devoted to venting women's bitterness at being denied what they feel entitled to—at the very least, the support of other women. As Hewlett tells it, feminists refused to acknowledge that mothers might require special consideration in the workplace, and antifeminists refused to acknowledge that some mothers might need to work. But she is particularly disappointed, as an early convert to feminism, by the failure of the women's movement to fulfill the expectations it engendered, making neither child rearing in absentia easier nor working fewer hours less punitive so that mothers might compete on equal footing with their childless peers. "Motherhood is the problem that modern feminists cannot face," Hewlett declares. "The modern women's movement has not just been anti-men; it has also been profoundly anti-children and anti-motherhood."[5]

The Feminists Cry Foul

Sympathizers though we may be, if we resist joining Hewlett in her tirade against the women's movement it is because Susan Faludi, author of *Backlash: The Undeclared War Against American Women* and feminist heir apparent, so convincingly indicts the promulgators of antifeminist propaganda. Women today feel like the rug's been pulled out from under them, Faludi contends, precisely *because* of saboteurs like Hewlett, backlashers who undermined feminist initiatives such as the Equal Rights Amendment, lobbied against no-fault divorce laws, and continue to blow smoke clouds around the real antimotherhood crusaders—New Right leaders, conservative politicians, and corporate executives "who not only ignored mothers' rights but attacked them."[6] A key point that Hewlett and like-minded critics overlook, notes Faludi, is that "when feminists pushed for women's rights in other areas—employment opportunities, pay equity, credit rights, women's health—mothers and their children benefited, too."[7]

If women are living compromised lives, it is not because feminism has let them down, she insists, but because they have compromised themselves—because, in short, they have bought the backlash. When the media aired erroneous statistics showing "man shortages and barren wombs," Faludi writes, women allowed themselves to be badgered into marriage. Brainwashed by Hollywood and Madison Avenue, they allowed themselves to be exploited and harassed by their spouses and employers. Intimidated into silence by the right-wing God squad, they permitted themselves to be divided and conquered. As a result, she points out, women have been divested of power in government, in the workplace, and on the home front, *hence* their lesser life. The backlash, while not a conspiracy, succeeds in robbing women of their gains because women believe its propaganda to the contrary. Indeed, what makes this phenomenon so insidious is its implication that feminists are to *blame* for women's sorry postrevolution predicament.

But who, really, is to blame?

The Politics of Choice

Most of us raising children in the '90s are sorely divided in our loyalties. We can certainly relate to Hewlett, a capable woman who, inspired by the women's movement, pursued a successful career until motherhood compromised her ability "to be superwoman and succeed on all fronts."[8] But unlike Hewlett, who graduated from college giddy with the possibilities feminism had proffered, we do not expect to "have it all." The generation of women before us who rushed to fill the corporate ranks altered our expectations of what working motherhood could be, tempered our ambition, and exploded the supermom myth many of us held dear.

Faludi would insist, of course, that we're mistaken: Women *can* have it all, and indeed, during the early '80s, came darn close before the backlash convinced them otherwise. She goes to great lengths to prove that our recollection of the beleaguered, barren baby boomer is plain wrong, an image sown by the media and based on flawed research and specious reasoning. There was no "marriage crunch," no "man shortage," no "infertility epidemic," no "birth dearth," she maintains. If women of the '80s were single or childless, it was because they *preferred* to be.

Faludi marshals a mountain of statistics, polls, and studies to corroborate her thesis. Single and career-bent or married and working, with two kids at home, the women I know who've read her manifesto concur that it's a blood-boiler. But Faludi, who is single and childless, does not—*cannot*—grasp what has alienated some of her otherwise supportive audience: the unnerving fact that many mothers have *chosen* to compromise their careers, have even *allowed* themselves to be "mommy-tracked." As Faludi's good friend and fellow Pulitzer Prize winner Anna Quindlen says of her, "I'm not sure, as good a reporter as she is, that Susan is fully conscious of how many of the conflicts in the lives of women arise naturally out of wanting to be in two places at once. Society doesn't project on us these contradictory feelings we have after we go back to work after having a baby."[9]

When my generation stepped up to bat, we felt we deserved to play in the major leagues, but we didn't want to have to hit a home run to prove it. Superwomen we are not, and superwomen we have no desire to be—and not because the media have brainwashed us with erroneous reports about the high costs of having it all, but because motherhood, in all its complexity, has shown us a different set of priorities. Certainly we expect to maintain both a career and a family, but we expect excellence in one role will come at some cost to the other. Certainly we would like to think we're entitled to the house with a master bedroom suite, luxury sedans, private schools, and Caribbean vacations, but we're chastened by our minimal savings and the specter of our husbands losing *their* jobs. Certainly we want issues such as child care and family leave to be perceived as problems affecting all of us, not just women—but we recognize, too, that we must then *all* bear the burden of paying for them and making them work for the businesses upon which our economic survival is based.

Limitation, to our generation, is not a gender-specific condition. "I don't think we're leveling the playing field so much as life is getting unfair for men as well as for women," postulates Ethel Roskies, a professor of psychology at the University of Montreal, who has studied life satisfaction levels among various groups of married and unmarried professional women and who teaches seminars on coping with the current employment environment to men and women. "Women discover early on that being nicer, better, smarter, or more efficient won't necessarily control the outcome; they recognize they're dealing with a system whose rules don't accommodate them and never have. But now men are finding that not only will they not become CEO, they'll be lucky to keep their jobs. Most people have no idea how to deal with the current job environment, because running faster and working harder just isn't working. All their effort won't necessarily pay off. The rules they grew up with don't apply anymore.

"I teach people to run marathons," Roskies says, "because life isn't a sprint."[10]

So unlike Hewlett, and despite Faludi, we're not all that surprised to learn, midrace, that it's a long and grueling one in which individual will and endurance count most. Or to return to the baseball metaphor, my generation will settle for a base hit—confident that eventually we will indeed tour all the bases and cross home plate to score. It is not so much that we have *lowered* our expectations (a sure signal that we've been manipulated by the backlash) but that we dismiss any quick fixes, painless remedies, or "have it all" credos as unrealistic. Even irresponsible.

Which is why many of us writhe in our chairs when motherhood's presumed representatives—women like Beverly LaHaye, president of Concerned Women for America, or Phyllis Schlafley, head of the conservative Eagle Forum, or Marilyn Quayle, deposed mouthpiece for all the women standing behind great men—talk about our fundamental obligation, as caretakers of the next generation, to raise our kids to be emotionally secure, morally responsible, educated contributors to society. When Beverly LaHaye notes that "the women's movement really hurt women because it taught them to put the value on the career instead of the family,"[11] many of us are inclined to nod in agreement: Part of our "essential nature" wants to go home and tend our children and husbands. None of us are against family values. As much as we may despise the women of the New Right for their blatant hypocrisy (putting in 70-hour workweeks jetting around the world to extoll the virtues of staying at home), we don't denigrate or care to devalue motherhood or child rearing.

I can recall, while listening to Barbara Bush at the 1992 Republican National Convention, actually pining for those simpler times she described, for Fourth of July picnics, Little League games, backyard barbecues with neighbors, and weeks ritualized by scout meetings and church suppers. Looking at the Bush clan assembled on the stage, I couldn't help but wonder if indeed theirs was a span of generations uniquely privileged, spared the ravages of drugs and AIDS and random acts of violence. Their faces belied any tragedy or misfortune, as though growing up with a mother at home and a father who supported them was all that was necessary to ensure their prospects for material success and marital bliss.

Choice, portrayed against this tableau of tradition, smacked of something degenerate, the sort of freedom that had mired our lives in tragedies such as abortion, single parenthood, substance abuse, and unemployment. Choice had given us opportunities at the expense of our children's. Choice indulged our selfish motivations, and hence choice was to blame for our fractured families, dysfunctional children, and morally bankrupt society.

Despite the conservatives' compelling appeal for the return of the '50s, I voted, as apparently 46 percent of all women voters did, "against" family values.[12] I would have liked to have voted pro-choice *and* pro-family, believing, as I do, that the freedom to be self-determinate needn't be exclusive of motherhood, but the political arena offered me no such alternative—however viable Ross Perot at one point appeared as a third-party candidate. I would have liked, in the end, to have voted *for* someone and for some positive vision rather than against the group and ideology I found most abhorrent. But as a woman I was courted as a co-victim, a voter likely to sympathize with the most wronged, the longest-suffering. Was it working mothers, harassed and under-paid and unaided in their struggle to earn a living and provide for their families, or the underappreciated, much-maligned, often overlooked stay-at-home population, sacrificed on the altar of our children's future? I had a hard time deciding. (*Should Hillary have baked more cookies?* I wondered. *Or should Marilyn have given up on Dan's career and concentrated on her own?*)

One thing is for sure: Women are oppressed, even victimized. Sylvia Ann Hewlett shouldn't have been forced to work during her difficult and painful pregnancy, shouldn't have been forced to return four weeks postpartum, shouldn't have had to choose between nurturing a premature infant and keeping her job. Susan Faludi shouldn't be made to feel like a second-class citizen because she is single and in no hurry either to marry or to have children. And women who agree with Beverly LaHaye shouldn't have to feel like lepers for wanting to stay home and raise their own children. We should all—men and women—be able to be who we want to be and not be penalized for who we aren't. We should all be free from the expectations of others, free to deter-mine the family/work commitment befitting our individual priorities and values. We should all be free, in short, to be ourselves.

But this isn't our current reality. While we are either passively awaiting or actively fighting for a more responsive administration to take office, for a more flexible workplace to take shape, for a more equal-minded man to evolve, we must grapple with our only-human husbands, our profit-driven employers, our inefficient bureaucracies—and our immediate need for some kind of balance, some sense of satisfaction for our labors, some reassurance that our prospects aren't hopeless, imperfect though we and our world may be. Tomorrow may well dawn a better day, but it's today we've got to get through. We would like to know what *we* are empowered to do, *right now.*

Solutions—or Pipe Dreams?

Hewlett's not entirely sure women are in a position to do anything. Her own repeated efforts to make "women's issues" economic mandates for new legislation failed, she acknowledges, in large part because policymakers continue to harbor "a residual hostility toward working mothers."[13] In *A Lesser Life,* she vests her hopes for change in the trade unions, despite the fact that they have "not yet adjusted to the labor-market realities of the 1980s,"[14] let alone the '90s: "The fact that unionized women workers earn, on average, 30 percent more than nonunionized women workers speaks for itself," she wrote in 1986.[15]

But apparently it didn't speak loudly enough, because in her more recent book, *When the Bough Breaks: The Cost of Neglecting Our Children,* she's back to advocating that private industry and government, not workers themselves, step in and fix things so the workplace can accommodate working mothers' need to properly rear the next generation—her own experience with recalcitrant policymakers conveniently forgotten. Ultimately, Hewlett determines women need do nothing but wait, as the "demographic realities" of the '90s and beyond—a population deficit of qualified white males—will force employers to provide the benefits and services that make for a "family-friendly" workplace.[16]

Susan Faludi suggests no specific action; she merely reminds us that we must act collectively, that as individuals seeking redress we will only ensure our further demise. "Women need to be armed with more than their privately held grievances and goals," she cautions. "To instruct each woman to struggle alone is to set each woman up, yet again, for defeat.

"In the past," she elaborates, "women have proven that they can resist in a meaningful way when they have had a clear agenda that is unsanitized and unapologetic, a mobilized mass that is forceful and public, and a conviction that is uncompromising and relentless."[17]

For Beverly LaHaye, the answer is as simple and unequivocal as the need for the species to reproduce. "Women must put family as their top priority," she says in an interview with Faludi. "If that means giving up the career, then so be it. It's just the natural way. It's built into us as women."[18]

A Feminist for the '90s

So to whom, if not our elected representatives or religious leaders or academic mouthpieces, can we turn for inspiration, for an image of ourselves that is neither victim nor superwoman? Who speaks for us, if antifeminists cannot appreciate the lure of the workplace and feminists cannot understand the primacy of motherhood? How can we make choices when all around us insist we are leading a lesser, compromised life that denies us choice, that we are victims of our gender differences and "feminine" predilections? How can we begin to help ourselves when it has become politically expedient to plead helplessness?

Consider the case of Connie Lezenby, an architect and mother of three who abandoned her partner-track position with a predominantly male firm to go out on her own. Being self-employed, she will tell you, was not one of her original career goals; on the contrary, she had very much enjoyed the salary, prestige, and projects that came with corporate employment.

Now that projects are no longer coming to her automatically, she finds her workload—and income—significantly reduced. Nonetheless, this is her choice, because the costs of staying on at her firm, she determined, were intolerably high.

Ultimately, what was required to make partner was something she wasn't willing, or even able, to give: time. "Commitment was measured in sheer hours," she explains. "Never mind that I was handling more projects than anybody: I fell into the trap, as women usually do, of compensating by doing things better and faster, hoping to be rewarded on the basis of creativity, talent, and the ability to delegate." With kids ages 6, 10, and 12, Connie wasn't about to try to compete with her male peers on the basis of 14-hour days and six-day workweeks.

But what actually catalyzed her departure was outrage over the discrimination levied against her female co-workers, discrimination that ultimately cost them their jobs. It all started when an outside consultant, hired by the firm to troubleshoot inefficiency, encouraged each employee to discuss what was wrong, unproductive, or wasteful about the way business was conducted. Each female staffer shared with Connie, the senior woman on staff, the ways in which she felt thwarted, the reasons her performance suffered. Unequal pay, as it turned out, was but one of their "horror stories."

"What they were talking about—partners making sexual remarks and promotional threats, partner-track projects always going to the men, raises that weren't comparable—just blew me away," recalls Connie. "I'd always thought it was just me." It was then Connie's job to report back to senior management. Within a matter of weeks after she confronted the partners with her staff's accusations, every woman but herself and two secretaries was laid off.

"After that I couldn't possibly stay," says Connie. "It was a moral choice. Of course, I could be working there still, but in effect I would have no longer had a job: I wouldn't have been given the projects; I wouldn't have been given the recognition for bringing in clients."

To even the most conservative eye, Connie's story is one of blatant job discrimination: She didn't choose to go out on her own—she was *driven* to it, at great loss of financial security and career advancement. What happened to Connie is emblematic of the oppression Faludi so well documents; what happened to Connie is what the women's movement is all about. She is a victim, powerless to claim what is rightfully hers, powerless to fulfill her potential.

And yet, remarkably, that's not how she elects to see herself. A victim of sexual discrimination, yes. But powerless, voiceless, and robbed of what she wants and deserves most—not at all. "I have really grown," says Connie of her experience. "I have more self-confidence because I know now that my talents are my own—something you don't necessarily discover in a group. I'm still angry I don't have the income I did, but I'm confident I will: I know this is a lull in the economy and my business will eventually pick up—if I want it to. The truth is, I don't feel so driven anymore. I have a sense of relaxation about who I have to be, what I'm trying to prove."

Looking back on her corporate employment, Connie says she's come to see the "whole attitude—that work is paramount and family should suffer because that's the way the world is"—as unhealthy, an attitude damaging both to women *and* men. Now that she's not putting in all the hours away from home, her husband, also in business for himself, has started to cut back, participating in his children's school activities and taking the occasional day off. "I'm as happy as I've ever been," she says of her new arrangement. "I have control over my schedule. I have less stress, more energy. I'm a lot more available to my kids, and I've got more time for my husband. And I'm learning to see the value of being at home; I'm finding I can be just as creative there as at work." She's discovered she has an artistic side, and now enjoys painting and writing. She's also become "much more resourceful" as a result of having to run her own business, and much more sympathetic about "what other people go through" as entrepreneurs.

Perhaps most importantly, says Connie, "I've come to realize I have choices: I don't have to do things in a certain way." Ever the good girl, always one to keep quiet and stifle her anger lest she "rock the boat" or make herself "undesirable," Connie did an about-face when her female cohorts lost their jobs, determining she would no longer put up and shut up, whatever the immediate costs in the way of favor or approval or even career advancement. If more talented women were to "vote with their feet," Connie believes, sexual harassment and discrimination might be discontinued as private industry came to realize it was not only bad behavior but bad for the bottom line.

"If things don't improve for us [women]," says a newly outspoken, self-determinate Connie, "then we have really only ourselves to blame."

The Silent Majority Speaks

To look at our talk shows and tabloids, you would think anyone who stood up for herself and took personal responsibility for her life was a freak, and victims of every conceivable abuse and injustice were the norm. A week of watching *Geraldo, Oprah,* and even segments of the nightly news (a typical "News Extra" topic: "Sex Addicts: Are You Getting the Help You Need?"), and anyone who was not molested by their father, beaten by their husband, raped by their employer, or sued by their children would have to conclude she is either the only such woman on earth or is "in denial," having failed to perceive her own dysfunction. The victim bandwagon used to be reserved for the genuinely downtrodden, notes historian Charles Sykes in *A*

Nation of Victims, but now everybody—millionaire artists, Ivy League students, the obese, children of addicted parents, homosexuals, American Indians, the elderly, the disabled, and *women*—is jumping on in record numbers, eager to be spared the arduous journey of walking unaided and independently.[19] Since women alone account for 51 percent of the population, a clear majority of Americans are victims. Who indeed has not claimed, or cannot claim, some sort of handicap that compromises his or her chances for complete happiness? Who doesn't deserve a leg up, if not a free ride?

The women who've triumphed over the obstacles tripping up the rest of us presumably number so few we have to keep recycling their images on the covers of our magazines. Our current breed of role models tend to be media luminaries like Kathie Lee Gifford or celebrity moms like Demi Moore—as though contending with late limo service or surviving a movie that bombs were hurdles with which we could all readily identify. "All these celebrities you read about have such an easy time balancing their lives," notes Elizabeth Woodman, a mother of two who helps her husband run a business, "but their world doesn't have much to do with the real world, and their lives certainly don't have much in common with mine."

Certainly none of them appear to pay any price for their fame or fortune: hubbies (rich, handsome, brilliantly successful) adore them, kids never suffer separation anxiety, friends have nothing but nice things to say, and their health and good looks never betray a lack of sleep or a steady diet of low-calorie soft drinks and microwave pizza. We know such flawless portrayals are unrealistic; we stay interested almost out of a perverse delight in awaiting the inevitable breakdown. (Donald Trump, as we anticipated, is leveraged up to his eyeballs, and Princess Di's prince turned out to be not so charming.)

In contrast, the Connie Lezenbys of the world are everywhere, working in every walk of life, confronting and overcoming all manner of setbacks largely on their own steam. And yet we do not see their faces splashed across the supermarket racks, do not hear their stories on the nightly news, and rarely see their lives dramatized on a sitcom, precisely because we buy magazines and watch television to see not ourselves but an idealized image of ourselves. Advertisers wouldn't be able to sell a jar of eye cream, a can of hair spray, an ounce of perfume, or a single size-six bikini if their models even remotely resembled us. Relying on the media for a sense of ourselves is like packing a loaded gun for protection and having it go off in our face: On the one hand, we are flattered to think we could look like the Guess jeans girl and cavort on the beach with our hunky boyfriends, but on the other, we are frightened to find ourselves portrayed as little more than objects of desire, victims of sexual harassment and exploitation, passive, powerless, and voiceless. The world the media would have us inhabit only exaggerates our vulnerability, peopled as it is with a frightening assortment of date rapists, serial killers, abusive husbands, sex-crazed employers, murderous pro-lifers, witch-fearing preachers, criminally violent policemen, corrupt officials, and utterly impotent politicians. Where in such a landscape would we hope to find women like Connie—vocal, confident, resourceful and self-determinate?

But there is growing awareness of an alternate reality out there, one in which women do not cower and allow themselves to be exploited but instead assert themselves and make a measurable difference. Recently *Redbook* surveyed 1,000 mothers, 70.3 percent of whom worked (45.1 percent worked full time and 21.4 percent part time, and 3.8 percent generated income while staying home), and to everyone's surprise found that most mothers (54.2 percent between 30 and 40 years old, 70.4 percent with some college education, and 49.2 percent with two kids under 18) are feeling very good about their lives, despite the media's portrayals of them as depraved or victimized. Ninety-four percent said they're managing "quite well" juggling work and home.

A full 85 percent said they believe there are advantages to being a working mom; 57 percent said they'd work even if they didn't need the money. Most (87 percent) feel they're doing a *better* job as mothers than their moms did. (Their kids think so, too: 76.7 percent of the women hear no complaints about the quantity or quality of time they're spending with their children.) Even more (89 percent) feel they're better wives than their own mothers were; only 8 percent worry that work is adversely affecting their marriage. And virtually *all* (98 percent) feel they're setting a good example for their kids.[20]

Like Connie Lezenby, these women perceive themselves as neither victims nor superwomen. Those surveyed attribute their success to *doing less,* particularly in the way of housework and meal preparation. Many give credit to their husbands for easing their load: One in four working moms even leaves her preschoolers home with Dad. And if husbands don't help out enough, kids, relatives, or baby-sitters are recruited to pick up where Mom cannot. These women are confident enough to delegate; they don't need to prove they can do it all in order to feel worthy or desirable. Supermom-dom, it could be argued, is the ultimate victimization: These women, for all that they cannot change, are remarkably self-determinate, choosing what they want to do well and what they want to do just well enough and what they don't want to do at all.

But what makes them warrant our attention is that *their* goals are *our* goals. They want well-adjusted, secure children who contribute to society rather than burden it; a relationship or marriage that will weather time and hardship; a pursuit outside the home that not only earns them a salary but allows them to flex their talents and discover new ones; an identity forged not by what they do or who their kids turn out to be or how other people perceive them but by who they are. And despite gross social inequities, a persistent wage gap, and the utter negligence of government, they are meeting these goals, compromising not on the ends but on the means.

Shocking as this portrait of working mothers would appear against the more typical tableau of beleaguered stoics the media offers us, the *Redbook* survey is hardly singular in its findings. In all of my random cold calls, I noted that the more reason my interviewee had to feel sorry for herself, the more adamantly she resisted. Take Jill Mallory*, the divorced mother of a five-year-old. The divorce, which her husband filed for ten months after she gave birth, wasn't her idea; working full time during her daughter's toddlerhood would never have been her choice. Yet she focuses on time she can make, actions she can take.

"Since I make money by the hour, the more I work, the more it improves my income," says Jill. "But I don't have to make a *spectacular* income. I don't have to jump out of bed and drive my daughter crazy to get to work earlier. I can have a nice breakfast with her, walk her to school, get to my office after nine. I'll only get this chance [as a parent] once—I can't pick it up 20 years from now. I'm not going to spoil it, or risk her emotional health, feeling bitter about what I tried to fix but could not."

And then there's Pam Retseck, a mother of a ten-year-old and a six-year-old, who owns her own paper-recycling business but could just as easily have caved in to her husband's expectations that, like his mother, she stay home baking cookies, taking care of the house and his needs and rearing the children. "There have been some hard years being an ambitious woman with a man who never had that kind of mother," Pam remarks. "But I'm more confident now that what I'm doing is important. I think I know that being home would be too constraining: If I had to put all my energies into my children, I'd make them crazy. They're healthier for not being my only focus.

"I've always been eager to please," she reflects. "Eager to please my husband, my family, my extended family, the people in my community. But I've been standing up for myself a little more. I'm not going to be pushed around as much, trying to please everybody and winding up living the kind of harried lifestyle I truly question."

I heard lots of variations on the same theme: Motherhood overloaded the circuits, but on the brink of burnout, it was motherhood that sparked the lifesaving epiphany. "I don't have to make myself miserable trying to meet everyone's expectations," says Kathy Kaufmann, a lighting designer with two toddlers. "I probably should have gotten further along in my career, but that's lack of drive on my part: My priorities have shifted. There's nothing I feel I'm *owed*."

In short, what distinguishes this current generation of multi-role women is not their goals but how they choose to attain them. For while the idealogues and zealots define ever more narrowly the qualifications for membership in their elite club, the women they court pretty much like who they are, see successes in endeavors too small to be recognized, let go of goals that make them counterproductive or crazy, make time for enjoying their lives and their families, and are driven by their own very idiosyncratic values. They're not willing to postpone fulfillment for that future day when the playing field is perfectly level and life is fair. Neither are they self-indulgent: While previous generations sound the alarm about the effect on our children of a "parental time deficit,"[21] our generation is devoting more time than any generation in the twentieth century[22] to ensuring that our children are not shortchanged by the failing educational system, bankrupt social services, or faltering economy we inherited. Success, for a great many mothers who have to or want to work, is an ongoing process of compromise.

Without fanfare, without an audience, without government assistance, and without a lawyer, many of us are making a positive contribution by resisting the very ideals that have rendered us a society of choiceless victims and insatiable crybabies. A few warrant our attention not because they have the answer but because they have rejected the mentality that insists there must be one answer. What makes them role models is not how much or how little they work, how many or how few hats they wear, but rather how well they understand, and accept, that for all rewards there will be commensurate sacrifice; for all gains, some loss; for any pleasure, some pain.

A Paradigm for Nonvictims

Which underscores for me a curious irony. Over and over I was impressed with the *resourcefulness* of my interviewees; whatever the roadblock, their attitude was "I'll find a way around it." One woman opened our dialogue with the declaration that she never felt herself to be a victim, never once felt it wasn't in her power to effect positive change—a declaration that seemed all the more impressive when I learned that her son, at the age of five, was awaiting open-heart surgery, his eighth operation since birth. Others asserted they weren't superwomen and then proceeded to describe a life so jigsawed with demands on their time and energies that they made Katie Couric look like a slouch. These were women not handicapped but *empowered* by the sudden limitations motherhood imposed on them in their struggle for self-actualization. If feminism, as Faludi defines it, "asks that women be free to define themselves—instead of having their identity defined for them, time and again, by their culture and their men,"[23] the working mothers I met were all paragons of feminist virtue, role models the women's movement might well celebrate.

Yet these are women who, in Faludi's estimation, have compromised, have bought the backlash, have buckled under the pressure exerted by men, the media, Madison Avenue, Pennsylvania Avenue, the religious right, the Republican party, shrinks and support groups, employers, and parents. These are women apparently too stupid to note they are being manipulated and exploited. These are women so wimpy they'd sooner give in to what others believe they need than fight for what they really want.

"Instead of assailing injustice," Faludi writes, "many women have learned to adjust to it. Instead of getting angry, they have become depressed. Instead of uniting their prodigious numbers, they have splintered and turned their pain and frustration inward. . . . Millions of women have sought relief from their distress, only to wind up in the all-popular counseling of the era where women learn not to raise their voices but to *lower their expectations*" (italics mine).[24]

Anything short of having it all smacks of women *being* compromised, not women *choosing* less, as Faludi sees it. Having no children of her own, she cannot conceive of limitation, cannot imagine the trade-offs inherent in parenthood. Hence she assumes any trade-off we're living with cannot possibly have been our choice, must certainly have been imposed on us against our will or knowledge. Any suggestion that we chose our imperfect predicament is heresy: Our salvation depends on acknowledging our victim status. Money and political clout don't get channeled to self-determinate, individually empowered women but to women who can prove themselves objects of a society-wide oppression.

So the Champions of Choice, ironically enough, would insist we have none. (The antifeminists at least credit us with having engineered our own misery.) As Faludi describes us, we're by implication victims of our chromosomes, hormones, and maternal nature; we're too deferential to male authority, too needful of male validation, and too subject to innuendo and misrepresentation to resist exploitation. The only active role we might play in our destinies, the only choice she sanctions, is to claw our way to the top where we belong, thus proving unequivocally our equality and merit to all who might otherwise doubt it. Whether we want to be there, whether we like being there, whether we're willing to endure the process of getting there or willing to make the personal sacrifices necessary is irrelevant. Accepting anything short of what we know we deserve and all that men owe us signals betrayal. To compromise is to contribute to the backlash, to further our own oppression, to undo 35 years of struggle. To lower our expectations or temper our ambitions or accommodate anybody else's agenda ahead of our own is a choice we are not permitted.

Make no mistake: There is a backlash, and it has cost us dearly in the form of job discrimination and sexual harassment, limited wage-earning potential and financial security, limited choices in birth control, and limited political representation. But let's suppose feminism were to overcome this backlash and secure, at last, the economic security and freedom of choice for which its adherents have long struggled. Let's imagine the playing field were suddenly level and that all employers treated, promoted, and paid men and women strictly according to merit. Let's fantasize about having our child-care crises resolved, our housework halved, our "second shift" shared equally with our mate, our second-class status abolished. Surely this is what the feminists of any generation might consider "having it all."

But would we find, in this utopia, our internal conflict between home and office suddenly assuaged? Would our decisions regarding how we spent our time (and with whom) be any less agonizing? Would we find, once all obstacles were removed, that we no longer lived with trade-offs, that we never again needed to compromise?

And most importantly, would we feel any more secure in our choices, any more at peace with our shortcomings, and any more fulfilled by our lives?

CHAPTER TWO

Expecting to Have
It All

When I was 24 years old and still under the impression that life was a meritocracy, I worked with an ex-con in North Carolina who spent much of his spare time conducting a rehabilitation class at a state penitentiary. One of the texts he used was called *We're All Doing Time,* written by an inmate serving a life sentence. The premise was that each of us lives behind some kind of bars—whether they be made of iron or iron-clad beliefs, responsibilities, fears, or handicaps—but we're prisoners *only* as long as we focus on our limitations.

I could appreciate his insight, yet I was untouched, at the time, by its potential relevance. His philosophy seemed clearly to be the outgrowth of rather singular circumstances, a means of coping with permanent incarceration. The rest of us—myself, certainly—could hardly be said to be "doing time." I was single and zealously pursuing a career in journalism with no barriers in sight, convinced my female attributes were an asset, not a liability. Having been blessed with a supportive and loving family, an excellent education, and the backing of an entire generation of women who had fought for—and largely won—my opportunities for me, I felt quite confident that persistence would win me the success I envisioned. I never doubted that my future was self-determined: Freedom of choice concerning my body, my relationships, and my occupation was for me a fundamental right, not a politically protected privilege. The realization of my own dreams, I believed, depended on the same commitment of will and application of skill that had led me to graduate at the top of my class. I could not imagine being forced to acknowledge that some hurdles, regardless of my ability or perseverance, might prove insurmountable. I could not perceive any consequences that weren't somehow the result of my own actions or that might suggest that life was fundamentally unfair.

Only with motherhood did it dawn on me that I did not, and could not, exercise unlimited choice or control all outcomes, that I would not be given all that I was entitled to, that I might not be rewarded according to what I deserved. During most of the 15 months that my son was an only child, I felt like I was "doing time." Only after I had two children did I come to see how *liberating* limitation could be and how fulfilling I might find meeting certain goals halfway.

When I got pregnant (a rigorously planned and chosen course of action) I decided to rewrite my five-year plan as a magazine editor to build in some time at home as a full-time mother. I could afford a pit stop in my career, I reasoned, certain I was far enough ahead of the competition to sit on the sidelines for a bit. I would have my baby (naturally, of course), breast-feed for about eight months (as my mother had done with me), and, when the child was in some sort of preschool program, resume editing part time, or do some writing on the side. Maybe I didn't even think that far ahead; throughout my textbook pregnancy, I knew only that I was going to be a good mother, as I had been a good editor.

But on the very threshold of parenthood, control was wrested from me. My son arrived not by the fruits of my labors but by cesarean section. I did not nurse him eight months, but barely four—and not exclusively, as I had hoped, but with supplementary bottles at every feeding. He wasn't even three months old before I took on a writing assignment, and very quickly I came to the fearsome conclusion that maybe I wasn't going to be a good mother after all. Not good enough, anyway. Because no matter how I tried, nothing went according to plan—not the birth, not the breast-feeding, not the happy domestic scenario.

For all my constant activity, I seemed to be running in place, or even slipping backward past the milestones I considered significant. At four weeks, Chase weighed less than he did at birth because I was trying to nurse him while proving to the world that, despite major surgery, I could resume all prebirth activities and obligations immediately. My milk supply and his weight thus became a source of constant anxiety: Even in my dreams I saw his open mouth and heard his pitiful cry, searing reminders of my stupidity. Everywhere I looked, in fact, I saw an indictment of my poor mothering skills, from the dishes that sat in the sink to the laundry that amassed in front of the washer to the rash that persisted on Chase's bottom. Somehow, somewhere, I had gotten badly off track. I'd made some terrible mistakes, all my education and preparation notwithstanding—and this innocent and utterly dependent new life paid for them. I dearly wanted to start over, wipe the slate clean of my faulty judgments. I fantasized about just walking out the front door, free of the baby, the stroller, the diaper bag, and the shroud of anxiety that I wore night and day as a new parent. Not that parenthood was tantamount to incarceration, but certainly in those first months I behaved like someone handed a life sentence.

What made it all the more difficult to bear was the contrast between my new life and my old. Gone were the lavish lunches, the first-class plane tickets, the presidential suites in five-star hotels, the insider passes to every sight worth seeing the world over. A distant memory were the remote, privately owned Fijian islands my husband and I had enjoyed while "on assignment" for the magazine for two glorious weeks. Other destinations had included Hawaii and Mexico, most of the Caribbean, Europe, and Asia. I had even journeyed to the "Rooftop of the World," trekking to 18,000 feet on the Tibetan side of Mount Everest.

From such heights I fell into the numbing routine of changing diapers and sterilizing nipples, my most far-flung destinations the supermarket and dry cleaner's. I couldn't look forward to returning to my job because I'd given it up. My husband and I had agreed that I would resign after my paid leave expired, primarily because we concurred that mothering was and should be a full-time job. My staying home was a luxury we could then afford. More importantly, for my husband it represented an opportunity to give to his child what he had been denied: a mother on hand all the time. And with my mother's example of total devotion to six children shining before me, I could hardly insist on returning to work, however much I loved it, however much satisfaction it afforded me.

So why was this decision so hard to live with? I had *wanted* Chase, chosen to have him, reveled in his reality and delighted daily in his infinite possibility. I seemed only to have underestimated the consequences of my action, the costs and trade-offs associated with the privilege of parenthood. Why had no one told us? Or had we been unwilling to listen? Or did we believe we would, somehow, be different—better organized, better read, better prepared? And what excuse did I have, the only daughter among six children? I had watched my mother; surely I had a better understanding than most of what enormous amounts of energy and devotion were required to rear a family. My mother, during the two weeks she spent with us to help out with Chase, was clearly in her element; I was clearly out of mine. Had I failed to inherit some essentially female nature? Or had I failed to grasp how much of my identity I derived from work? Was I a poor nurturer for not wanting to stay home, or was I a poor feminist for not insisting on returning to work?

Just as every woman emerges from childbirth convinced that her labor was more excruciating than average, I blundered through Chase's infancy certain that I was singularly ill-equipped to adapt to motherhood, let alone rejoice in it. I found I couldn't read *What to Expect the First Year* or any other baby-care bible without feeling panicky about what I wasn't doing, or worse, what Chase wasn't doing. His growth percentile became the measure of my skill as a mother, largely because of my failure to notice he wasn't getting enough during those early weeks of nursing. I found myself studiously avoiding women who had never condescended to a bottle. What I could not avoid were the inevitable, no doubt innocuous, comparisons other mothers made between our children, driving the stake of guilt through my heart. "He's six months?" they would ask, incredulous. "At his age, *my* son was twice his size."

My fixation on Chase's percentile (an index all too reminiscent of standardized tests and SAT scores) diminished, however, in direct proportion to the number of free-lance projects I took on in order "to keep my hand in." When he was ten weeks old I accepted a writing assignment that necessitated an emergency baby-sitting visit from my mother so that I could meet the deadline. Finishing it—despite what it cost me in terms of exhaustion, guilt, and tarnished maternal image—gave me a rush akin to an addict's. I was not willing to withdraw from my work habit; I couldn't give up the gratification it afforded. So while my mother congratulated me on being a stay-at-home mother, I solicited more work and arranged for regular day care, albeit in my home.

I was so ashamed of this "double life," so fearful lest I disappoint my mother, renege on my promise to my husband, or, God forbid, deny my child in some life-scarring way, that I adopted a chameleonic existence in order to please all and offend none. During the months I was caring for Chase and pregnant with Kathryn, I kept house and set up a business; took my son to the park and paid a woman to do it for me; trotted back and forth to the pediatrician's and commuted into the city on editing assignments; and wore either career or family hat depending on the expectations of the people with whom I socialized.

By the same token, I felt the need to constantly apologize for my shortcomings—for failing to be both a mega-editor and the perfect homemaker—depending on whose company I felt cowed by. Inevitably, however, this schizoid view of myself manifested itself in gross hypocrisy. I could, for instance, condemn my corporate lawyer neighbor for relinquishing her children to a nanny 70 hours a week and then turn around and take a five-day free-lance job in the city, rationalizing that we needed the money. I could listen to my mother castigate my sister-in-law for putting her three children in day care and never once point out to her that my kids, while in my home, were in surrogate care most of the week. I lost track of where I stood myself: Was I a good mother because I was *still* home? Or was I a good feminist because I was *still* working?

Motherhood afforded me choices, but I couldn't see them, blinded as I was by my failure to adhere to certain ideals concerning child rearing and a career in journalism, hobbled by my need to *prove* to others that I could and would do it all. My working at home I perceived as a temporary departure, a habit I was ashamed of, one I would kick as soon as I got better at mothering. Whether a colleague called to revel in her prestigious assignment or a friend shared her triumph in toilet-training her two-year-old, jealousy consumed me. I wanted not only to run in both races; I wanted to *place*.

And I know I wanted someone to make it possible, to make it easy for me to have both my child and my former life. Where once I had perceived personal challenges, I saw then only barriers, barriers perversely erected to keep *me* back, to prevent me from "being all that I could be." Where once I had looked within myself for solutions, as a new mother I wanted solutions ready-made and served up to me. Why should I have to give up my happiness to ensure my child his? Why did it have to be that

Chase's well-being was inversely proportionate to my own? I had worked hard; I deserved better.

Examining Our Expectations

What do women *want*?

For all his ground-breaking insights into the human psyche, Sigmund Freud purportedly did not have a clue. But he must not have asked too many women, or at least, not too many *normal* women, because when I've posed the question I've been read chapter and verse. Working mothers, in particular, seem to be consulting the same hymnal.

"Every administration's full of talk about caring for children," observes Yvonne Kearney, president of her own executive search firm and mother of two preschoolers, "but over and over fails to foster any sort of child-care system. We've got to recognize the importance of our children and address child care on a major level; it's not just 'a woman's issue.'"

"Maternity leave in this country is a joke," notes Maeve Fegan, a decorator supply rep and mother of two. "We're in the Dark Ages compared with most European countries, where mothers get not only job security but five or six *months* of paid leave."

"We've got to support mothers and fathers so they can be the best possible parents," adds Connie Lezenby, whom I introduced in the preceding chapter. "Both parents must have their own life, their own outlet for expression, as well as self-esteem for supporting a family. I envision a society where both parents can stay home for a year, then both can work part time; it's not like it's a lot of time before kids are ready to be in groups, so until then, caring for them should be our top priority."

Are these unreasonable expectations? And if they are reasonable, why are we so far from realizing them?

There are basically two schools of thought to account for the gap between our current reality and our wish list. One we have already explored: Women are victims of a society-wide backlash that robs them of voice, power, and collective action. The other, promulgated by most self-help programs and theorists, holds that we're held back by our lack of self-esteem—not a uniquely feminine ailment, to be sure, but a potent undertow dragging us from the shores of deliverance. Women don't fight for what they want, or haven't succeeded, because they don't consider themselves *worthy*.

And it seems empirically true: Our self-esteem barely registers on the scale. We lack not only "situational" self-esteem, the kind that comes from knowing we compare favorably with others and meet their expectations, but also "characterological" self-esteem, a belief that no matter how we perform or how we measure up to external standards of excellence or beauty, we are lovable and worthy creatures, deserving of good fortune and the fulfillment of our wishes.

The roots of this malaise—why *women* are so particularly prone to a poor opinion of themselves—go far deeper than I'm qualified to explore, but the symptoms, for my generation, are so widespread that everyone from New Age savior Shakti Gawain to old-school feminist Gloria Steinem is cashing in by offering an antidote, if not an explanation. Gawain, best-selling author of *Creative Visualization,* asserts that the cure for this fundamental unworthiness is found through "affirmations," positive, self-loving mantras such as "I am beautiful and lovable/ I am kind and loving, and I have a great deal to share with others/ I am talented, intelligent and creative/ I am growing more and more attractive every day/ I deserve the very best in life." Talking to yourself this way, insists Gawain, is "especially effective because much of our negative self-image comes from being convinced in various ways at an early age by other people that we are bad, stupid, or inadequate in some way."[1]

Steinem, whose *Revolution from Within: A Book of Self-Esteem* hovered at the top of the best-seller lists for most of 1992, suspects there's a bit more to it than that. Her message, too, is wholly positive: Adults denied a sense of intrinsic worth as children can always go back, determine what happened, and "re-parent" themselves. It's never too late for a happy childhood, she posits, never too late to journey back in time, painful though it may be, to "relearn" who we are, to cherish ourselves as perhaps our own parents did not, simply for being us. Building on that foundation, we might then trust our inner voice in order to become that person whom we dared not believe in or hope for—a process of affirmation not altogether unlike that which Gawain promotes. Indeed, writes Steinem, "If our dreams weren't already real within us, we could not even dream them."[2]

Yet that process cannot begin until we "un-learn" our education and examine our assumptions, however routinely corroborated by science or the establishment. Steinem focuses on the anomaly of high academic achievement and low self-esteem: Study after study shows that women's self-esteem erodes the *more* they are educated and the *better* they perform academically. Even more alarming, women emerge from college more self-critical, while men whose grades were lower graduate with their intellectual and interpersonal self-esteem intact or even strengthened. Steinem's interpretation of the results: Good grades mask what women are *really* learning, and that is that the female gender *must not be worthy* of greater opportunities because they find no such role models to convince them otherwise.

"The difference seemed to be," she writes, "that with each additional year of higher education, the women saw less of themselves, and less chance of being themselves. In the academic canon and in the classroom, their half of the human race was underrepresented in authority, often invisible, sometimes treated with contempt, perhaps treated as if success were 'unfeminine,' and denied even the dignity of a well-recognized suffering. And since the great majority were in coeducational schools—and studies report that male classrooms are more 'competitive' while female classrooms are more 'cooperative'—women of all races were having to function in an alien and often hostile culture."[3]

According to Steinem, then, we *learn* poor self-esteem—because we are taught it by racist, sexist male authority figures and because, for lack of evidence to the contrary, we begin to believe it. Our poor self-esteem then cripples us in our quest for personal fulfillment as well as in our campaign for societal change—for equal rights, better child care, job security, and family support. Hence the "revolution from within" furthers the same agenda as that other revolution Steinem is credited with leading, the women's movement.

It's a rather seductive solution: Love thyself and thou wilt become empowered to change what thou dost not love. But it's also true that we're keenly motivated to effect social change as long as we're keenly unhappy with our personal lot. If we were to become utterly content with ourselves as we are, we wouldn't be embarking on any revolutions, within or without. For the women's movement to succeed as a catalyst for social change, and for the self-help movement to profit as a catalyst for personal improvement, we need to remain fundamentally *unhappy*; we must continue to believe our expectations have not been met and we as individuals could always be made *more* likable—thinner, or younger looking, or more successful. The carrot must always remain just out of reach, lest we lose our incentive to participate in some larger social agenda.

Note the paradox evident in Gawain's advice to those with physical problems they'd like to overcome—those who are overweight, for example. "Through affirmations and loving energy, start learning to love and appreciate yourself more *as you already are,*" cites step Number One. *Simultaneously,* she adds, "Through creative visualization and affirmations, start creating yourself as you *want to be*—slim, trim, healthy, and happy. These techniques are extremely effective in making real changes."[4]

In other words, in order to become who we want to be and who we have the power to become, *we must not entirely succeed in liking ourselves as we are.* Far from "curing" us of poor self-esteem, the argument could be made that any improvement program or "revolution"—personal or social—succeeds only to the extent that it *fosters* poor self-esteem. No one seems to question the underlying assumption that women are unhappy, unfulfilled, and denied the full flowering of their self-potential. But what if the current generation of women, with one foot in the work-place and the other squarely planted at home, were actually to be perceived as having all that it takes to be happy? Most certainly we do not have everything Faludi or Steinem believes we deserve, but is perfect freedom to do whatever we please and guaranteed absence of penalty prerequisite to fulfillment? Are we not then condemning ourselves to a lifetime of disappointment and self-denigration, in that our expectations are purposefully unrealistic, unattainable? If we're not entirely content, is it because we have yet to move the social mountain in our favor or is it because we already have and *it's still not enough?*

No one seems to question the reasonableness of our expectations: If we want something, then we must have it, because in having it we will be happy. When we get it, and happiness doesn't follow, we reposition the bar a couple of notches higher. Right now the bar for women is arguably higher than that for men. Yet however high we leap—and we working mothers have outdone ourselves—it is never high enough.

So I'll ask the question anew: What *do* women really want?

Mixed Messages and
Male Role Models

"I'd like to stop having to prove myself," sighs Madeline Wilson, a fine-arts photographer with two girls, five and three, who devotes three days a week to her work, shooting or developing or hanging her latest gallery showing. "I feel like I'm shortchanging my kids working this much, and yet I feel like my professional colleagues don't take me seriously, working 'just' three days a week. I'm so *sick* of feeling this way."

Over and over I hear these sentiments, frequently expressed by women who, to all appearances, seem to have worked out the kind of balance most of us crave. Whatever we're doing, whoever we are, *it isn't enough*. But it's not what we do or who we are that causes us distress; it's what we're *not* doing and who we *might* be that torments us. Little wonder we have trouble finding role models to guide us through these shoals: No one less than God Herself could be all the things we'd like to be to all the people we'd like to feel approval from.

Which begs an important question of all who would bewail the absence of any decent role models. What would this inspirational creature look like? How would she juggle career and family in today's workplace and social environment? What would her values be? Her priorities? How would she view herself?

One can't help but imagine "she" would look and act a lot like "he." That is, the feminist "ideal" would have to be somewhat modeled on men, who, feminists contend, *are* unhindered in their ambitions and *are* enjoying all the rewards and none of the penalties. Indeed, the ideal would perforce incorporate such male "virtues" as competitive spirit, egocentric drive, an unwillingness to compromise, and a predator's survival instinct. These would be coupled with those few "female" imperatives such as— such as, well, giving birth. The result would be a genderless amalgam, a tough and tender, aggressive and yielding hunter and gatherer who happened to bear children. It would be a bizarre enough demigod to ensure that none of us ever succeeded in emulating it, but compelling enough to goad most of us to try.

The role models my generation grew up with weren't all that different from this ideal. I'm not speaking of whom we might have been exposed to in school or in our families, but of whom we watched and with whom we identified on television, that cultural homogenizer we all embraced. If anybody was vulnerable to brainwashing, it was we, the children of the '60s and '70s who spent our youth in its glare. Wasteland though it may have been, television was our common ground, a landscape at once fabulous and familiar, peopled with characters we could adore or despise but never forget.

I'm appalled to find that I can remember the theme songs, with complete lyrics, to *The Beverly Hillbillies, The Jetsons,* and *The Brady Bunch* but get confused as to how the second verse to "The Star-Spangled Banner" goes. I'm alarmed to be able to recite the first and last names of all the characters on *Bewitched, Gilligan's Island,* and *The Waltons* but unable to remember the names of former best friends in whose weddings I was a bridesmaid. I am sickened at some of my spending habits, dictated not always by value or need but an unfounded fondness for brands whose advertisements seized my youthful fancy. (To this day I pass over the store-brand frozen vegetables for the more expensive Birds Eye and Green Giant products, after being swayed as a child by packaging that seemed to promise *their* vegetables would look a whole lot more appetizing than what my mother served.)

For better or for worse, my career goals and vision of my adult self were shaped, if not dictated, by this medium. "I want to be an astronaut," I confided to my junior high school guidance counselor when asked my future ambition. And I zealously did, not because I'd seen the Apollo moonshot (televised to my third-grade class in conjunction with our studies on outer space), but because I was absolutely addicted to *Lost in Space, Star Trek,* and, later, *The Six Million Dollar Man,* shows whose male leads, in my gender-blind, prepubescent perception, I identified with and dreamed of emulating. My childhood library contains 16 volumes of James Blish's *Star Trek* serial fantasies and only two Nancy Drew mysteries. My early diaries are filled not with accounts of boys whose affection I pined for but plots from *The Six Million Dollar Man,* whose bionic protagonist I did not want to marry but rather dreamed of *becoming.*

Antagonism toward these goals—or lukewarm encouragement—came from other sources closer to home. After that interview with the guidance counselor, my mother asked me if I had mentioned my culinary skills (almost entirely in the cookie-baking genre) or the fact that I was sewing my own ski jacket. I can remember my horror at having failed to address these key topics, my shame at having shared an ambition the counselor no doubt must have thought ridiculous. Whatever made me tell him I wanted to travel to other planets and find new life forms?

I asked Madeline Wilson what she recalls from her years spent parked in front of the television. "*The Man from U.N.C.L.E.,*" she responded without hesitation. "That was my absolute favorite show. And *Lost in Space*—I identified with Will. Oh, and *That Girl*—except she was always hanging around with that ditzy boyfriend of hers." Other women I put the question to mentioned *My Three Sons, My Favorite Martian,* and *The Dick Van Dyke Show.*

Not that we don't remember shows with female leads or extant mothers or working women: Madeline watched *Family, Eight is Enough,* and *The Brady Bunch,* as I did, but together we could not recall Mrs. Brady's first name (Carol), what happened to Tom Bradford's wife that left him raising eight kids by himself (the actress died of cancer after five episodes and was written out of the script), and what, if anything, Kate Laurence did in *Family* outside of raising Nancy, Willie, and Buddy (no one seems to know or care). *Family Affair* also stumped us: What was bachelor Bill Davis doing with a male valet and three kids? (Answer: Trying to raise his orphaned niece and nephews.)

If female leads were secondary in the television we gravitated to—mothers dead or otherwise written out of the script, working women absent or secretarial, and young girls boy-crazed or marriage-fixated—then it would appear we had little choice, if we aspired to be leaders, but to identify with the male stars. Contrary to the current feminist thinking, we were not 'programmed' with the inadequate, stereotypical, bimbo-or-victim female images that did crop up on our screens, precisely because they weren't wonderful enough or likable enough to seize our youthful imagination. Certainly children are inclined to identify with their own sex, but only to the degree that they're made conscious of gender as a distinguishing trait: Prior to puberty, children recognize only the most obvious physical differences in themselves as girls and boys, unless they've been taught by sexist adults to discriminate prematurely on that basis.

Television's few leading women weren't marketed to us anyway, but rather to adult men whose tastes were apparently limited to sex symbols and women who were utterly chaste. Witness heroines such as Wonder Woman, who flew around saving the day in high-heeled boots and a satin merry-widow suit, her cartoonish bust threatening at any minute to spill over and distract Super Foes—and the Flying Nun, airborne only in full habit and wimple. Other women who were "special" were always special in one way, and that was in their ability to please their man: There were Charlie's Angels, pinup private eyes Sabrina, Jill, and Kelly, hired to do the instant bidding of their mysterious boss, and Major Tony Nelson's Jeannie, in harem pants and bustier, locked up in a bottle when she wasn't granting her "master's" wishes. Women who actually held a respectable job in a man's world got there by being either the blond broad—remember Jennifer Marlowe, the buxom secretary on *WKRP?*—or the sexless automaton (the Bionic Woman, after all, was half machine).

If we failed to aspire simply to the role of wife and mother, perhaps it was because we didn't like what television showed us of women who did. Partnerships offered up to us as "modern"— meaning the women were liberated—always ended in divorce or separation. Sonny and Cher split up; Marie split from her Mormon family, her brother, *and* her husband; Mary Tyler Moore's costar Rhoda dissolved her marriage to Joe nearly as quickly as she began it; cousin Maude was working on her fourth husband; and Mary, poor single wretch, was too liberated to attract any man in the first place. Women who did make it to marriage were rather helpless, resourceless souls. What else were we to have understood from characters such as Shirley Partridge, whose solution to widowhood and insolvency was to become her talented brood's bus driver? (She looked to a man to actually manage the rock-and-roll act.) What were we to have made of Carol Brady, who had Alice cooking and cleaning full time, except that Mrs. Brady was utterly overwhelmed by her new responsibilities as mother to six? And however we might have waxed toward the weird and self-possessed Morticia Addams, we couldn't possibly conclude she was good mother material—her kids, after all, were monsters.

Livvy Walton, strong and maternal as she was, consisted of pure nostalgia, a woman we couldn't look forward to becoming because she raised her seven children 40 years before the women's movement, divorce, and the sexual revolution forever altered our future. In fact, I can recall only two strong, attractive, self-actualized women in happy relationships on television in the late '60s and '70s—the era in which women were presumably breaking out of their chains and stereotypes. There was Agent 99, Maxwell Smart's intelligent and poised girlfriend (later wife) in the spy spoof *Get Smart,* and Samantha of *Bewitched,* Darrin

McGavin's sexy spouse, who had more than a few tricks up her sleeve to keep boss Tate happy, the neighbors from getting too nosy, and her warlock relatives under control. Ultimately, Samantha was even a mother, to Tabitha, who inherited the witch genes, and Adam, who took after his all-too-human father. Both shows were, interestingly enough, highly successful: *Get Smart* ran 138 episodes, from 1965 to 1970,[5] before going into syndication, and *Bewitched,* with 252 episodes, ranked as one of ABC's longest-running sitcoms before also going into syndication.[6]

Yet both of these women, likable as we may have found them, communicated to us a highly mixed message. Samantha was a witch: Evidently no mere mortal woman could expect to be a mother *and* wear the pants, as she did, or do the things she did or say the things she said and expect to get away with them. And if Agent 99 was so clever and accomplished, what was she doing as a nameless sidekick to a dimwit like Smart?

Twenty years later, we are still assaulted with TV shows in which women are either utterly absent or represented in such loathsome ways that we turn to cable or our VCR (also wastelands, for the most part, but we can at least be more selective). There are exceptions, of course: Murphy Brown and Roseanne Arnold are sassy working mothers who better reflect both who we are and who we might like to become, and their ratings would seem to indicate our approval for such ground-breaking characters. But for all the evil brainwashing we reputedly suffered and continue to suffer at the hands of the white males who programmed our sets, we have emerged, ironically enough, along the lines of that feminist ideal I described earlier: both tough and tender, aggressive and yielding, ambitious but grounded, "male" but unapologetically female too. We became astronauts (women, that is, with better math aptitude than I), artists, and entrepreneurs. We built enduring relationships based on mutual respect. And we became mothers—mothers who nurture, clean house, and cook meals, mothers who support their husbands, remember to buy birthday and wedding presents, and send out Christmas cards *in addition* to working outside the home.

That is, as much as the ideal man-woman can be realized, we're it. The only problem is in our attitude toward what we have accomplished: We're still hopelessly "female" in our lack of self-esteem. The inadequacy is not in who we are but how we see ourselves, because we continue to regard our split loyalties, our ambivalence, our male-female, yin-yang duality as manifestations of *imperfection*. We persist in concluding that we are not good enough because we are not flawless in performing the many roles we have perforce adopted. We expect more from ourselves, or we think others do.

What we want, now, is a different set of expectations. What we want, now, is to enjoy who we are and who we have become, to feel pride in our considerable accomplishments instead of anger or frustration about what we perceive as our shortfalls. We want to stop having to prove ourselves. We want to be good enough *just the way we are.*

Reevaluating Expectations

While I waited for the workplace to accommodate my "disability" (that's how maternity was classified by my employer: as a form of workers' compensation), for some government policy to compensate me for my loss, for my employer to level the playing field, and for the feminists to fix everything, my daughter Kathryn arrived—unplanned but welcome—barely 16 months after Chase. Kathryn was, thankfully, perfectly healthy, but unlike her brother cried for hours every day and evening for virtually four months. Attending to her left little time to dote on Chase exclusively, and he couldn't understand how his parents could so suddenly split their loyalties. And just when I thought the physical and emotional rigors of our days and nights couldn't get any worse, my husband lost his job.

It was not a time in my life I would care to repeat. And yet, despite Kathryn's colic, Chase's two-year-old temperament, and our financial worries, for the first time as a parent I was strangely at peace. I lived moment to moment, utterly clear on what I needed to do and what I could do. Attending to Kathryn took first priority, as none of us could think or function while she was crying. Chase got more of my attention than he had for months, simply because I involved him as much as possible in his sister's caretaking. And while I could not make the house a quiet and orderly haven for my husband, I could make sure I was a good listener, receptive to his thoughts and supportive of whatever actions he deemed necessary.

Virtually overnight I stopped thinking about the future, not only because I was so preoccupied with the present but also because I could no longer imagine, let alone control, what lay ahead. We were living in a rental, a house that was comfortable enough and in an overtly friendly neighborhood, but one that I had hoped to occupy only as long as it took us to find that 4BR dream house with FP and EIK on half an acre, close to schools, shopping, and transportation and within our budget. Indeed, whenever I used to despair at my permanently discolored kitchen linoleum and grapefruit-colored stair carpeting, I consoled myself thinking it was only temporary. When it became possibly permanent, I had to change my coping skills. So I focused instead on the freedoms our rental afforded us: We had no mortgage hanging over us, our landlord took care of all maintenance and appliance failures, and if the kids took the finish off the floors or drew on the walls, I didn't have to care.

And living in the present, tied 24 hours a day to two babies, proved remarkably liberating. I felt oddly free of my old angst, my former terror that I was letting slip some phenomenal opportunity to better my future; it was all I could do to tend to my immediate family. The housework, aside from the need to battle bacterial growth in the kitchen and bathroom, was ignored; relationships with friends and family were suspended; and free-lance projects were shelved for when I could more confidently leave Kathryn with a sitter. I couldn't worry myself about what other people thought of me or my dirty house or my stalled career.

The irony of the situation wasn't lost on me. Never had I fewer options open to me, and yet at last I knew just what I wanted to do and how to go about doing it. Circumstance beyond my control forced me to jettison all my idealistic notions of how motherhood *should* be and concentrate instead on how I could do my best given the boundaries imposed by time, money, and situation. Despite my limitations—or indeed, because of them—I was able, suddenly, to discern between goals that were important and those that just didn't warrant the sacrifices I'd have to make. It finally occurred to me that my future would be shaped by countless unforeseeable, unplanned, and possibly unfair events—as in fact it always had been—and my success would be based not on how well I resisted them but rather how well I accommodated them.

For the first time in my life, I felt absolutely free to do as I saw fit and make apologies to no one. Hounded always by the expectation of excellence on all fronts, I learned where and when excellence really mattered. And rather than hide my compromise as a weakness, I began to flaunt it as my strength.

But I'd be a colossal hypocrite if I were to insist that this credo of compromise—accepting what I could not change, changing what I could not accept—has made me over into a working-mother-at-peace. It hasn't, largely because 30 years of striving to be a good girl is hard to shrug off. I grope daily for a balance that affords me satisfaction; rarely do I manage to walk the high wire of working motherhood unswayed by maternal devotion or workaholic drive. I'm still an impatient perfectionist, eager to please, dependent on others' approval, and easily frustrated by people or events not going my way. My work and my children force me to live in the present moment, but when I'm not tending to my kids or tapping at my keyboard, I'm assailed by the "What if?" harpies. (*What if Ken were never to get another job?* I have wondered at 5 A.M. *What if one of my children were hit by a car and killed?* I ponder frantically when the house is quiet and they are playing with the sitter outside.) And if I'm not worrying about the future, I'm kicking myself for screwing up in the past. "If only . . ." whines the little voice, the insistent one perched on every perfectionist's shoulder. *If only I hadn't left the scissors within Chase's reach! If only I hadn't taken on that assignment!*

The immediate present, I've found, is a razor's edge, a difficult place to stand very long without teetering into an abyss of unmet expectations—either past moments never seized or future catastrophes never to be averted. Becoming a parent—becoming a working parent—burdens us so heavily with responsibility and stress that balance would appear well nigh impossible, and peace of mind hopeless. If those who claim to speak for us say we're living a lesser life, we're inclined to believe them. If those who champion us insist we're beleaguered and oppressed, we're inclined to agree. But it is child rearing and our work, ironically enough, that offer us salvation, because doing both jobs well demands we walk that razor's edge and not succumb to the "if only" and "what if" scenarios that so readily paralyze us from taking action in the present. It's our expectations, not our perceived shortcomings, that deny us the fulfillment we so desperately seek.

A Credo of Compromise

"Years ago I thought compromise was a dirty word, a word that described someone as a cop-out," notes Elizabeth Woodman, mother of two boys, six and eight years old, whom I mentioned in the previous chapter. "Now I think of it almost as a religion, something which keeps me spiritually and emotionally sane and healthy."

Parents, intimately acquainted as they are with limitations, are the archetypal compromisers—and not because their goals are any less lofty than those of the rest of society. Their essential contract with their children is inviolable. They're always held accountable for their actions, imperfect judgment notwithstanding. And they must behave responsibly, because their offspring invariably suffer the consequences if they don't. Only children are convinced they can, and should, have it all; the ability to make hard decisions and live by them is what distinguishes adults. Because they can't have it all, they must choose; in order to choose, they must prioritize; and in order to gain, they must sacrifice.

Yet one might hardly guess we were a society of parents, given our litigious outrage over failed expectations. Government must give us jobs while erasing the deficit, insure us against catastrophe but not charge us an arm and a leg for health care, do something about our crime-congested streets but stop handing out money to able-bodied indigents, and solve our child-care problems without taxing away the income we earn to support our families. Our legal system must protect our liberty to do and say what we please but also protect us against any injury we may sustain as a consequence of those words or actions.

We insist on having our cake and eating it too: We want to be free to make our choices—but we don't want to have to live with them, or pay for them, if we don't like the way things turn out. The papers are replete with stories of civil cases that ten years ago would have seemed too preposterous for the courts even to consider; today, they set legal precedent. A Princeton undergraduate is injured when he climbs atop an electrified campus train for a stunt and sues the university on the grounds he should have been protected from his own recklessness.[7] Parents of an AIDS victim sue their son's lover on the grounds he knew he was infected with the virus and didn't take proper precautions to prevent contagion.[8] A woman signs away her right to sue a moving company for damages and then sues anyway, arguing that she was too eager to let the weary movers go home to read the contract properly before signing.[9] With jury awards for personal injury hitting all-time highs of $127.7 million,[10] the incentive to disregard personal responsibility and let the courts decide who's to blame is nearly irresistible.

But as participants in this society, we will pay—literally, to the tune of $184 billion per year in "tort tax," according to one study[11] or, if not in measurable dollars, then ultimately in terms of individual freedom. Financially strapped colleges, for example, will reinstate in loco parentis policing of students, essentially treating them as children in need of constant supervision, limiting extracurricular activities or dispensing altogether with some that may prove too great a liability for the institution. Those who may be at risk for HIV aren't likely to get themselves tested, or say anything to anybody should they test positive, if such knowledge makes them liable to be sued. And contracts may as well not exist—making everybody vulnerable to the whims of others—if signing them fails to make them binding. These are restrictions to our freedom we should not tolerate. This is an authoritarian society in which we are governed, and treated, like children, denied choice because we cannot handle responsibility.

If, however, we were to acknowledge that our expectations of what life owes us may be unrealistic—if we were to admit that real, constructive change is not a matter of our courts being more efficient, our legislation more far-reaching, or our regulations better enforced—then we might begin to grant ourselves the privilege of real choice, however "compromised" our circumstances, however lacking we find the workplace, the child-care system, or our own husbands or families.

To be sure, as women we have been unfairly discriminated against, unfairly burdened; we are frequently victims of those whose power is contingent upon our subjugation. It's very difficult *not* to play the blame game, when so many of us have just cause. But we are, in the process, too frequently paying out precious self-esteem for what we perceive as just compensation. If we allow ourselves to be numbered among the addicts helpless to correct their addiction, the victims not to be blamed for their own victimization, the children not to be held accountable for their actions, then we cannot possibly hope to be given the responsibility to choose our own destiny. If we join hands as victims to gain political power, we can win recognition only as dependents.

If we feel victimized as mothers, then we must examine our expectations—expectations fostered by everyone from our non-working mothers to our career-bent single sisters, expectations fueled by everything from television and the movies to our political affiliation and our justice system, expectations that, more often than not, we cannot possibly hope to meet. We have looked to government, or the women's movement, or our husbands to compensate us for bearing children, for being competitively handicapped (who can we sue for this biological accident?), for being denied the full flowering of our potential. But if we see only limitation, vulnerability, and injustice in the privilege and miracle of motherhood, what salvation do we imagine possibly exists?

What Women Want

The women in this book understand that victimhood is a two-edged sword: If we insist that others recognize how we have been exploited, oppressed, and duped, we must perforce concede we're passive, weak, mute, and stupid; if we manage to win society's pity, we cannot hope to view ourselves with dignity. The women in forthcoming pages are not waiting, passively, for deliverance—for their children to grow up, for their employers to become flexible, for the workplace to be gender blind, or for men to change. However much the idealogues may damn them for their decisions—to stay home, to be workaholics, to select a "mommy track"—they are at least *making* them, consciously choosing the trade-offs these decisions may entail. However unacceptable the feminists may find their compromises, these women are striking them, meaning they have options and feel empowered enough, and confident enough, to choose among them. However bleakly activists paint their future, they're the ones who recognize they have to live there—and they're the ones doing something about it.

Contrary to the image the backlash perpetrators (television, the movies, the news media, and the fashion industry) project, most women ultimately seek compromise as a means, not an end: They're not *lowering* their expectations but simply weighing more carefully what they're willing to pay for what they want. Instead of harping on what they cannot change, they are focusing on actions they can and will take. Instead of seeing all options as equally vital to pursue, they're exercising real choice by prioritizing, by letting go those pursuits that serve only to gratify other people's unrealistic expectations. They don't eliminate roles they enjoy simply because they cannot perform them perfectly: Achievement, for them, *is* balance, attained not at unbearable cost but by making acceptable trade-offs. They expect it is not their societal due to "have it all" but rather their individual prerogative to choose what they want.

And what they want, above all, is peace of mind, a suspension of inner conflict and doubt. "I just want to stop having to prove myself," I heard over and over from the women I spoke with. "I'd just like to know I'm doing the right thing," was the other refrain. "Whatever I do, no matter how well I do it, it's never enough," most women agreed. They don't want life to be easy; they just want to feel like they are making it better. They don't want to be perfect; they just don't want to be expected to be.

What they want is to be *good enough*.

CHAPTER THREE

The Unadorned Truth About Full-Time Motherhood

L et me introduce you to my friend Gail Gallagher*, a full-time mother with three children ages four, three, and one. She and her husband, Phil, just moved into a six-bedroom home to accommodate their expanding family; Gail is already talking about number four, despite Phil's insistence that three is the limit. Seven days a week, 24 hours a day, she is on call for her children, although twice a week a sitter relieves her so that she can volunteer at a local hospital, whose fund-raising committee she chairs. What little leisure she has she's currently devoting to getting the new house fixed up—making curtains, buying furniture, replacing the bedding—but she looks forward, with her two older children in school part time, to pursuing some of the craft projects she enjoyed before the birth of her third child.

That mythical '50s mother—the one we keep insisting no longer exists—*does* exist, despite 25 years of feminine mystique–bashing, and Gail is her most recent incarnation. Husband Phil earns all the income; she is the devoted wife and mother, homemaker, and charity volunteer. Unlike Donna Reed or June Cleaver or even her own mother, however, Gail is not home because society expects her to be. On the contrary, she has consciously chosen a role increasingly *un*representative of women, one that her peers both envy and denounce. She acknowledges that her choice is an economic "privilege," given the fact that in most households today two incomes are a necessity. But marrying a man whose salary obviated the need for hers was not merely good fortune: Gail clearly envisioned her homemaking role and chose someone who could make her dream a reality.

And this is her dream. With four years of college and an M.B.A., she certainly isn't raising her family for lack of better career options. Nor does she stay at home, with two children 13 months apart and now a toddler to supervise, because it's any easier: Few would contest that caring for and playing with very young children day in and day out requires Herculean endurance and the patience of Job. Add to this the fact that Gail takes care of even traditionally male chores—from taking out the garbage to getting the car fixed—and one must conclude she does it all because she wants to, because she derives great satisfaction from her role, and because she firmly believes her full-time presence is, for her children, a benefit for which there is no substitute.

"If you're not there more than at the very beginning or very end of the day," explains Gail, "your kids are going to know their nanny better than they know you. Sure, once in a while you find somebody wonderful who really loves your kids, but I've seen plenty of nannies who sit there in the park, with the kid in the stroller, and they don't say a word. There's no interaction.

"I think it's awful. I think the kids suffer," she comments. "And I think we'll see it when they're adults."

The Mommy Wars

Admit it. Already you don't like her, and not just because she's got a husband who supports her and three beautiful children (because you just know they are) and matching towels in every bathroom. You find her contentment vexing because you know darn well how relentless and even boring caring for young children can be—and yet she seems to take it in stride. Or you find her choices threatening: Does nothing about the workplace entice her? Is she not compelled by centuries of hard-won opportunities for women to take advantage of any of those opportunities?

But most of all, you find that her moral superiority—her unassailable belief that a good mother is one who stays home—just makes you bristle. What does she know about your caregiver, or your child's needs? Never mind that you've already judged *her*: *How dare she condemn you (and your children) for your choices!*

Sensitive to the fact that you may be working because you have no choice, she wouldn't dare—except perhaps in the privacy of her own home, among her stay-at-home friends. Ask her and she will admit to harboring rather passionate convictions about mothering. But with her working friends (or friend—she has one who works) she typically "dances around the issue."

"We're very cautious about what we say because we don't want to insult each other," observes Gail, noting that her friend works because she *prefers* it to staying home. "So I say, 'I think it's good you recognize that it's better for you and the kids to be working, but I just wouldn't be comfortable.'"

Oh, to be so politic! But that's how we '90s moms are, ever smiling and publicly tolerant, despite the fact that we're locked in mortal combat over how we choose to raise our children. And we thirtysomethings do exercise choice, don't we? Our mothers had to stay home; we don't. Women ten years our senior had to uphold the feminist cause; we needn't. We may choose to have babies, or we may choose to remain childless careerists. We can have it any way we like. Right?

Okay, so maybe the majority of us have to work. So maybe now we're handcuffed to the vacuum cleaner *and* the briefcase. So maybe our entire life hangs by a thread, a thread our caregiver may cut at any given moment by not showing up, getting sick, getting deported, taking a better situation, or quitting on a whim. So maybe on some days there appears to be only the Right Choice and the Wrong Choice. And on those days, even though working may not have been our choice to make, women like Gail make us believe we chose wrong. Nobody has it all, we know; we've been told a thousand times. But Gail so embodies the Good Mother image most of us carry in our box of cherished fantasies that we wither in her presence, as though flashed with a silver cross.

What makes it even worse is the tendency of the Righteous to (publicly) harbor no hostility toward the Damned. Gail maintains she feels "almost sorry" for her working peers; she senses not hate from them but envy. And it's true, you don't *hate* her. Some days your hat's off to the full-time mothers for being able to endure the relentless routine and incessant policing seven days a week instead of two. But on other days, merely the image of this woman crafting a brontosaurus out of sugar paste and sheet cake for her two-year-old's birthday drives a stake through your heart. You dread running into her at the playground, fearful of engaging in one of those subtle games of one-upmanship over whose kid goes to bed without hassle or whose refrigerator contains more foods rich in beta-carotene. You can't help scrutinizing her for signs of superior mothering skills and hoping for evidence of deficient ones. Yet you're supposed to be above all this pettiness: The Mommy Wars, after all, are over. That sort of mutual intolerance was an '80s thing, an outgrowth of women's insecurity at embracing "new" roles while trying not to impinge on the old ones.

Certainly the press has covered it to death, the public has made it cocktail-party banter, and the political climate is one of tolerance, tolerance, tolerance (or you'll be sued). But the Mommy Wars continue to smolder like the Cold War before disarmament, and they are most certainly not a guilt-induced, paranoid figment of the working-mother imagination: Full-time mothers may insist they feel no guilt for staying home and not a trace of defensiveness for being 'only' a mother, but question them closely and you will find their politics anything but neutral. Kelly Courier*, who quit her job a year after her son was born so as not to miss out on another moment of his childhood, has, like Gail, one friend "who's into working." That would be okay, she says, if her friend were happy, but according to Kelly, working has put a lot of pressure on this woman's marriage, pushing the relationship almost to divorce, and has exerted an entirely negative influence on the woman's five-year-old son.

"I have so much compassion for her," says Kelly. "I almost feel sorry for her, although I don't like to put it like that: It's just that I know she's not happy. And now that she works full time, I can see the repercussions in her son. He's practically in kindergarten, and she's still sleeping with him to get him to go to sleep. She lets him get away with murder.

"I guess we're competitive, slightly," Kelly concedes. "In simple things, like my trying to get my two-year-old to share and her trying to get her five-year-old to share. I know she probably does envy me. My husband's in construction, so our house is bigger than hers, and she doesn't have a truly happy marriage; I know she's fighting to make it work, having the added pressure of her full-time job. We don't have a whole lot in common, as far as raising kids; we're bound to be different. But I need to be careful about what I say, because she's still one of my best friends. So I'll say something like, 'I remember letting Kenny get away with that . . .'—and I'm probably out of place throwing out these little jabs—but I can really see the difference between our children. Looking at her son next to mine, I think there's nothing more important than staying home."

Stay-at-home mothers, their numbers shrinking, their self-esteem constantly assaulted, their image slurred by a society that devalues a mother's role, are ever more fervently concerned that their offspring turn out better so they won't have to stoop to say "I told you so." Working mothers, their numbers imparting no solidarity, their self-esteem corroded by guilt, their image forever undermined by a society that continues to worship a feminine mystique, are praying *their* kids turn out functional so they can stop being defensive and apologetic and instead assert "See? I did do it all."

The Unadorned Truth

"A generation or two ago, mothers were home," notes Valerie Buickerood, a member of Mothers' Network, a support group for stay-at-home mothers. "Today, half of all mothers are in the work force and the other half of us feel we're being looked down upon."[1]

"Often our value is based on what we do," says Joy Bier, addressing her peers at MOMS (Moms Offering Moms Support), another support group. "Have you ever been at a party and someone asks you what you do, and although you love being at home, you wish you could say something like 'I just won the Nobel Prize'?"[2]

"My husband is a perfectionist, and occasionally he'll tell me, if some errand wasn't run or dinner's not ready, 'You're home all day. You should be able to do that,'" explains Kelly Courier, who quit her job against the wishes of her husband, who felt they couldn't afford it. "I feel myself boiling, thinking the whole time that if men stayed home, they'd see!"

"When my son brings in the newspaper from the driveway 'for Daddy,' he says, that sends a strong message home to me," comments Karen Cooke, who chose to be home with her two sons rather than work part time for her husband's business. "It says I'm not the one sitting down to find out what's going on in the world; I'm expected to be making dinner."

"Every day there's something that drives me off the wall," admits Trish Rachlin, who's expecting her third child, "and I can't stand being that way, I can't stand that point where I yell and scream and act like a maniac."

A shortage of patience, too much isolation, and too little appreciation, understanding, or support—these are the short-term costs of staying home. If the number of support networks mushrooming around the country in response is any indica-tion—groups such as FEMALE (Formerly Employed Mothers at the Leading Edge); MOMS; the National Association of Mothers' Centers, with its own hotline; Home by Choice; Mothers at Home, which publishes *Welcome Home* magazine; Mothers of Pre-Schoolers; and GEMS (Group to Encourage Moms)—electing to be Mom is tantamount to martyrdom. Ask any woman who chooses to work and she will apologize for lacking the saintlike qualities she perceives among women who devote themselves to full-time child rearing. It's hard work. There's no leisure. There's no letup, no backup, no escape. And the payoff can be years down the road, if ever. "The hardest part," says Mary Schnog, who has been home for almost four years, "is that you're not sure what the end result's going to be—if this all worked, if I did the right thing."

To be sure, if we were to focus solely on those serendipitous magical moments—first steps, first words, gleeful exchanges, mimicked expressions—that full-time mothers are privileged to witness, staying home would seem an undeniable luxury. Yet child rearing, on day-to-day examination, seems hardly the kind of job any woman would really covet. "If I were to be perfectly honest," confides an editor friend of mine, "when my daughter was very young and still sort of a lump, it was very easy to leave her. The office was kind of a refuge." Now this woman has tremendous difficulty leaving her two-year-old but has no doubt that caring for her daughter full time, if it were financially feasible, would be far more stressful than going to work. So why does someone like Gail, who admittedly struggles to get her husband to help out, who toils daily at so many tasks that will be undone moments later, who yells just as much and gets frustrated and exhausted just as much, and whose kids aren't even perfect—why does she bug us?

Because, for starters, she's so enviably clear about what she wants and what she's doing. (Remember the sense of instant loathing you felt upon seeing anybody wearing a button that said "I've Found It!"?) She has no doubt that working is incompatible with good parenting. "One of the problems I see with my sister-in-law and her husband, who both work," Gail confides, "is that their daughter, who's two, gets away with everything. When they get home at night, they're exhausted. They haven't had any time to themselves; they haven't had any time with their child. She's not having any limits set on her because they're too tired, and the little time they do have with her they don't want to ruin.

"Parents who aren't with their kids that much, they feel guilty, so when their child's giving them a hard time, it's just easier to give in," Gail says. "But that doesn't help in the long run."

Gail's confidence, compared to ours, is unshakable, because all those whom we annoint "experts" in child care *also* think she's doing the right thing by staying home. "You can tell a baby who's been responded to, who, when he cries, gets picked up and held instead of being left to scream," she notes, echoing the scientific establishment. "All the research that's been done indicates that the more children are responded to, the more optimistic they become as people and the more they have a positive impact on their environment."

And finally, Gail gets under our skin because she comes darn close to a real-life Perfect Mother, someone who, unlike our own mothers, we can't dismiss on the grounds that she's a throwback to an aberrant generation or in denial or somehow being smoked by a societal conspiracy. She doesn't feel she's sacrificing the best years of her life, but rather that she's living them. Most enviably of all, she appears to be incredibly untouched by true hardship, by having to make agonizing decisions, by having to give up anything of value. She has what we so desperately want: peace of mind.

What Fuels the Illusion

Rationally, of course, you know this to be a fallacy. But there's good reason why you cling to it, to the Apotheosis of Motherhood: the weight of scientific research, the opinion of countless child-care experts, and even the voices of the media declare the Good Mother formula as prescribed by Gail a panacea to our modern malaise.

As a pseudo-stay-at-home working mother and incorrigible fence-sitter, I make it a habit to track what academic circles are saying about my lifestyle choices, just in case they might suddenly offer information that will make up my mind for me. I'm always on the lookout for research "proving" that women who work are a) in the majority (because misery loves company); b) raising more, not fewer, Nobel Prize winners or Olympic medalists; and c) not handicapping their children emotionally, let alone screwing them up for life, because they need or want to work. Yet ingrained as I am with a formidable body of evidence from my own youth suggesting that staying at home is what makes for superior children, I'm just as sensitive to reports suggesting that surrogate care is harmful. My own kids now experience "nonmaternal" care 40 hours a week and have since my youngest was nine months old. On most days I feel confident we're all doing just fine. But then I pick up the newspaper and doubts are sown anew.

In 1986 a professor at Penn State by the name of Jay Belsky made quite a stink by asserting that the effects of extensive, early nonmaternal care resulted in "insecure attachments" and "heightened aggressiveness, noncompliance, and withdrawal in the preschool and early school years."[3] His study, based on how children behaved in the "strange situation" of being left first with a stranger and then entirely alone in a room, was but one of several, yet it attracted a good deal of press because he quantified what many of us feared or suspected. Mothers needed to care for their own offspring during the first year of life or their kids would turn out to be social time bombs.

Belsky has since attempted to clarify his conclusion, saying his research pointed up the need for better parental leave policy and job security, more part-time job opportunities for mothers of young children, and more affordable, high-quality care for infants and toddlers—but he holds to his theory that early, extensive day care is harmful to infants.[4] More recent studies seeking to amass all strange-situation data show "a significant association between the likelihood of insecure infant-mother attachment . . . and the experience of nonmaternal care," although the magnitude of the effect proved rather small: While 71 percent of children cared for exclusively by their mothers tended to be securely attached, *nearly as many* (65 percent) of the children whose mothers worked were also deemed to be securely attached.[5]

Methodological loopholes such as widely varying care experiences, homogeneous socioeconomic backgrounds, and the validity of the strange situation itself have given disbelievers plenty of ammunition, but the sheer volume of evidence seems to solidify the stay-at-homers' stance. Perhaps the federally funded study now under way, touted as the most comprehensive, in-depth study of young children to date, will provide more conclusive results come 1996, but I'm not holding my breath: Given the fact that no study will ever be able to take into account *every* variable in an issue as complex as child care, and given the degree to which we've politicized the whole issue of day care, it's bound to be hopelessly equivocal in its conclusions.

I've slowly come to realize that the child-rearing experts are also fundamentally allied with the full-time mothers. When it came to caring for newborns, Brazelton, Spock, Sears, Arlene Eisenberg, and Penelope Leach all won my undivided attention with their Mothering Manuals for Idiots. On issues such as whether to nurse, how to discipline, when to toilet train, and what to do about sibling rivalry, they were lifesavers. My standard present at all baby showers was a copy of Leach's *Your Baby and Child,* because in the middle of many nights and many crying jags it never failed me.

But their sympathies are decidedly lacking for mothers who graduate from infant care to a job that denies them ongoing bonding and breast-feeding opportunities. T. Berry Brazelton, the nation's child-care guru and author of *Working and Caring,* was quoted in *Esquire* as saying, "The only kind of really bad mother, the only kind who can harm her children's develop-ment, is not the mother who spends time away from her child, but the one who doesn't care about her baby."[6] But then in an interview with Bill Moyers he said a child's first year should really be spent "bonding" with his mother or he'll become a delin-quent, a social outcast—a terrorist, even.[7] So much for caring for workers.

Penelope Leach doesn't even try to walk the line. In her impassioned essay in *Parenting,* "Are We Shortchanging Our Kids?," she makes it wrenchingly clear that we as a society will pay a huge price for passing off our children to other caregivers. "The parenting journey . . . has already carried many mothers and fathers beyond doing what is best for their children and on to doing what seems least harmful," wrote Leach. "Not being able to see the negative results makes it dangerously easy for parents to assume there are none; to believe other people's assurances that a course of action in child rearing that feels uncomfortable is perfectly fine; and to follow that same course again with subsequent children." Even stay-at-home mothers blanched at their potential inadequacies: who hasn't wondered if maybe she couldn't be a more dedicated, insightful parent? Leach went on to conclude, "The plain truth is that most infants and toddlers would be better off if it were practically and economically possible for parents to do the bulk of the caring themselves."[8]

A friend of mine who had to return to work six weeks after her daughter was born confessed she sobbed after reading Leach's manifesto ("It is clearly best for newborns," writes Leach, "to have something close to full-time mother care for several months at least—conveniently linked with the period a baby is breast-feeding. . . ."[9]), "as if I had any real choice," she said. After all, we can forgive ourselves mistakes regarding our own destiny, but jeopardizing our children's future (particularly when we think we're securing it) is untenable. No mother could conceive of doing so consciously, and what Leach did was raise consciousness. More than that: She, the undisputed authority, had said in no uncertain terms that good mothers are mothers who stay at home.

And the media, presumably unbiased but historically sympathetic to working mothers (too sympathetic, says Leach), ultimately dispense "expert" opinion according to the current fad perceived among their readers. "You Can Go Home Again," *Child* magazine asserted in one of its headlines, citing as evidence of this going-home trend the fact that the percentage of women ages 20 to 44 in the labor force dropped from 74.5 percent to 74 percent[10]—a staggering half a percentage point! Never mind that most mothers with young children work and will continue to work: This is old news. When it comes to selling magazines, any statistic, however insubstantial, can be massaged to support the more provocative thesis.

Given this bedrock of societal support, is it any wonder Gail seems immune to the bouts of crushing doubt, paralyzing insecurity, excess guilt, or negative self-esteem that the rest of us suffer? Is it any wonder we accord her the moral high ground? Is it at all surprising we want what she has?

Gail, predictably enough, doesn't see herself as a perfect mother living anywhere near a perfect life. And while she feels rewarded, she doesn't feel she's getting off easy.

"Sure, you can have a career, you can have a happy marriage, and you can have kids," Gail concludes, "but not all at the same time. I want my daughter to have choices open to her, but I wouldn't want her to fool herself into thinking that she can have everything and do everything, because that's crazy; something's eventually going to break down. There are compromises."

Exploding the Myth

I went to high school with Gail. Back then, I would never have guessed her destiny to be that of committed wife and mother; I thought that was my destiny. My own mother and grandmother were stalwart proponents of the sequential-reward philosophy: that you can have everything, one thing at a time. Exclusively dedicated, as they were, to raising children, their expectations for their offspring were very high—and pretty clearly communicated. For daughters it was understood that the highest achievement, the only success that really counted, was Motherhood. It was a woman's raison d'être, it was the backbone supporting a host of inviolable family traditions, and it was the means by which each generation honored the sacrifices made on its behalf by the last.

Until my mother's older sister, Anne, came along, all the Whitaker women had embraced this responsibility and carried out their biological duty with puritanical dedication. Anne had four children and adopted two, but relocated at a tender age to the opposite coast and quickly established herself as a business-woman par excellence. Tales of her exploits, her money-making schemes, and her complete lack of maternal instinct colored our dinner conversation for most of my youth. Her character was often most damningly portrayed by her own tongue: Very matter-of-factly, she would describe how she conned a dying woman (Anne was, among other things, a registered nurse) into selling Anne her diamond ring for a fraction of its worth. She told these stories, no doubt, just to see her mother and her sister writhe in horror. We found her irresistible: It wasn't that she was immoral so much as amoral, a species rare and exotic in our rigorously sheltered environment.

Anne was the proverbial black sheep, the rebel who found her cause not to be mothering—at least not exclusively. The censure and criticism she endured would have withered my mother, Joan, who, only 15 months Anne's junior and educated as her twin, was forever trying to smooth the waters between sister and mother. In family movies, Joan is always attempting to get Sister to smile instead of smirk at the camera, to behave, to smooth down her dress and look presentable, or to stop fighting with her brother. Ever focused on motherhood, Joan graduated with a music degree from Mount Holyoke in 1949, eager to get married and get on with the real business of her life. After a few health setbacks, she had her first child in 1956, at perhaps the apex of America's infatuation with total domesticity. Indeed, my mother was nearly solely responsible for the Baby Boom, with ten preg-nancies in 11 years. She embraced child rearing and homemaking with the zeal of a crusader, and she excelled at both.

To be sure, Joan didn't have six children solely to compensate for her sister's deviance or to court her mother's approval; she really wanted a big family, long before the feminine mystique ensured its popularity. In tenth grade, she told me, she was fantasizing about having babies of her own to care for, and to this day she is fond of reminding us we are her most rewarding accomplishment. We grew up, however, sharing a driveway and several acres with her parents, who figured daily in our lives and, of course, in hers. Though they now live a mile away, such chronic parental scrutiny may in part explain why my mother continues to be driven to heroic levels of achievement.

It wasn't enough to birth, nurse, nurture, and guide us through the shoals of adolescence, even while she herself endured paralysis in both legs after back surgery when her youngest was still in diapers. She literally made our home, braiding some 20 rugs, piecing nearly 30 quilts, knitting upwards of 200 sweaters (by her own conservative estimate), and tending, seasonally, to about 200 houseplants and an acre of garden. When my youngest brother was in school, she wrote a book about how to grow herbs and salad greens indoors that ultimately sold nearly 100,000 copies—an achievement she dismisses by pointing out that the book was a hit among college students growing marijuana in their dorm rooms.

The book yielded her a consistent guest spot on local television and radio shows, and she abetted sales by lecturing and teaching horticulture. Those classes, sellouts for nearly 20 years, currently furnish a roster of clients for her burgeoning landscape architecture business—a business she's been building while pursuing her degree at Temple University. For five years she's been laboring feverishly at her drafting board, learning how to draw on a computer, gutting out required curricula in engineering, physics, and chemistry, teaching horticulture once a week, playing mini piano recitals at her parents' retirement community, organizing her garden club, and being, still, the good homemaker and wife to my father.

My brothers and I are immensely proud of her. Yet our attempts to remind her of what she's accomplished, to acknowledge her many talents and shower her with praise, fall somewhat upon deaf ears. (She is legendary for declaring, not minutes after someone has complimented her on her cooking, "I've overcooked the beef.") Our appreciation is never enough to assuage her doubts about whether she is good enough. My mother, at 66, is still trying to live up to the expectations of others—primarily those, not coincidentally, of *her* mother. Never mind that the world perceives Joan in a superhuman light: So long as her mother withholds final approval, she cannot ever rest satisfied that she did the job and did it well.

Textbook, isn't it? The proud legacy of full-time motherhood also frequently happens to be a legacy of low self-esteem, a condition not easily corrected, even if you grow up to be Gloria Steinem (who is still rectifying her poor self-image). Perhaps my grandmother, yanked out of college by marriage and saddled as a very young woman with three children, did not always grin while bearing her responsibilities. Motherhood was expected of women of her generation, taken for granted as the sum of a woman's self-worth. An athletic woman with a passion for nature, art, and literature, perhaps she chafed—then—at being so narrowly defined. Years later, how could she not envy my mother, living a life seemingly richer in possibilities and studded with accomplishments? With her own child-rearing days past, she could no longer compete. Perhaps, having felt at one time responsible for and in control of her children's future, she could not accept the role of powerless bystander. Perhaps unconsciously she adopted her own mother's unyielding stance: She could not relinquish authority; she would not. Hence to this day she holds my mother hostage by communicating only the martyr-dom of her own insatiable expectations.

My mother maintains that no one can appreciate the constric-tion of this tie to her mother. What everyone sees instead is the grandmother I know, the enthusiastic and ebullient matriarch who is enormously proud of her 18 grandchildren and 23 great-grandchildren, the mother who is profoundly grateful that her focus in life was her family. She was my constant companion when I was growing up, a woman whose interests became my own, a grandmother who nurtured my proclivities and rejoiced in whatever I did, bubbling with praise and encouragement. Yet even as a little girl, I was struck by her constant self-deprecation. Exceedingly knowledgeable as she was about antiques, she never answered a question about a museum exhibit or piece of furni-ture without prefacing her comment with a disclaimer like "I'm such a stupe—my friend Chris Batdorf could tell you so much more. . . ." We never played a game together without her profess-ing her "stupidity." She never broached a discussion about an article in *Smithsonian* or *The Atlantic Monthly* without reflexively denigrating her comprehension of it. Self-effacement was more than an expression of modesty; it was a pathology.

So I begin to understand why my mother's radar is so sensitive to criticism. She still treads the well-worn ruts of her youth, when her impression of her mother was of a woman hard to please, frequently negative, and rarely satisfied with anyone—least of all herself.

Come the Empty Nest

Gail, certainly, is by no means laboring to fulfill her mother's expectations; I've no doubt she's exceeded them. Nor is she struggling to define herself as "more than just a mother," because she chose this definition, narrow though it might be, over others. The rewards, fortunately, of full-time motherhood are immediate and apparent to Gail, not contingent on her kids turning out to be more successful than her neighbors', not marred by an unspoken competition with her mother or anybody else.

But there are trade-offs to being a mother exclusive of other roles, trade-offs Gail may well have in common with generations of mothers in my family. Nothing so vicious, say, as having children who become drug addicts or high school dropouts; nothing so inevitable as divorce or financial ruin or a nervous breakdown. (Nothing so calamitous as what working mothers in their weakest, most vindictive moments have wished might befall their detractors.) No: The occupational hazard of doing anything so devotedly is being unable to stop doing it, as one's identity has come to be utterly defined by it. Being able to indulge in the pursuit of one role over all others means achieving a level of mastery so close to perfection that it becomes impossible to believe persistence won't pay off. Total mastery is not only possible, it's *obligatory*.

Gail fears that she won't be able to let go of her children. Like her mother before her, she is the end-all, be-all, omniscient caretaker and provider for her husband and children. She jokes that if she were to die no one else would marry Phil because she has made him so entirely dependent on her, from scheduling his social life and ironing his golf shirts to anticipating, interpreting, and answering his children's physical and emotional needs. "My family is so dependent on me," Gail muses, "that when I'm dependent on them, emotionally, can I say goodbye and let them lead their own lives?

"That's my biggest concern," she continues. "If I were working, I wouldn't be quite so dependent on their feedback. I'd have something else to fulfill me. I know my mom is still searching for that. For her, right now, this empty-nest period is the most difficult, far more difficult than when we were little. She's having a really hard time making the transition. I know if we were to move to California she would be heartbroken. I hope that I'll be able to let my kids go and do their own thing and not make them feel guilty."

Big deal, you say. Menopause and an empty house are a long way off; what haunts working women are fears about tomorrow, not that day 20 or 30 years down the road. Except that what Gail's really talking about is losing control over who she is by dint of losing control over her children—allowing them to individuate. Control is an issue with which we're all intimately familiar, something we all grapple with every day, whether we're working or not, because everyone looks to us to impose control. It's absolutely essential to making our lives work. Yet we hardly resist the responsibility; if anything, we fantasize about having total control, about having our lives run like a Swiss watch. If we were to have more control, we would have less disappointment. If we were to have more control, we would be less disappointing to others. We would be cherished; we would be heroic. And finally, we might be really happy with ourselves.

As parents, however, our ultimate responsibility is to let go, to have done our job well enough that our children won't need us. Thus, letting go of our role as nurturer, if indeed that's our primary role, means opening up a vacuum of purpose in our life, not to mention triggering an identity crisis. That black hole, for Gail, appears to be 18 years distant. But in fact the dependency that today, with very young children, she looks forward to shrugging off, she will be fighting to retain tomorrow. As our mothers continually remind us, children grow up awfully fast.

Enlightened Despots

Ask Linda Miller, a former nurse with a nine-year-old daughter and a six-year-old son. Linda claims she's no control freak, and yet she daily despairs at the erosion of her influence on her children. She frequently finds herself "nearly exploding with anger" because she's being "tuned out"—whereas her husband, upon making the slightest request of his children, commands immediate attention and response.

"Where, when, did I lose this power over the kids?" she muses. "It annoys me and angers me, being taken for granted: 'Mom will pick it up. Mom will do it.' Mom's part of the scenery, part of the woodwork. That's the major trade-off [of staying home]— the lack of appreciation and respect."

Linda jokes that she's somewhat accustomed to being underappreciated, as her profession before full-time child rearing was nursing—a job looked down upon by her feminist peers as "a woman's profession," one "not tinged with much power." But she has been happy in both "thankless" roles, largely because she derives a sense of accomplishment from being able to juggle four or five balls at the same time. Problem is, should one ball fall to the ground, she feels like a failure. Trying to keep all the balls in the air, she admits, qualifies her as a supermom contestant. She feels she has to take care of the house, run her kids wherever they need to go, and still be able to respond to her husband at ten o'clock at night in order to prove, mostly to herself, that she's doing enough, that she's worth supporting financially, that she is no slouch for not bringing home a paycheck.

"How my family perceives me is very important," she admits. "I don't get crazy about it, but now that my son's in school, which he finds hard, he comes home and asks me what I did today. 'Did you work very hard?' he wants to know.

"Now that my daughter's older, I realize my kids think I've been lobotomized," Linda continues. "She had a homework question she asked me, and I gave her an answer, and then I heard her ask her father the same question—and he gave her the same answer. Being at home, I'm oversensitive, perhaps, but my kids' criticism does jab at my self-worth. Criticism from my husband is even more devastating, because I've always been fearful of not being taken seriously intellectually. And the longer I stay at home, the more I fear he thinks my brain has gone to mush."

Lack of appreciation and eroding self-esteem are two factors contributing to Linda's decision to go back to work part time. Not that nursing is full of pats on the back either, but for Linda it was a job she did well and a social interaction she misses. Yet she hesitates. She needs a refresher course, she says, and that won't start until next spring. Also, she feels she's playing a key role in her son's adjustment to first grade, although she admits that staying home is probably making it harder, not easier, for him to break the apron strings. (Her daughter, during whose toddlerhood Linda still worked, had no trouble adjusting to school, Linda notes.) And her daughter is getting to the age where she's discovering just how hard it is to say no, how difficult it is not to cave in to peer pressure. Linda feels it's terribly important that she be on hand for discussion, to keep an open dialogue. Recently her daughter rode her bicycle along a stretch of road Linda has repeatedly warned her not to travel and then went swimming, unsupervised, with her friend—whose mother thought it was okay.

"She was lucky," says Linda. "I've asked her to just call me in the future, put the decision on me, tell her friend she has a crazy mother. But the incident also made me realize I can't control everything."

Linda admits that she "often feels the urge to put [her kids] in a bubble" to protect them from all that would threaten their well-being. Herself the product of a changing neighborhood in Chicago, she made a conscious decision to raise her family where there wouldn't be the crime or hassles associated with living in a big city. Yet because she also fears her children growing up with prejudices, she volunteers at a soup kitchen and takes her daughter there with her in order to teach her that "people are people, whatever their color, religion, or thoughts."

"I'm trying to give our children a not-too-skewed view of the world," she says, "but I realize they're country kids; I'd be very uncomfortable taking them to Washington, D.C. I don't want neurotic kids, but I do want to control their exposure."

Linda acknowledges the importance of letting children make mistakes, or make decisions that may result in mistakes, as they get older. She realizes she didn't always make the right decisions, that some had the potential to hurt her, and that in some ways, allowing her children to be hurt emotionally would be doing them a favor. On the one hand, she resists letting go because she fears the consequences of error in today's world may be far more damaging and permanent, even life-threatening, than when she was growing up. On the other hand, she's willing to concede that every parent in every generation suffers the same paranoia.

"My mother was very wise in knowing how to let go when she needed to," she recalls, "and it must have been very difficult, because I was an only child and born late in life. Yet as I get older I realize, in not doing things for me, how much she did for me. I hope I'll be able to let my children learn. I do try to control them, to regulate their lives and their exposure to alternative lifestyles. I guess I try and control them more than I care to admit."

The Fight for Independence

That's the hard part about being a mother. You're expected to be omniscient and prescient when presented with a totally helpless newborn; through the toddler and preschool years, your vigilance must be unflagging. By the time you've gotten really good at it, having won the bedtime and toilet-training battles and having met all the logistical challenges posed by taking the kids on vacation, having dinner parties in their company, and shopping with them in tow, it's time to surrender.

Ideally our children will wean us from our habit of making decisions for them, but we're more than aware that we made our own parents go cold turkey—by not soliciting, for example, so much as their opinion when it came to decisions like where (or whether) we'd go to college, whom we'd marry, and what we intended to do with the rest of our lives. It's not an easy evolution for any parent, of any generation. We're damned if we do—control our kids, that is—and damned if we don't.

But while being a mother is admittedly a lifelong preoccupation, it cannot, should not, must not be a lifelong occupation, if indeed we can all agree that the only real measure of our "success" as mothers is the extent to which our children can stand on their own, physically and emotionally. Our ultimate charge as parents is to prepare our children for independence. So for the mother who has opted to stay home, the question remains: Having perfected her role as caretaker, can she abdicate control to less practiced individuals? Having put all her identity eggs in one basket, can she hand over the basket freely? Having put aside her own ambitions, can she resist imposing them on her children? And having set one example, can she teach another?

Becky Piper, who's been a full-time mother of two girls for six years, is of a mind that where her own example is lacking, she can create one; where her own ambitions have been thwarted, she can teach her daughters to believe they can achieve anything. At 35, Becky reports that she's undergoing something of a midlife crisis, or "reevaluation," because it's clear to her that in electing to stay home she has traded in her opportunity for a successful career. Not that she can't get a job in her field, but she's anticipating "having trouble getting my foot in the door," having lost her contacts and the requisite competitive edge. Indeed, when she left her part-time job she had only just earned her master's degree—had never really started her career.

"Not that having children and staying home to raise them is a total strike against me," says Becky, "but an employer's a professional first and will likely choose someone who's been working for a while." Accepting an entry-level position when her working peers have long since ascended the ladder would be a somewhat bitter pill for Becky, who since childhood has been accustomed to excelling. "Nothing I do is half-assed," she says, "and when it is, it stresses me out."

Becky says she chose to drop out, chose not to add the stress and struggle of building a career onto raising a family. But circumstances certainly helped cement that decision. Her father, who with no sons pushed her and her sister to achieve, suddenly changed his tune when she got married, insisting that she allow her husband's career to come first. Her husband, a radiologist, did earn more than enough to support her and the kids. And while she had every intention of keeping her hand in, when she found herself pregnant with number two, the family relocated to Pennsylvania. "Who was going to hire someone who was obviously pregnant?" she reasoned.

But the price she's paid, says Becky, is that people tend to judge her stereotypically, by what her "rich doctor" husband does or what stay-at-home wives traditionally do. Total strangers—such as a workman who innocently asks if her decision is final or will she be deferring to her husband—press her hot button when they assume that, because she's home, she must be a subordinate housewife. Her professional peers perceive her as "not being intelligent, wasting away home with the kids." Even her husband, she says, occasionally "regresses" and looks at her as "a robot with a perfect house and children" instead of his equal.

"It makes me mad as hell, because I manage everything and make all the decisions," says Becky. "It's a conscious choice we made, my husband and I, that I wear the pants in the family; he benefits. I do the checkbooks, I run it all, and he turns it over to me. He's not a control person, and I am.

"But I also have to deal with things that smack of being the very traditional wife, and every time I get pushed into that role I feel diminished, and I get resentful. It's the biggest self-esteem lowerer."

To ensure that her family and friends would perceive her in a "multidimensional" way, Becky began to spend her spare time volunteering. In that environment she quickly found people looking to her for answers, reassuring her that she still had plenty of skills to offer, not backing her "into that corner where I feel I have to blurt out I have a master's degree and go down the whole line of accomplishments." By and large Becky feels she has purged the insecurity demons that at first plagued her. She no longer suffers, she says, from low self-esteem. "In some ways the most stressful job has been staying home, balancing the whole act, being the best mother, the best wife, the best multidimensional person," she explains. "Subconsciously I must really appreciate being at home or I wouldn't have stayed."

Quite consciously, however, she's haunted by the goals and desires she felt so passionately as a graduate student. "I still think about that young woman," Becky concedes. "When I'm an old woman, will I still be thinking about her? How realistic her goals were, I'll never know. How much regret I'll have—that will be the big question mark. If the kids turn out well, that question mark will fade. If they turn out to be worthless people, I'm sure I will question things in neon letters. I hate when people measure their self-worth by how their children turn out, but if that's what you stayed home to do, then you can't ignore that."

So Becky is making a concerted effort to impress upon her daughters that the sky's the limit. She's made a point of taking them to female doctors, exposing them to friends who are female professionals—trying to counter their impression that their dad is the only one who can achieve. At the same time, she finds she has to remind her daughters (and, on occasion, her husband) that she, too, has achieved, that she, too, is intelligent. She finds herself needing to adjust her older daughter's expectations, pointing out that the comfortable lifestyle she enjoys must be earned, that she must go to college and work hard if she wants to maintain a similar standard of living. Her daughters, Becky explains, are used to having things, and she doesn't want them to think it all comes easily—via marriage, for example. "I've worked very hard for what I have," she insists, "and I won't apologize for it. My husband tells the girls we both work, and that the money is ours, not his."

Whatever their perceptions of her, however her kids turn out, "I'm comfortable with who I am and what I do," Becky reiterates. "I'll know in my heart I did everything everyone else did; I gave my children every opportunity. I can't say I've done anything wrong, because I've done things according to what I thought my parents did right."

Indeed, Becky's daughters are growing up much as she and her sister did, with "horses and things other kids didn't have and a dad who plays with them and loves them." But in one respect Becky hopes she has deviated from her parents' example.

"We had to be perfect children," she explains. "We could not misbehave; our dad used to spank us to a degree that bordered on abuse. Our spirit was broken. I've gained a lot of self-determination and learned to be an independent person, and my daughter's like that. But I must be careful to guide her to use her energy in a constructive way and not beat her down."

The Legacy We Leave Our Children

The shape our children assume as adults is molded both by the genes they inherit and the environment we provide. The jury is still out on whether nature or nurture prevails in terms of influence, but certainly we like to think that, as parents, we're doing everything humanly possible to enhance, or mitigate, the chromosomal factor. How best to play our role then? Are we most effective when we teach passively, by our example, or actively, by inculcating a set of values we consider ideal, selecting exposures we consider instructive, and ardently screening out influences we fear might be destructive?

David Elkind, author of *The Hurried Child: Growing Up Too Fast Too Soon,* outlines four schools of thought on how parents socialize their children. One theory is "modeling," wherein adults can expect their children to be law-abiding, hardworking, honest citizens if they themselves are; another, advocated by behaviorist B. F. Skinner, is "behavior modification," wherein parents mold a child to conform by imposing a system of rewards and punishments. "Social cognition," espoused by Swiss philosopher and psychologist Jean Piaget, holds that rules parents impose are most likely to be heeded when they are adapted to the child's level of understanding. And finally, there is Freud's "identification and internalization," the process by which a child incorporates the values and beliefs of a parent only to the extent that he or she identifies, emotionally, with that parent.[11] Of these four theories, two hold a parent more or less responsible by example; the other two imply that parents play a far more active, deliberate role in fashioning the end product.

Not terribly surprisingly, mothers who elect to stay home with their kids to the exclusion of other caregivers tend to favor the more proactive approach, modifying behavior and setting rules. Conscious of how much children learn merely by observing adults, these mothers try to control this passive imprinting process by limiting their children's exposure. Mary Schnog keeps her kids' universe to herself and their father, leery of what nonfamily sitters might pass on, however unconsciously. "If it weren't me, it'd be somebody else they'd be mimicking," she explains.

Indeed, every full-time mother I interviewed reiterated that she was glad to be home not so much because day care was evil but because she wanted to control the imprinting process, to be both passive example and active teacher. These women felt strongly about the primacy of their own values, their own memories, and their answers to questions others might answer differently. "I want my child to have the benefit of my background," says Carey Furillo*, "as opposed to that of some other caregiver to whom this is a four-dollar-an-hour job. If my son were to ask where clouds came from, I don't know what some caregiver's going to tell him. I'd say God made the clouds, but maybe that caregiver doesn't believe in God so she wouldn't say that. And that's a very important difference to me."

Undeniably, during the early years, when exposure to outsiders is limited, a parent has the option to mold, rather than merely guide, her offspring—an option Elkind would support. The bottom line on good parenting, he maintains, is that children should be permitted to grow at their own pace to be their own person and not the extension, or surrogate, of the parent. Because helping a child achieve that independence demands, argues Elkind, a constant monitoring of his or her intellectual, social, and emotional development in order to gauge what freedoms are appropriate to the exercise of responsibility, all too many harried, distracted, and overworked parents choose to short-circuit the process in order to make life easier on themselves. Poor parenting "hurries" children into adult roles with adult responsibilities before they're ready to accept those responsibilities. If parents award freedom regardless of whether their children have demonstrated an ability to handle it, children never learn to see a clear link between responsible behavior and adult privileges.[12]

A tall order for any parent: to be sensitive enough to a child's development to neither expect too much nor too little, to neither discourage independence nor grant too much of it too soon. Among parents who are too distracted and too stressed, with too little time to treat their child as anything more than a stereotype of known characteristics—working parents, typically—Elkind notes a particularly disturbing tendency to ask too much of the child in demanding that he conform to adult schedules or adopt adult responsibilities. But he also points out that nonworking parents are just as capable of "hurrying" their children, insensitive to their offspring's developing identity because they are preoccupied with their own unfulfilled ambitions.[13]

The effect, perversely, of hurrying these children to be more successful versions of their parents is to prevent them from ever really growing up, from ever being independent of their parents' expectations. Authoritarian parents may withhold support for certain activities, or friendships, or course selection in school in order to extort achievement in areas of their own choosing. "Achievement overload" often occurs, notes Elkind, "when young people assume that parents are concerned only with how well they do, rather than with who they are." Children who sense that achievement is for the parent, instead of for themselves, either "eventually give up or go into achievement overload to assure continuation of parental support."[14]

Elkind postulates that full-time mothers, denied the attention and respect they feel to be their due, may be inclined to manipulate rather than monitor their children to ensure an outcome that will bring them, vicariously, that attention and respect.[15] Ironically, it is these mothers' refusal to abdicate responsibility, to allow their children to live their own lives free of a chronic sense of debt or guilt or expectation, that makes them guilty of the insensitivity characteristic of "negligent" parents.

Can the Ringmaster Retire?

Not that all full-time mothers fail to perceive their self-worth and must perforce exploit their children for it. Yet the problem of invisibility, the incredible deficit of self-esteem that full-time mothers describe, seems to come with the territory. Day in and day out, the feedback from their spouse and kids suggests they are part of the woodwork, with no intelligence to illuminate a homework question or share any insights on politics. The more they're taken for granted, the more balls they incorporate into their act in hopes of garnering attention. When no one recognizes or applauds their amazing juggling act, they perforce derive their sense of self-worth from being ringmaster—someone not necessarily talented but indisputably in charge.

Mothering hence devolves into an all-out campaign to "run the show," to manipulate external influences—influences, by definition, out of one's control. Becky Piper cannot control what people think of her; Linda Miller cannot control what fates befall her children. Who we are, what we make of our lives, what example we make of ourselves—this is the only outcome over which we have a modicum of control, despite the illusion (a life-sustaining one for many stay-at-home mothers) that the home and all its occupants comprise a universe in which Mom is God.

Consider the legacy of our parents—what we remember fondly and wish to pass on to our offspring. I'd wager it is not what our parents "taught" us but how they conducted their lives, not what they "made" us into but what they made of themselves. We don't thank them for having tried to screen us from objectionable exposures or for choosing our course of action for us; on the contrary, Linda Miller attributes her sensitivity toward others to having grown up as one of the only Caucasians in an urban neighborhood (an experience, interestingly, she doesn't trust to have the same effect on her children), and she's grateful to her mother for allowing her to get emotionally hurt when she was still young enough to bounce back and learn from the encounter.

Nor do we thank our parents for trying to make us perfect:

Becky Piper is determined to avoid repeating this aspect of her own upbringing, fearing she will reflexively quash her daughter's spirit in trying to mold it to her own notions of achievement.

Ultimately, in fact, the degree to which we appreciate our parents is the degree to which they have let go of us and their expectations for us. If there is a price to pay for the privilege of spending the early years of child rearing in the driver's seat, it is our reluctance, our inability, to tolerate being demoted to the backseat. Spurred by our success in programming our children during the preschool years, we may find it difficult to forgo in later stages the level of control that once afforded us so much satisfaction.

Nor will our families tolerate our slacking off: For full-time mothers such as Gail and Linda and Becky, the years spent tending to every need and fixing every problem engender, they admit, not gratitude but expectation, not independence but a false sense of security. "Mom will always be there," sighs Linda. And indeed she must if she is to have any sense of her own value. Should she fail to protect her kids from the consequences of their own immature judgment, she can only conclude she has failed as a mother. Gail says Phil is quite appreciative of all she does, saying, time and again, "I don't know how you do it"—but she doesn't leave him alone with her three children for more than a couple of hours because she's convinced he would flounder and she would be a failure, in his eyes and her own, for not having made it easier for him. Becky is pleased to report that her husband "likes the way I handle things" but is depressed to think that "if anything happened to me, he couldn't step in and take over." He's so dependent, she adds, "it frightens me." An all-too-familiar observation.

And yet there is no obvious way out of the vicious cycle of control breeding the need for more control, near-perfection breeding the drive to reach for even greater heights. Says Karen Cooke, "We all suffer from PMS—Perfect Mother Syndrome."

The Handwriting on the Wall

My mother has in her bedroom a counted-cross-stitch aphorism no doubt familiar to every mother of her generation: "There are two lasting gifts we can give our children: One is roots, the other, wings." As students of the feminist movement, having wings was the goal my peers and I were schooled to value most, but as mothers, we fear the family-values backlash of denying our children roots. Imprinted with both feminist and antifeminist values, we can't decide whether to postpone our identity crisis—and risk disappointing or alienating those whose approbration we live for—or have that crisis now, in front of the children, and hope everybody emerges more self-determinate for it. We'd like desperately to liberate ourselves from unfulfillable expectations—those that we feel are imposed by society, by other women, by our mothers and possibly spouses, and by our own fantasies—if only to ensure that we don't saddle our kids with the same desperate need to please.

No one, of course, knows which is the better course: not Gail, not Penelope Leach, not the National Institute for Child Health and Human Development, not even our mothers, despite their insistence that we turned out so well precisely because they stayed home. How easy, how wonderful, if indeed there were one infallible set of rules for us to follow! We would never know the horror of having our children denounce us as abusive parents before a television audience of millions. We would never suffer knowing we fueled our child's ten-year dialogue with a psychotherapist. We would never waste another day examining our choices for poor judgment or a life-threatening lack of foresight. How perversely liberating to have but one option!

But instead we must acknowledge that there are many options, many ways to rear our children, either because we don't have the privilege of copying our mothers or because we have chosen to nurture, through working, our own potential. And no authority—church, state, parent, or pediatrician—can offer us the kind of insider information that might guarantee our particular investment strategy will garner the returns we anticipate. We alone can examine the balance sheet and determine which assets incur liabilities we can live with. Motherhood in all its guises and permutations is more art than science, however eagerly we look to science to quantify the trade-offs. The art is in choosing those trade-offs that, as Gail acknowledges, we're ultimately comfortable making, regardless of payout. If staying home full time were an option, would we take it? If we were to adjust our fantasies for reality, temper our memories of our own mothers with more honesty, and weigh the day-to-day costs against the rewards we imagine, would we happily carve for ourselves a more traditional role?

For my friend Gail, the importance of giving one's children roots necessitates clipping one's own wings—a cost she can live with, but clearly not one celebrated by her feminist peers, despite their insistence that each of us choose as we see fit. For the rest of us, giving our children wings would seem to necessitate keeping our own, the better to show them how to fly. But are we ready to acknowledge the cost—to our children, our husbands, and our peace of mind—of asserting our independence?

CHAPTER FOUR

The Trade-Offs of Reaching the Top

"BAG THE GUILT," ran the headline in *The Wall Street Journal* about a study showing that working and nonworking mothers devoted about the same amount of time to performing such parental duties as bathing, dressing, feeding, and helping with homework. "Married mothers spend about 10,500 hours on 'primary' child-care activities when raising two children through age 18, whether they are employed or not," summarized the *Journal*.[1]

On first inspection, a stunning finding, given the almost universal perception that stay-at-home mothers dote on their children all day long. The study's authors, Keith Bryant of Cornell University and Cathleen Zick of the University of Utah, wanted to see just how much time parents spent actually assisting their children in light of research showing a direct correlation between the amount of attention given to children and their developmental and educational outcome. Citing Sylvia Ann Hewlett's proclamation that today's middle-class offspring may be increasingly "at risk" because of an employment-induced "parental time deficit," Bryant and Zick amassed statistics dating back to the 1920s to compare not only hours working and nonworking mothers spent in child care but also hours present and past generations spent.

The raw data offer some rather surprising insights. During the years 1924 to 1931, child care amounted, on average, to .85 hours per day; in 1981, the figure improved slightly, to .87 hours, whether mothers were employed or not (estimates were weighted for variables such as family size and education and represent the *average* of hours allotted to child rearing per day over an 18-year period). In other words, directly tending to a child occupied less than an hour a day—clearly more than that during the preschool years, much less during adolescence. Married employed women spent fewer hours caring for their children than their stay-at-home counterparts while the children were very young (3,161 vs. 5,037 hours for the first three years), but more than compensated in the later years so that by the time their kids were 18, they had actually put 101 *more* hours into child rearing than full-time moms. Moreover, the study found that "husbands of employed women spend more time in direct family care than the husbands of stay-at-home wives"—about 430 more hours over the first three years of the child's life. Other caregivers' contributions were not measured.[2]

Zick and Bryant concluded that, despite alarms sounded by child-care experts that modern families have failed their children, "the facts with respect to the time parents spend on direct child care do not square with these allegations."[3] They also noted that while families are accused of relinquishing their responsibility for their children to the schools, "the data seem to indicate that married women, even after accounting for their employment, spend more direct time than they did fifty years ago caring for school-aged children."[4]

Quality, Not Quantity

But before all working mothers stand up and rejoice, vindicated at long last by the academic establishment, let us ask: Is this what parenting boils down to? A quantity, rather than a quality, of commitment that can be measured in man-hours spent bathing, feeding, dressing, and helping one's offspring with homework? Sure, we'd all like to bag the guilt—put me at the front of the line—but is time an accurate measure of our involvement?

Working mothers are more than entitled to some pats on the back for scraping together all those hours for their kids. Few, however, would care to insist that the "primary" child-care activities examined by the study comprise the essence of mothering. When Martha Eden, a financial analyst who laments she could not afford to stay home with her two boys, notes that "good mothers are those who spend a lot of time at it," you can bet she's not deriving much comfort from her bottom-line score, however many more hours she's racked up in active child-care duty. If it were that easy to define our value as parents, then our bookshelves wouldn't groan with the literature of experts trying to explain what, exactly, makes a good parent. Guilt, that ball and chain shackled to virtually every working mother, may be an unjustified burden we carry around—but chances are Zick and Bryant's argument won't be the key that liberates us.

Acknowledging Our Responsibility

It's going to take more than a mountain of research to dislodge our guilt because some of us have reason to feel guilty. Some of us, against our better judgment, choose priorities that can only ensure we will wallow in guilt. We're not ready to have some study or survey soothe us because we know in our heart of hearts we're *not* achieving a good balance. We even know why. If pressed, we might just admit that it isn't the hours our employer demands or the time our household chores eat up or the fact that we have so little help. We might just concede we're our own worst enemy.

Popular wisdom and feminist ideology would insist I'm mistaken. Women who have to work, they would chide me, may not be making choices that are good for themselves or their families *because they have no choice.* On the other hand, women who leave their children every morning because they *want* to work— they're the ones who bring guilt upon themselves, and they're the ones who are in a position to do something about it. Those who aren't so lucky deserve my unconditional support—or so the politically correct canon reads.

I can recall having invited one of my neighbor's kids to an egg hunt we held in our backyard one spring Saturday afternoon. When neither my neighbor nor her daughter showed up, I called to see if perhaps she'd forgotten or something had come up. "Sarah can't make it," she told me rather curtly. "I work at night and nap in the afternoon, so her father's got to bring her, and he's not here right now." As though this explained why she hadn't even the courtesy to respond to my invitation one way or the other.

Knowing how beleaguered working mothers truly are—knowing because I am one of them—I am still amazed at how one need only say "I work" to be forgiven all expectations, to be assigned almost a handicapped status that no decent human being would burden further with demands. "I work" has become the universally accepted excuse, invoked as an all-purpose explanation for bowing out, not participating, letting others down, or otherwise behaving inexcusably. I have used it myself when the March of Dimes or the American Heart Association calls me at 6 P.M. to solicit not funds but my help in mailing out letters to my neighbors—"I'm sorry," I say, "but between my job and the kids I just don't have time." There is implicit in this cop-out a silent accusation, one that says 'life has been unfair to me because I have no choice but to work.'

But when I speak of choice, I'm not talking about working or not working. The overwhelming reality is that work is not a choice, not for men and not for very many women. Choice is how we structure our lives around the immutable laws of existence, one of which is that adults must labor to survive. Work though we must, our jobs do not automatically determine our priorities concerning our marriages, our children, our social life, or even our health. It's still our life, constrained as it may be by limited disposable income or leisure time, and we're still responsible for making it something we enjoy or endure. Guilt enters the picture when we ignore that responsibility. Guilt arises over emotional decisions, not from actions circumstance dictates. And for most women, a job is *not* an emotional decision but a financial imperative.

Disease or Symptom?

That said, to be a mother and to work—for whatever reasons—is a surefire recipe for anxiety, however decent the child care, however supportive the husband, however flexible the job. Historian Barbara Berg set out to determine why in her book *The Crisis of the Working Mother* by surveying hundreds of women and soliciting input from scores of clinical psychologists and academicians. Her conclusion was that internal conflict—not the logistical struggle of accommodating work and family—accounted for her subjects' chronic malaise.

The guilt oppressing working mothers is, says Berg, entirely unwarranted. She spends the bulk of her book showing the many ways in which we allow this unnecessary guilt to sabotage our lives. We let it get in the way of hiring the best caregivers for our children. We let it ruin our careers. Goaded by it, we spoil our children, become workaholics, and wreck our marriages. Why? Because, she argues, we are at odds with our primary role model: our mothers. Guilt arises *not* from the dual pursuit of career and motherhood but from "the decision to be different."[5]

For starters, argues Berg, having internalized our mothers' standards of child rearing, we were doomed to feel like failures when we could not, for socioeconomic reasons, adopt them. Yet we were also going to be different not simply because we had to, but because we *wanted* to—because, in all likelihood, we also internalized our mothers' "intense unhappiness with the very role we were to emulate."[6] For Berg it is somewhat of a given that our mothers were intensely unhappy, at least some of the time, at least subconsciously. Hence our separation, she concludes, is painful and difficult because "it implies rejecting the ideals, values, and standards of that primal identification."[7]

Berg's thesis seems entirely plausible if you consider how many of us do, indeed, labor against the legacy of a stay-at-home mother. Jane Watkins, a senior-level manager for a state pension fund, might take considerable pride in her accomplishments both at work and at home were it not for the fact that her mother lived her life according to a different and, in Jane's estimation, *better* set of priorities. Never mind that Jane is the primary breadwinner in her family and cannot choose, as her mother did, to stay home. She is racked with guilt, tortured by the possibility that any day now she or her husband or her son is going to pay the price for this state of affairs.

Six months pregnant with her second child, responsible 24 hours a day for managing the pension fund's investments, and currently orchestrating the relocation of her company to another office complex, Jane feels she's walking a tightrope, one from which the slightest wind might make her fall. "I don't know what we'd do if we had health problems," she says of herself and her family, adding that "normal people wouldn't even try to do all this," let alone a pregnant mother. Jane is fretting about what the addition of a second child will mean to her already precarious balance but admits it will fall to her husband to work it out, since he picks up most of the child-care duties at home. Some nights, if she's lucky, Jane gets home before her two-year-old falls asleep.

Jane's mother, a one-time nurse and mother of five, never returned to the workplace after her children were born, even after her youngest was in school all day. "She can't understand why anybody would work, or want to work, and not be home with her kids," sighs Jane. "She was a very good caregiver, very attentive: She went through all the motions, from cleaning the house and making the beds to taking us to the doctor for inoculations at the right time and cooking good, nutritious meals."

Despite the fact that Jane has little choice but to leave her son five, even six days a week, her mother accords her little sympathy. "I work far longer hours than my four brothers," says Jane, "yet she would understand why *they* work overtime—but not me."

When she can, Jane tries to do some of the things her mother expects of her, mostly domestic details—just to get the guilt demons off her back. "I guess it's hard for any daughter raised by a traditional mother to get her out of her system," she says. "I thought my childhood was normal and healthy, so if I'm not home I have to worry that my son's childhood won't be." Still, she cannot generate the slightest interest in maintaining her house; she has never derived the least bit of satisfaction "from ironing or cleaning or looking right or any of the girl things" her mother tried to impress upon her.

Indeed, it was her father, an entrepreneur, whom she emulated because "everything I did he thought was great; the things he admired, like being a good student, were things I enjoyed doing," she explains. And despite the pressures at work, Jane enjoys what she does and wouldn't want to do less, even if her level of responsibility were to allow it: "I'd feel just empty, to not work, and it'd be miserable for my son if I were home because I'd be so unhappy." Her choice, she feels, entails accepting chronic guilt as a condition, something that just "comes with the territory."

Jane's is the sort of guilt, Berg might argue, that devastates her happiness for no legitimate reason. It's simply an outgrowth of her conflict with her mother. It should, and can, be excised, perhaps with a little psychotherapy. If surrogate care inflicts no damage on children of working parents—and Berg offers proof by quoting experts such as Margaret Mead and T. Berry Brazelton on how children adjust best to society and become more independent and less sexist when they're the product of several caregivers[8]—then guilt must be eradicated before it becomes a self-fulfilling neurosis. "While working in itself does not seem to bring harm to our children," she writes, "the guilt that we feel over it certainly does."[9]

What Berg does *not* address, however, is the possibility that guilt may be a red flag more of us should heed. She so readily pins every conceivable compulsion, self-destructive behavior, and familial tragedy on this angst and worry we needn't feel that one must wonder why we haven't shed it by now. Eager to reassure her readers that guilt is a disease rather than the symptom of a disease, Berg glosses over the fact that working mothers are just as prone as full-time mothers to compulsive behavior that renders peace of mind impossible. Working mothers are just as likely to want to conform to a standard of perfection—and just as likely to suffer from their failure to meet it—as their stay-at-home counterparts.

Indeed, the pressure is on working mothers to be *more* Perfect Mothers, to prove that work hasn't the slightest deleterious impact, in addition to proving to their superiors that mothering hasn't the slightest deleterious impact on their work. Perversely, they must appear more in control the less they *are* in control. These are compulsions they choose, or don't choose, to heed, sources of guilt they choose, or don't choose, to adopt. Berg is right to point out that guilt arises not because work and family are mutually exclusive priorities but because we *perceive* them to be, a zero-sum equation forcing us to choose the "right" one over the "wrong" one. But guilt is just as likely to arise from our inability to prioritize at all, to expect ourselves to perform 100 percent in each role and consequently punish ourselves when we fail—as we inevitably must.

Because by and large what limits choice for working mothers is the tendency to regard all roles as morally or ideologically critical, and therefore equally important. This is called juggling, an apt term since it implies all the balls must be kept in the air and the juggler can never rest—she is doomed, in fact, to keep everything in perpetual motion without ever having the satisfaction of getting somewhere or finishing anything. Should the juggler tire, or relax her concentration, the act culminates in failure: The audience pays attention to the juggler only as long as she defies the inevitable.

For example, it is the rare mother who, given an evening either to help her son finish his science project or to complete a project for her boss, actually prioritizes one over the other: "I'd just stay up all night and do both," says Sylvia Simmons*, a biology professor and mother of one. We can't say no to anything, because without our commitment and involvement, an endeavor might fail and we would have only ourselves to blame. We can't bear to choose for fear of failing or disappointing someone else, someone in whom we vest our image of self-worth. Enslaved to uphold the expectations that are imposed on us by others (or that we internalize as our own), we hold ourselves personally responsible for all outcomes, however little real control we may exert over them.

True balance requires assigning realistic performance expectations to each of our roles. True balance requires us to acknowledge that our performance in some areas is more important than in others. True balance demands that we determine what accomplishments give us honest satisfaction as well as what failures cause us intolerable grief. Women who have struck such a balance may still be at odds with their mothers but no longer have cause to fear the consequences of their differences. The very presence of guilt, let alone its tenacity, implies imbalance: Something, we suspect, is getting more of our energy than it warrants, at the expense of something else, we suspect, that deserves more of our energy than we're giving.

The Drive to Excel

"I've started to feel really horrible about my daughter," says Helen Rice*, a senior editor with a national magazine. "It's hard for me to believe this, but she's actually begun to suffer because I'm spending so little time with her."

Recently Helen accepted a book contract in addition to her responsibilities at the magazine, and since she can't cut back any more at work, she's had to cut back on her time with Courtney. Never has she felt such strain, noting that the simplest errand— having to pick up her blouse from the dry cleaner's—becomes the proverbial straw on the camel's back. As though mornings weren't difficult enough, trying to pry her two-year-old from her knees merely to get out the door, and as though evenings weren't agonizing enough, deciding anew whether her job or her child should get the extra half hour, Helen is now working every Saturday in order to produce the book on deadline. Her husband, a real-estate broker whose weekday hours are long and erratic, typically works on Saturdays, so Helen recruited her mother, who fortunately lives close by, to watch Courtney.

"She'd be happy to see Grandma," Helen observes of Courtney, "because she thought we were all going to stay. When we'd leave, there weren't just the usual histrionics—I can tell those, and this was way beyond that. She was truly angry. And she was pissed off at me when I got back as well.

"I began to feel unbelievably guilty," she says. "You start to think, what the hell could possibly be the point of having a child if you're only going to see her an hour or two each day and then on weekends for just a few hours more." Helen recalls condemning her landlady, a woman who went to great pains to adopt a child, for hiring a nanny and returning to work immediately; at the time, Helen was childless. "I remember thinking, my single self, 'What's the point of getting this child and then having someone else take care of her?'" she explains. "I've since learned it's so difficult being a parent, being a mother, whether you are full time or part time or whatever, that everybody really has to be allowed to make their own way and do whatever they feel works for them."

Yet Helen admits she is not doing what really works for her. "For the record," she notes, "I'd never do this again: The book was a big mistake. I paid more attention to what other people wanted out of me and basically agreed to impossible circumstances and deadlines. For the first time I've truly felt completely overextended, and it's not a good feeling for someone as obsessive as I am about deadlines. It's terrible to realize you can't possibly make it no matter how hard you work.

*　*　*

Nina Decker*, successfully self employed as an investor relations consultant, asserts she feels no guilt: Everything is in perfect balance because she's in control.

Her business is thriving precisely because it is her own, not subject to the vagaries and injustices of corporate life, with which she's more than familiar. After eight years on Wall Street as a financial analyst, she was "swept out of her job by a man"; after a stint with an investor-relations firm where she resisted bilking clients by overbilling them, she was laid off. Three months pregnant and saddled with a huge mortgage on a "money pit" she and her husband had just purchased, Nina felt so stressed, overwhelmed, and bereft of control that she "kind of tuned out" and collected unemployment.

Two weeks before her baby arrived, however, she elected,

despite her swollen condition, to go to a conference several states away, where it dawned on her that, with her connections, she could start her own investor-relations firm. She landed her first client that day, delivered her son on time, and two weeks later, cesarean surgery notwithstanding, met with her client in the city. She is not one, Nina notes with evident pride, to allow such normally cataclysmic events to knock her off track.

"My time is now my own, and it never has been," she says, pointing out that her business has ultimately vindicated her by proving to be quite lucrative. She'd like to expand her client base, but, she sighs, three things hold her back: living in and working out of a 200-year-old house under constant renovation, and her roles as wife and mother. Not that these aren't also her choices, she's quick to add: They're all her "job" too, things she wanted, a lifetime of demands she opted for, and a diversity she feels lucky to have, even though on some days she feels emotionally stretched. "Keeping all three areas in life [career, marriage, child] in balance is not easy," explains Nina. "What I need to do is organize my time better so I don't perceive them as demands."

Efficiency, organization, and attention to detail are skills she prides herself on, skills that have paid off handsomely in at least two of her jobs—her career and motherhood—granting her the control she feels is necessary to excel at both. "I want to make sure *I* raise my child," she asserts. "I want the decision-making process to be mine. If I'm here, I can monitor the nanny, see how she does it, make sure she listens to me." Nina highlights the fact that her son has had the same nanny from birth, a consistency of care that was "very deliberate" on her part. There's no revolving door at her house, she maintains, because she took care to hire the right person in the first place and takes measures to ensure she stays.

Likewise, she attributes her success in business to staying on top of things: Word of mouth has brought her most of her new clients. She finds being in charge of the direction and outcome of her career "liberating," akin to giving birth in that she and she alone pulled it off. "I'm fed up with trusting people," she notes. "I've always wanted to be able to rely on myself completely. My mother waited hand and foot on my father, and I was sent to boarding school to travel in the same direction. I finally decided that wasn't going to work for me, that I had something to contribute to the world."

As for her own marriage, Nina will not discuss it, except to note that her second husband has turned out to be as unsupportive as the first, unwilling, she says, to help out on the home front and unable to "grow up." "I most certainly don't wish I were someone else to meet his expectations," she says. "So much of what he expects is not on my important list; they are things I don't prioritize. It's not that I refuse to do them, but I'm too exhausted. I feel he should be doing them if he wants them done that badly."

To meet each other halfway is going to require, she knows, a lot of work. But Nina doesn't hold out a lot of hope that such work will take place. She explains that she's always been "ready and willing to be available, to listen, and be accommodating" but that she's not going to be manipulated by a set of expectations that she doesn't respect. Prior to marriage, she explains, she never was one to feel the pressure to conform to others' expectations; now, because she does everything from raising their son to running her business to getting the house renovated, she feels if anyone deserves to be accommodated, it's her. But her husband does not share her perspective, and, Nina observes, she cannot make him.

"In a marriage, it's not just yourself you have to work things out for but another adult, with feelings of his own," she says. "If you have a husband who's not completely mature, or at all competitive, or not as helpful as he could be, the distance in such a situation requires a lot of emotional energy to pull together." Psychologically, says Nina, she's preparing herself for the marriage to dissolve. "The baby doesn't deserve to be in a household full of turmoil," she reasons, believing she might easily handle—even prefer—the demands of single parenthood because she wouldn't have to rely on anybody but herself and the help she hired.

"I see women in similar equations to mine," Nina continues, "and their problems are usually with their husbands, not their careers or children." Reflecting on her own parents' marriage, she claims the only part she envies is the fact that her mother "ran the house like a Swiss watch."

"Some people seem to have rather charmed lives: They have total control," Nina observes. "But I've never been that person."

* * *

Barbara Hahn, a marketing executive for a major Manhattan bank, makes no apologies for putting her job first, over her family—and not because she's the breadwinner, either: "If you were to grill our accountant," she concedes, "you'd figure out I probably don't *have* to work." She resists being labeled a workaholic but admits she enjoys working hard, enjoys excelling at whatever she chooses to do, and enjoys the rewards and extra challenges associated with doing her job well. Hence when she was recently passed up for a promotion, she suffered for months, trying to understand why and trying both to accept and overcome her setback.

"I have plenty of friends who say, 'Well this just goes to show you . . . ,' friends who consider the child comes first and who could therefore write off the whole thing [as further evidence that business refuses to recognize the primacy of the family]. I can't say that's true of me; if it were, I'd feel more peace of mind than I do now. I wouldn't feel that I am shortchanging myself as much as I do. If family came first, I'd work even shorter hours, wouldn't take work home with me—a thousand things I don't dwell on but could enumerate."

What really burns her, says Barbara, is the fact that she never

even had a real chance at the promotion because since her pregnancy she has not been given "some of the more visible, more
important projects, those crisis projects that would necessitate
dropping everything and working undignified, uncontrollable
hours"—the kind of projects she might well have managed to do,
her shorter hours notwithstanding, but for her boss's *assumption*
that motherhood had compromised her commitment to her job.
"People's perceptions are very shallow," explains Barbara, "and
they were looking at the fact that I live outside of the city and
had a kid." Looking back, she realizes her role in the "stellar"
projects had been secondary or tertiary at best—not in the lead-
ership capacity that might have earned her the promotion. "That
begins to mean more to you when it's withheld," she notes.

As the only mother in her department, Barbara has tried to
downplay her reduced availability, and she insists that, while she
can no longer stay at work until 7 P.M., she compensates—maybe
even overcompensates—by coming in earlier, working through
lunch, and avoiding water-cooler chitchat and other social
luxuries. She can't help but notice, however, that "people's
expectations are not in keeping with what I can deliver and
what's been proven I can deliver."

Yet Barbara would also concede that motherhood itself—and
not just her boss's perception of it—does compromise her competitive edge at work. Unlike other obstacles Barbara has faced
and overcome, "you can't make this one go away; you can only
hope to minimize its effects." Meetings at which she feels her
presence is critical seem inevitably to take place late in the afternoon, forcing upon her the really hard decision of whether to
call her caregiver and ask her indulgence for another two hours
or breeze out of the meeting to make her 5:30 train.
Increasingly, she feels she's not making choices so much as having them foisted upon her. For Barbara, a self-avowed "control
freak," losing control over any one aspect of her life bothers her
because she must then contend with the domino-like sequence

of disasters it triggers, whether it's missing a train or having to miss a meeting.

"I'm not unrealistic that things will work smoothly," she says, "but I organize them to at least run. When things get way out of kilter and you have to spend energy rescheduling, it becomes a different sort of burden. *Because* there are so many areas where I'm not in control—and never will be—I don't like relinquishing what little I have." People now make choices for her, she notes, whereas she used to feel privileged to make them for herself. In her view she's been "mommy-tracked," despite the fact she herself would have chosen to put career first.

Perversely, such a work ethic has not only failed to reward her at the office but has caused her to endure unfavorable judgment outside it—a hostility she senses from other women who conclude her priorities are skewed simply because she doesn't *have* to work. "It bothers me because it's so unfair," she explains. "I know what I'm doing is the right thing to be doing. It sounds like the greatest cop-out of all, but I believe and know absolutely that my child is much better off without me taking care of her full time. If that doesn't sound like a big lie, it sounds incredibly callous. But having spent lots of time with her, I know pretty close to real what it'd be like to stay home all the time, and I'm telling you it would not be good; I'm too impatient, for one thing.

"It comes down to knowing yourself," says Barbara emphatically, "and I know I'm not cut out to be a good full-time mommy." This conviction would give her peace were it not for the nagging suspicion that *other people* expect more of her, whether they voice it openly or criticize her behind her back. "I'd just like to feel I am doing the best I possibly can both at work and at home," she muses. "What will help is if I feel I have enough under my belt for increased confidence; what will help me gain that more than anything else is having everybody measure me favorably and regard me in a favorable light. But since that's impossible, it means I'll have to reorient my thinking to care less what other people's assessment of me is, be it the comments of my peers or the rewards from my job.

"I can't expect other people to change their perception of me," notes Barbara with awesome insight. "I can only change the degree to which their perceptions affect me. I've got to change within myself the importance that carries so I can reduce the whole unnatural strain, the need for control which I can't have, the need to excel which I may not be able to maintain. My self-worth has to come more from me. I recognize this is where we make it even tougher than it has to be, because when you're doing something difficult solely to satisfy someone else or someone else's opinion of you, then something's wrong."

Achievement vs. Compulsion

While I cannot, like Barbara Berg, absolve these women of responsibility for their woes, I most certainly empathize with each of them, because their compulsions are my own. Like Helen, I cannot resist taking on projects that amplify my sense of self-worth even as they cost me the embrace of my family; like Nina, I am impatient with those who interfere with or even sabotage my plans because they resist my control; and like Barbara, I have been known to prioritize according to whom I can least bear to disappoint. Indeed, for much of my life compulsion has been so rewarded I find it incredibly hard to regard it as destructive behavior. Before motherhood, not only did my drive bring me recognition, approval, and privilege, but it seemed to cost me relatively little—a night's sleep, a missed meal, a momentary misunderstanding. I was the middle child in a family where excellence was so taken for granted that the only way to stand out was to continually top the last achievement. My role models were a mother who by all accounts could have held down the presidency in her spare time and a father who pined so for perfection that he used to chide us for using the stairs because we'd wear out the carpet. Achievement came cheap in our house: It was failure that carried unimaginable costs.

In *Perfect Women: Hidden Fears of Inadequacy and the Drive to Perform*, author Colette Dowling makes very clear the long-term costs of compulsive achievement, the kind that sacrifices any and all that is dear to the attainment of perfection in some chosen pursuit. When Dowling's daughter Gabrielle was awarded a scholarship to Harvard, Dowling rejoiced in having the world recognize her firstborn as a flawlessly bright and beautiful woman—until Gabrielle suddenly dropped out of Harvard and out of school entirely, abandoned responsible behavior, and became bulimic. Willing to see herself in her daughter only as long as her daughter reflected back perfection, Dowling was suddenly forced to confront the possibility that she herself was flawed and that her achievements reflected only her intense drive to mask those flaws. No amount of accomplishment, she recognized, would ever fill the black hole of her insecurity: Instead of feeling joy at her celebrity status for having written an international best-seller (*The Cinderella Complex*), Dowling felt instead depressed and anxious lest her future work not be deemed "good enough." Her daughter's "failure" helped her identify the flywheel of her own drive, that only repeated flawless performances could keep at bay the specter of being a "nobody."[10]

From her personal journey and the experiences of the many women she interviewed, Dowling postulates that most of us are running on empty in terms of self-esteem and in search of fulfillment flog ourselves "to appear competent in every way" because "good feelings tend to be attached to achievement and achievement only."[11] Like junkies in search of a fix, we try to do more, have more to show for our efforts, squeeze more time out of a finite day, be better organized or more efficient or more in control—essentially to prove ourselves superior lest we be "found out" as imperfect and thus unlovable. "A belief in the possibility of perfecting ourselves is the chief illusion seducing women today," writes Dowling.[12]

And while the illusion of gain incurs considerable pain—insomnia, irritable bowel syndrome, debilitating muscular tension, headaches, exhaustion, ulcers, pneumonia, failed marriages, insecure children—we tend to endure it all as the price of glory. The fact is, Dowling observes, the majority of us who complain that " something's got to give" have not *the slightest intention of giving up anything.*[13] The job, our husband, our kids, and our bodies must be perfect, must reflect back that we are perfect, so we can feel good about ourselves, because "there's nothing warming us from within."[14] We have no sense of true Self, Dowling concludes: "It is from our image in the mirror and our reflection in the eyes of others that we try to derive a sense of security, some grounds for self-esteem."[15]

Dowling, like Berg, is of the firm conviction that our failure to individuate from our mothers—who, in turn, failed to separate from their mothers—is what accounts for this vacuum of self, for we have separated only enough to see that we are different and to condemn ourselves for that difference. Our internal conflict arises from wanting both to emulate and to rebel against our mothers. From this conflict arises guilt, and from guilt the compulsion to prove ourselves new and improved, if not perfect. We "do it all" simply to feel worthy and acceptable. We do it all simply so that we might perceive ourselves as *good enough.*

For all the hundreds of thousands of women who have tapped into therapy to resolve this oxymoronic relationship with their mothers, you'd think we'd see some progress: less compulsive, less driven, less exhausted working mothers, at least. Yet guilt is alive and well, Berg's book and Zick and Bryant's study notwithstanding. Our internal conflict continues to spawn a red sea of self-help books, television talk shows, therapy programs, support groups, and professionals dedicated to resolving it. Like a Hydra that sprouts new heads with every sword stroke, however, guilt seems to gain even more faces as all the therapists and Ph.D.'s and talk show hosts continue to hack away at it. Why can't we slay this beast?

Perhaps because, in our zeal to fulfill all expectations but our own, we continue to breathe life into it. Our mothers are not the only authority figures from whom we cannot individuate: Our societal analogues—religious and political leaders, feminist and antifeminist demigogues, bosses and husbands, anchormen and advertisers, neighbors and friends—all wield a similar parental power over us, telling us what to do because we somehow doubt the voice of authority within. Maybe we, as a gender, are "insecurely attached," because the more we sense these bastions of authority receding from us, or disapproving of us, the more we cling to them, devoid of the self-acceptance that allows children to venture forth in the world as contributors rather than dependents. We look to society, as we look to our mothers, for that "mirroring" that tells us who we are and that approves of us. Without that approval, we cannot bear to act according to our own instinct.

Is it any wonder, when the mirror urges us both to stay home to rear our children *and* to stay in the work force and resist the mommy track, that we are a generation uniquely confused, torn with internal conflict not readily assuaged? Is it any wonder we cannot figure out our own priorities, when validation exists only for those who opt either to renounce all roles but one or to renounce none and run themselves into the ground? Is it any wonder we can't find the middle ground when compromise is reflected back to us as failure?

The Pressure to Conform

When I was six months pregnant with my second child and working the drought-and-deluge schedule of a free-lancer, I happened across Deborah Fallows's *A Mother's Work* while feverishly researching an impending article. A book emblematic of the so-called "home movement," one tale of redemption among supposedly thousands (when women like the one portrayed by Diane Keaton in *Baby Boom* suddenly woke up to realize their life's work was raising children), it recounts the author's own conversion from career-bent prestige hound to laid-back mom and buddy to her two boys. How good it felt, Fallows wrote, to be out of the rat race, able to savor afternoons in the park and fun outings to museums whenever the whim struck her.[16] How enticing she made it sound, particularly to me then, when each day that I was on deadline meant a marathon of feeding and dressing and comforting my son, working according to my sitter's five-hour meter and Chase's two-hour nap, whipping through the supermarket for a five-pound slab of ground chuck and a case of toilet paper, burning dinner, bolting it down, and hustling my son to bed so my husband and I could plan the next day's race. By chapter two (all I had time to read) I was a convert to Fallows's Go-Home Crusade—until my husband pointed out that writing a book isn't typically accomplished in that half hour when one's children's naps overlap. Anyone remotely aware of what's involved in turning out a couple hundred pages of prose can tell you that Ms. Fallows had to have missed an awful lot of afternoons in the park in order to extoll the virtues of "dropping out."

Fallows, of course, wasn't the only one to open my eyes to the fact that the stay-at-home advocacy was full of hypocrites. Susan Faludi hoisted the worst offenders by their own petard in her interviews with such women as Beverly LaHaye, self-appointed lobbyist for submissive wives and mothers because "God didn't make me to be a nobody"[17] and math professor Margarita Levin, whose campaign to debunk feminists necessitates having her husband stay home to watch the kids.[18] And during the 1992 presidential race, there was the overt example of Marilyn Quayle, whose law practice and lecture circuit and political career-by-proxy didn't keep her from sermonizing on the importance of subordinating ambition to husband and family. Women like these gave homemaking a bad name.

But was I, or my peers, any less seduced by the image of women offered up by the feminists? Catherine Beekman*, a psychologist who practices three days a week so that she may spend the rest of her time with her four-year-old daughter, contends that she is finally free of caring about what other people think. But looking back, she's conscious of just how much pressure she felt at college to find a career outside of mothering. "Of course I'd work," she recalls. "Everyone thought that way; it was the height of the women's movement. I went to grad school and became a professional because that was the message of the movement: You have choice; now here, make *this* choice. My own mother stayed at home, didn't work. But my role models were the women I went to school with, who were working, who were fighting to have this 'choice.'"

The feminists, fighting to expand women's choices from either/or to all-and-everything, may have succeeded too well: Choice for my generation frequently feels like an imperative, a roster of obligations to be met lest we disappoint our foremothers. As Judith Posner notes in *The Feminine Mistake*, a follow-up to Friedan's exposé of "the problem that has no name," we have succeeded in shrugging off one set of chains only to adopt another—and have yet to figure out who we are, let alone who or what the problem really is.[19]

"Surely, the purpose of the contemporary feminist movement

was not to trade one form of monolithic identity and mystique for another," writes Posner. "Yet this appears to be exactly what has happened. In our rush to disidentify with the feminine, we have become too closely aligned with the work mystique and patriarchal ideology. We have lost the ability to listen to our own inner voice."[20]

It would seem that in looking for our identity as something "more" than mothers but not limited to our occupational association, we might arrive, after 30 years of "revolution," at a resolution celebratory of our many roles, both at home and in the workplace. But the pendulum of women's essential nature continues to swing far left and far right, never achieving the stasis point halfway between the extremes. Staying at home, as I've endeavored to show, is not all it's cracked up to be: It wasn't in 1956, as Betty Friedan documented so enduringly in *The Feminine Mystique*; it isn't today, no matter how "New Traditionalist" *Good Housekeeping* insists we are; it won't be tomorrow, even if the federal deficit miraculously disappears and the Moral Majority regains its political footing.

But neither is the high-demand, high-profile, time-intensive job that feminists would like to see all women hold as proof of their ability to be men any more of an arrival. "In our attempt to assert independence and autonomy we may have unwittingly reinforced the masculine notion that occupational status is the be all and end all," notes Posner, "as well as ignoring in a catastrophic way the accomplishments of mothers' work."[21]

Uneasy Compromise

Instead of culminating in a compromise, our pursuit of both "mystiques" has us gyrating wildly in an effort to prove allegiance to both. Those who rose to the challenge during the '70s and '80s tend to exhibit, as a result, an almost schizophrenic ambivalence toward their chosen pursuits. Consider the case of Martha Eden, now in her late 40s, whose intense desire to maintain her career is equalled only by her intense regret that she could not stay home to raise her two boys.

"I'm grateful I didn't have a daughter," she says, "because I wouldn't know what to tell her. What advice would I give her? Would I be doing her a favor, teaching her how to bat her eyelashes and be taken care of the rest of her life, or teaching her to be independent? I wouldn't have wanted to raise her to be someone like me, because it's been really hard—but I don't think I would like her if she went the makeup-and-hair route, either."

Martha maintains that "the world needs good mothers more than good financial analysts" and that women "should orient themselves to raising children." Yet women like Phyllis Schlafley, she says, "make me want to vomit; I have absolutely no respect for her." Feminism, too, is a philosophy she resists espousing.

"Feminism went awry," she explains, "in trying to dominate men, to say we're the same as men. There's nothing wrong with being a nurturer, or placater, or mediator. The world has a great need for that talent. Women are far stronger than men will ever be but could play an important role in the world by *not* trying to be dominating. If the Serbian and Croatian women played a role in the power structure, that war would have been over real fast. We should take our natural tendency, our 'weakness,' and give it more value.

"Nature won't change," she adds, "but how we perceive it could. How can we change how women's strengths are perceived when women themselves don't value their role as nurturers or placaters?"

Learning to Value the Image in Our Own Mirror

Anyone who's borne a child knows that women are not, thank

God, the same as men—we are stronger in some ways, as Martha observes, but in *different* ways. Yet it is against men, curiously, that we take our measure, as though men were the norm and women the aberration. Biologically speaking, all fetuses develop as females until the Y chromosome kicks in and modifies certain structures to be "male." But our profound bias, as a culture and as a gender, is to assess ourselves according to how closely we conform to a male standard—in physiological, behavioral, and emotional ways. This peculiar and crippling mentality is the subject of *The Mismeasure of Woman,* Carol Tavris's catalog of the ways in which women are not inferior, not superior, and not the same as men, but second-class citizens nonetheless because we cannot trust our own gender-specific definitions of success.[22]

Recently the press picked up on a disturbing income disparity between male and female doctors, a difference of 34 percent, or about $50,000, in median salaries. At the top of the money pile—doctors earning $400,000 or more—men outnumbered women five to one; at the low end of the pay scale, making less than $60,000, women outnumber men almost three to one, according to a survey of some 17,000 doctors conducted for *Medical Economics* magazine. Even in specialties where women are heavily concentrated, such as family practice and pediatrics, women trailed men in income anywhere from 27 to 34 percent. Such a disparity suggests to Margaret Hennig, dean of the Graduate School of Management at Simmons College in Boston, that medicine is evolving into a two-tiered system wherein men are "the chiefs." She cites as evidence the fact that women made up less than 4 percent of chest-surgery residents, 5 percent of orthopedic-surgery residents, and 8 percent of brain-surgery residents in 1991.[23]

Now, on the surface it would appear that women are yet again the long-suffering victims, denied not only equal opportunity but equal pay and professional respect. No doubt sexual harassment, sexual bias, and any number of other discriminatory crimes are committed on a daily basis in the halls of medicine. But while everyone—the American Medical Association, the media, and readers alike—eagerly pounces on discrimination as the explanation for women's perceived lack of success in the medical profession, no consideration is paid to the possibility that women might be *choosing*, to a degree, their "lesser" status, if not lesser pay. What of the likelihood that women don't enter all-consuming, 24-hour-a-day "macho" specialties such as surgery because they esteem family and personal life above money, status, and ego gratification? What of women like Peg Chapman, who turned down her father's highly successful ob/gyn practice in favor of pediatrics and rehabilitative medicine because, having grown up with a father who was forever running out to tend a patient, she knew all too well the toll such a specialty would take on her own family; or Diane Turner*, a dermatologist who elects to practice three days a week so that she can be with her kids and keep her hand in teaching; or Nancy Belser, a pediatrician who admits the group she chose to join might not have hired her if they had felt a need to build their practice, because she insisted on practicing part time?

Curiously, no one cares to note that many women may avoid specialties such as surgery because it doesn't allow them any kind of normal life (*normal* meaning, I think we can agree, time for spouse and children). As mothers and wives, they prize the flexibility to work part time above money or professional clout. A pay disparity between men and women working the same hours at the same job who wield the same seniority and carry the same qualifications is the sort of discrimination feminists rightly decry. But if there is a price assigned to added flexibility, many women would appear more than happy to pay it. Consider how the survey might otherwise be interpreted if we judged success not by how much money doctors made, not by how much clout they commanded, but instead by how much choice they exercised in pursuit of a career that allowed for spouse, children, and home life. Is it not *our* values, as a gender compelled to compromise, that should be recognized by society as worthy of support and esteem? We are so ingrained with the habit of measuring our progress according to male definitions of success that we cannot see how *well* we're really doing on a female-determined scale of priorities.

But without societal approbation, we seem incapable of trusting our values. The mirror we insist on consulting for a reflection of our true selves offers us instead a fun-house distortion. We see ourselves fat in all the wrong places, grotesque, unfit to be loved—when it is the mirror we should question, with planes so skewed only devout homemakers and career zealots look desirable. So long as the source of our identity is external— vested in how others judge our performance at work, or how others judge our children's performance, or how much money we make—we will find ourselves hopelessly flawed, forever short of the ideal.

We cannot control, as Barbara Hahn points out, how we are perceived; we can only change how that perception affects us. Still, Barbara laments never having enough confidence in herself to ignore what other people think of her, so she works harder; Helen admits she took on her book project out of "a sick need" for the ego gratification that comes from doing so many things; and Nina would rather hang on to her illusion of control than hang on to a husband whose imperfection threatens to destroy that illusion.

The toll needing to do it all takes on these women is akin to the toll taxing women who feel compelled, by staying home, to be perfect mothers. "I would just like to stop having to prove myself," says Barbara, echoing almost exactly the words of Linda Miller in the parallel universe of stay-at-homers. The gambit is that one's work, or one's children, will prove so superior that all personal sacrifices, however immense, will have been justified. Given the fact that we cannot control how others view our work any more than we can control who our children turn out to be, the odds are great that our sacrifices may *not* be rewarded as we envision they will be.

Paradoxically, letting go of the need to control is far more difficult than gaining control. Similarly, doing less is far more of a challenge than trying to do it all. Letting go and doing less necessitates tuning out the din of all the demands we've internalized in order to hear the tiny voice that is our own. Heeding that tiny voice requires feeling secure, and confident, that we indeed know what is best for ourselves and our families, that we can trust our instinct above the "expert" advice of others. Acting on our instincts means striving for goals no one else may recognize as worthy, for approval no audience may exist to grant, for status no political body cares to acknowledge. Having the confidence to act on our instincts means we've got to pretty much like who we are, make time for enjoying our lives and families, and respect our own very idiosyncratic values. The process of prioritization is, after all, highly individual, an ongoing personal reevaluation that demands we not confuse external influences with circumstances truly beyond our control.

Perhaps that's why so many of us, rather than perform the soul-searching required to prioritize, elect either to "juggle" our many roles (as though each were equally deserving of unflagging attention) or adopt just one—mothering, for example—in hopes of perfecting it. To compromise, and break from the ranks of those who would insist their priorities are the "correct" ones, is to risk losing what little identity we may have found. In a society that robs a woman of individual power by convincing her that she is a victim in a sea of oppression—a victim whose only hope of survival lies in climbing aboard a lifeboat of other victims—compromise is indeed a threatening credo, because it buoys the lone swimmer.

Not that acting as a group is without merit: Today very little in the way of policy changes without a formidable alliance of monied constituents united by self-interest. But without commitment to change on an individual basis, without acknowledgment that each of us bears individual responsibility for the choices we make, there can be no mass gain. "It takes very little energy to accede to one's imprisonment," remarked essayist Roger Rosenblatt, describing the 1989 Czech uprising, "but an enormous exertion of will to decide to want to be singled out, to be noticed, to make public the singular creature you know yourself to be. . . . To avoid a collective tyranny, one must learn self-rule, the idea that a democracy is made up of each separate individual, recognizing that he or she is a system on its own, frighteningly alone, magnificently alone in a crowd."[24]

PART TWO

Striking the Right Balance: Good Enough Mothers

What Makes a Mother Good Enough?

I've got a terrific interview prospect for you," my mother opened. "She runs her own business and she's got two young kids. I just know you'd really like her."

My mother was helping me scout role models. Except I didn't want her to be the judge: I wasn't sure what "role model" meant to her, but I could bet she would think I wanted to hear from women who did it all, dynamos like herself. "If she works and her kids are six or younger, I'll give her a call," I said with a sigh.

"Oh, she's perfect!" gushed my mother. "And such an *attractive* woman. . . ."

Already I despised this stranger; already I felt threatened. I didn't want to hear how she had managed to launch a successful business while nurturing her infants and probably breast-feeding them on the job. I didn't want to hear about her beloved nanny, who had been with her since her first child was born. I didn't want to hear about the perfect partnership she had forged with her husband, who cooked all the meals and took the kids for the weekend so she could get a break. And I didn't want to hear how she found the time to keep up with all her friends from college, do volunteer work at the local hospital, and get to the gym three times a week. "Don't tell me any more," I interjected. "I'll call her."

Perfect Compromisers

You won't hear from any perfect women in this book. I didn't find any, for starters, but even supposing such a creature existed, she's the last person I'd want to model myself after, the last person I'd tap for suggestions on how to make sense of the muddle the rest of us are in. The mothers I'm going to profile under the GEM (Good Enough Mother) rubrik throughout the ensuing chapters all work full time, all have (with one exception) at least two children, and have all had to wrestle their expectations down to the mat and pin them there. I chose to feature them because of all that's *not* perfect about their job or their marriage or their child care. Their circumstances differ wildly, but in their response to the struggle at hand they paint something of a consistent picture, inspiring me to believe that a resolution to the agonizing work/family conflict exists for all of us. Indeed, listening to their stories made me feel more positive in my outlook, more forgiving of my shortcomings, and more appreciative of what I've got and what I've accomplished. I chose them, in short, because they made me believe for more than a fleeting phone call that I'm *good enough*.

Each of these women, for her own reasons, *must* work. Wendy Lindman* is a single mother with no financial safety net; Verna Tweddale, a nurse and mother of three, has worked every holiday for the past 20 years to help pay the mortgage and save enough to send her kids to college. Elizabeth Woodman (whom I mentioned in chapter one) is not only her husband's partner but also their business's most vital employee; Christine Tauber* and her mate are individually pursuing risky new businesses in the hope and belief that if you do what you love the money will follow. Tina Lloyd*, gifted and "cursed" with artistic talent, must do what she loves or she will "explode." And Betsy Latham (whom I quoted in the introduction), whose husband supported her completely for nine years, can no longer afford to be a homemaker—not if she wants to hold on to her marriage, her self-respect, or her hopes for better-adjusted children.

And yet despite—or rather, *because of*—the limitations these women contend with, they've made their peace with who they are and with the cards circumstance has dealt them. Indeed, the worse their hand of cards, the more remarkable I found their outlook. "It's never the sort of journey you'd will yourself," notes Verna Tweddale, who gave up everything she prided herself on achieving in order to give her husband a critical career opportunity. "But it seems it's only when your back's up against the wall, and you have no choice but to walk through the fire, that you come to realize you've not only survived but emerged on a higher plane."

Each of these women, I think, has something to share that might give the rest of us the inspiration, and support, we need to find peace of mind in the many roles we have assumed as working mothers.

An Ex-Perfect Mother Returns to Work

One night a week Betsy Latham, 35, teaches a course at a local hospital on "positive living." The eight-week seminar addresses ways in which people who are fundamentally unhappy with themselves or their lives can effect positive change—if only in their outlook. Weekly topics range from the benefits of good nutrition and exercise to the importance of laughter. One whole night is devoted to discussing what Betsy calls the housewife worry syndrome, the tendency among women to obsess about things typically beyond their control. To help her students overcome their negative behaviors she uses relaxation techniques, incorporates role-playing and dramatization, and assigns lots of "homework" lest participants forget that they're really teaching themselves. "I tell them they can't expect to have happier lives after only eight weeks," Betsy says. "You can spend a lifetime working on this stuff."

Most of her students are women. Some are there because they think they're overweight or just aren't content with the way they look. Others are seeking better coping skills, ways to find that elusive balance so that they might feel less exhausted and overwhelmed. Almost all, Betsy reports, are trying to learn how to deal with their own anger and dissatisfaction more effectively. "I think that's a key point for women," she notes. "We're all trying to figure out how to care for our families, improve on our careers, carry all our responsibilities, and come out feeling fulfilled. But if women don't learn to be assertive, they're never going to get that balance right."

Betsy should know. For the last three years she's been on a quest to become more assertive herself, taking workshops, attending seminars, reading all the available literature. With a master's in human relations, she says, "you'd think I had it all figured out." But on the contrary, the course was an outgrowth of her own struggle to determine and then go after what she really wanted out of life. "Up until about four years ago, I didn't think much about anything—I just kind of went along with the flow. But something happens in your 30s; that's when people have a lot of stresses, a lot of bad times, maybe some losses. Then they get philosophical and start wondering what life is all about."

Betsy is a perfectionist by nature; balance has never been her strong suit. First she had to be perfect at her profession, which is teaching music and piano; prior to having children she managed to have a videotape of her techniques commercially produced. She quit her career soon after her daughter arrived because it interfered with her vision of being a perfect mother. So for nine years, until her son was in kindergarten, she stayed home, eager to be the best mother, the best wife, the best homemaker, the best piano teacher—the Most Super Mom she knew.

And for a while she was. She wowed her neighbors with her dedication to children—not just her own but everybody else's, too. There were always about 15 kids in her yard, Betsy recalls, because she was always organizing activities and coming up with rainy day projects. "My pleasure was in knowing that all the other mothers would say I was the perfect neighborhood mom," she recalls. "And, of course, my children loved it, because everybody wanted to come to our house."

For nine years she was also the unimpeachable child rearer, raising her son and daughter literally by the book. Having read somewhere that school-age children need ten hours' sleep, she used to dress her kids in their beds before they awoke, determined that the school bus schedule not encroach on their night's sleep. When she read that the best time to practice the piano was in the morning, she got her six-year-old daughter up at 6 A.M.—but put her to bed the night before at 6 to ensure she got the 12 hours' sleep Betsy understood to be best for kindergartners. "It wasn't just the books reinforcing me, either," she laughs. "My kids actually *were* perfect piano players, perfect students, and perfect children!"

And for at least five of those nine years, she tried to uphold her end of the perfect marriage by doing everything a stay-at-home mom was supposed to do: the cleaning, ironing, cooking, clothes shopping, and errand running that guaranteed her husband could never fault her for any inconvenience, want, or disorder in his life. She succeeded. But the relationship was far from ideal.

"I decided I didn't want to be married to him anymore," Betsy recalls. "But I didn't divorce him, and I'm glad I didn't, because we worked it out. I learned through counseling that it wasn't just because he was the most headstrong, bullheaded, male chauvinistic man you could imagine; I had to change, too. I had to change the way I think, the way I talk, the way I work—I had to learn a lot of different skills I'd just never been taught.

"The counseling just got me on the road to thinking," she continues. "I had to ask myself, 'What do I really want out of a marriage?' And I realized I want friendship. Compassion. Real communication. I wanted someone who was going to share my life goals, someone who was going to help me balance out my life."

Her husband had always been supportive of her professional goals, says Betsy, but he didn't know how to help her accomplish them. So she showed him: She posted on the refrigerator a list detailing the 50 or so tasks she performed in the course of a week and the three or four chores for which he was responsible.

"I told him, 'You've got to take half. If you're not going to help out, I'm going to hire a maid.' Well, he pitched a fit, claimed we couldn't afford it. I said, 'I can't afford to go crazy trying to do everything.' When he still didn't help out with the laundry, I took the clothes to the cleaner's and had them laundered. When he saw me come home dragging these huge bags of laundry, he just blew up.

"But I had come to the conclusion that I was important," says Betsy. "And I came to see that if I didn't take care of myself, nobody else was going to. If my husband didn't want to help out, then we weren't going to have a marriage; I had decided I was more important than that kind of relationship. The fact is, when you stand up for yourself and are assertive, when you respect yourself, men respect you a whole lot more. Most women don't think so, but it's true. My husband now puts me up on a pedestal, something he certainly didn't do when I was slaving away for him."

Every woman, says Betsy, has to learn to be assertive—for the sake of the next generation, if not her marriage. Betsy's own "bad habits" she attributes to growing up in an environment where all needs were met, all wants anticipated; she never learned how to discern what she wanted from what others expected of her. "None of us learned any coping skills," she says of her generation. "We were given so much, had such a charming childhood, that when we moved out and realized we'd have to work all day just to live, we just couldn't believe it. We were just overwhelmed. Our generation is probably the most depressed of the century, because we were so spoiled as children."

So Betsy, who used to equate being a good wife with being a maid and being a good mom with being a "slave," now expects considerably more from her family—and gets it. Her children perform 30 minutes to an hour a day of "real" chores. "Every time I feel like I'm going to revert to my bad habits," says Betsy,

"I think what I want for them: I don't want them becoming depressed adults. I'm not going to let them out of helping, of being a part of this world. When I look at my friends whose kids have everything under the sun, it makes me cringe. They're setting their kids up for such disappointment. How are those kids going to possibly afford what they had as children when they're in their 20s? Adulthood is going to be such an anticlimax."

What also helps keep Betsy from "reverting" to her doormat days, or letting her kids off easy, is her new job: She's teaching music to schoolchildren ages 4 to 14 four days a week, in addition to conducting her positive living course at the hospital one evening a week. It's what she enjoys, she says, something she promised she'd do for herself once her youngest was in first grade. Not that staying home was so bad: For a good many years, she thrived on all the "warm fuzzies" her labors earned her. But she found she lost her perspective on what being a good mother really meant. Most women of her generation, she observes, have but one image of good motherhood—the one their mothers embodied, waiting on their husbands, chauffeuring the kids around to Boy Scouts and ballet, running all the vital but thankless errands, and religiously attending PTA and other school functions. Anything done "for the sake of the children" justified, even ennobled, the mother's role. Motherhood was tantamount to martyrdom during that unique era when children were gods. Those who appeared to put their own needs first were castigated and shunned—the ultimate damnation for a gender trained to be wholly dependent on the acceptance and praise of others. "I didn't want anyone else to raise my kids," Betsy explains, not because she thought her children might suffer but "because that would have made me a bad mom in everybody else's eyes."

Unassertive and easily swayed by the dictates of her parents and her peers, Betsy found staying home cemented her perfectionist bad habits, locked her into doing too much for her kids and expecting too little from them—much as her mother had before her. Only when her marriage started to falter and threatened to dispel the image of perfection she had so carefully cultivated did Betsy begin to wonder if maybe there weren't other roads to happiness.

"I used to think I had no choices," she says. "Everyone does, particularly in the gray area: There are always little choices you can make that may affect the way you adjust to or even change the big choices that seem out of your control. Our generation tends to think in black and white, and so did I."

That is, she clarifies, if someone we marry isn't working out, then we divorce him for someone we think will be perfect. And if we fail to be perfect ourselves, then we conclude we must be worthless. "I have these women in my classes who think they're overweight, who are really unhappy about it," Betsy elaborates. "They're not fat; they just don't look like the models in advertisements. I don't tell them how to lose weight but rather how to be more accepting of themselves. There are some situations we can't always fix or change, but we can be less affected by what we feel we have to be or what other people think we should be. We all have to come to terms with being less than perfect, with *life* being less than perfect."

Betsy says her own expectations were so high that she used to feel "headachy" just thinking about them. What kept her going, despite all the pain and stress, was the praise and admiration she reaped from her parents, her teachers, her neighbors, and the experts whose advice she followed to the letter. "I was always taught that if I worked hard enough, I'd be rewarded," she says. It wasn't until she hit a "brick wall" in her marriage that she questioned where all her hard work was getting her—whether the payout of constantly meeting everyone's expectations was worth the stress.

Ironically, what prevented her from divorcing her husband was the perfectionist zeal that made him look so bad in the first place: "I couldn't divorce him," Betsy observes wryly, "because that wouldn't have fit into my perfect lifestyle of being a perfect mom or perfect wife. And my parents would have had a fit if I'd gotten a divorce: Then I wouldn't have been their perfect daughter."

Her mother lives through her, says Betsy, and thinks she's the most wonderful, flawless daughter in the world. "If I'm perfect and happy, so is she," Betsy explains. When Betsy was going through a rough time in her marriage and let her mother know it, "she was so miserable, she stopped calling me; she didn't want to talk to me, didn't want to hear anything negative, couldn't handle it." To this day, says Betsy, she has to steel herself for her mother's visits, because her stomach clenches at the mere prospect of having to live up to her mother's expectations or bear responsibility for her unhappiness.

But keeping up appearances wasn't the fundamental motive for trying to save her marriage, Betsy clarifies. She wanted it for herself, suspected she'd very quickly tire of the lonely and awkward quest for a new and better mate. She didn't want to hurt her husband that badly. And she wanted it for her kids. "In this case, all my hard work did get me what I wanted," she says, "because I worked harder on this marriage than any person known to make it right. I still do: I'm constantly thinking up new ways to improve it!"

These days Betsy is more concerned about her daughter, Jane, who at ten already feels compelled to be a perfect student—behavior reinforced, Betsy says, by the positive feedback of the entire school, the principal, the pastor, and the local media telling her how great she is for being such an achiever. "I'm the only one telling her she doesn't have to get a hundred on her math test," says Betsy, who's resorted to giving her daughter little gifts when she *doesn't* get a perfect score, to try to show her she doesn't have to perform perfectly. "Every Sunday I see her suffer an anxiety attack over the coming week, fearful she might slip up and disappoint her teachers. 'What if I miss one question?' she'll ask. So then we go through all the exercises. 'What's the worst thing that can happen?' I'll say. I talk to her like a psychologist. I'll say, 'Now what are the skills we know? You've got to lower your expectations—nobody can be that good. Think positive thoughts. No more what-ifs.'"

Betsy hopes she can reverse the legacy of perfectionism she has inadvertently passed on to her daughter; she hopes that by setting a better example herself—being assertive and less reliant on what other people think or say—she can spare Jane all the hard lessons and pain of her own youth. "I don't want her to be 30 before she figures this out," Betsy comments. "I changed; I hope that now that I'm acting differently, I can change all this I instilled in her."

But the behavior is so ingrained, and so constantly reinforced—"Jane's always being profiled in the newspaper for some achievement or other," says her mother—that Betsy feels like the lone voice of reason. "From day one we're pushing our kids to conform, to be people pleasers. The schools, the churches are notorious for it. When the boys don't snap to, and curse and fight, we excuse them. 'Boys will be boys,' we say. We're harsher judges of girls; we have higher expectations for them. As a society, as mothers, we send the message that it's okay for the boys to screw around, but it's not okay for the girls. Our love is more conditional for girls. They grow up believing you've got to please others to be loved."

So begins the vicious cycle of esteeming ourselves only as long as other people are satisfied. Self-respect that *isn't* derived from praise, isn't derived from being perfect, isn't dependent on the opinions of others is critical, insists Betsy, if we're ever to break out of the cycle that has kept women unassertive and depressed. For Betsy, overcoming the belief that "everything has to be happy and wonderful" is the biggest hurdle—the kind of outlook that can't help but clash with reality and thus guarantee feelings of betrayal and disappointment.

Thirtysome years of habit are hard to shake, she says, but at least now she recognizes when her expectations are creeping into the stratosphere, when her list of "shoulds" supersedes her list of preferences, when her challenges devolve into worries. When that happens, she says, it no longer "immobilizes" her; instead, she makes a conscious effort to catch herself, to do "a lot of positive self-talk." She looks her expectations in the eye and assures herself, as she reminds her daughter, that no one could ever live up to such standards. She practices relaxation exercises 15 minutes every day, *before* she feels overwhelmed and frazzled, before 9 P.M., when exhaustion threatens to unleash the harpies. And she's been looking around at her friends, talking to women in her class, and coming to the reassuring conclusion that nobody's marriage, career, or kids can be described as perfect.

The ability to compromise—without which we'd have war, says Betsy—is what she has come to pride herself on. But it hasn't come easily. "I've had to learn the hard way that you really can't love anybody else—can't yield, can't give of yourself—if you don't love yourself first," she asserts. "You can't compromise with others, meaning you accept their flaws, if you can't accept your own." Likewise, feeling compelled to be perfect really gives us no latitude and requires no real decisions: "I used to think I was in control only when everything was going my way, which is to say, perfectly," Betsy continues. "Now I believe you're in control only when you're making compromises or forced to recognize perfection is out of the question and you're going to have to make choices and work with what you've got."

These days, Betsy's content with her choices. With "an iron in every pot," she feels pretty well balanced. When she starts to feel overextended, she says, "I nip it in the bud: I say no beforehand instead of afterward." Priorities announce themselves—and they didn't used to. If she gets confused, she makes a list of all the things she considers important and then orders them according to the ways she *wishes* she spent time. She's forever paring down the list of priorities, not because she has trouble saying no to what she doesn't want to do but because she hates having to pass up "the next fun thing that comes along."

And she's made her peace with the past. "I see it all as a learning experience," she says, remarking on the irony that her wildly successful positive living course was an outgrowth of her own misery. She doesn't regret her years at home; for a while, the praise she got for her efforts was adequate compensation. People are still telling her what a great job she's doing, and "everybody respects me more," notes Betsy, but it's not their respect or approval that fuels her: She feels a lot better about herself.

"I'm doing something I enjoy," she reflects, alluding to her jobs teaching music to children and coping skills to adults. "I needed it for myself, but I like to think I'm making a difference in a lot of other lives. And I think I'm giving my daughter and son a good example. I want them to see they have choices."

An Ivy League M.B.A. Leaves the Fast Track

When 41-year-old Christine Tauber woke up from giving birth via cesarean section, her doctor told her to prepare to grieve.

Her son Riff was barely alive. Born with several congenital birth defects—a missing pulmonary valve, a hole between the ventricles of his heart, and an incomplete intestinal tract—that none of Christine's prenatal testing had indicated, he underwent anesthesia three times before he was six weeks old. He also had a rare allergic reaction to a hormone given to him as a life-saving therapy that caused his bronchial tubes to constrict, limiting oxygen to his brain and body. At 18 months he had open-heart surgery; at a little over two he had a colostomy reversal. For an entire year after the operations, he failed to gain any weight. By the age of three, when he had not uttered a single word, his parents postulated possible brain damage from oxygen deprivation.

"At every step of the way we faced the possibility that he might not make it," recalls Christine, an investment banker on Wall Street. After the first open-heart surgery, she and her husband celebrated Riff's "excellent" prognosis with a trip to Disneyland. The day after returning from the trip, his brother Jordan slipped and wound up in a full body cast.

"When everybody finally got to be okay, I fell apart," she

recalls. "I'd remained calm and was able to deal with all the crises, but they'd taken their toll. I needed to rest." For six months she concentrated on her family, and then she was lured back to work as a senior manager in an investment management firm with the promise of both job and time flexibility.

But three years later, when it appeared her son was going to have to undergo yet another open-heart surgery, Christine determined she needed considerably more flexibility than investment management could offer. When a former colleague called her and proposed she help him launch a new business, a national cable network targeting people with disabilities, she leapt at the chance. She took on the job as a consultant but found herself, as Riff recovered, increasingly committed to the enterprise. Meanwhile, her husband left his job in commercial real estate to return to his first love, documentary filmmaking. His camera lens, however, had a new focus: how families deal with children who have heart transplants.

"It sounds odd, but this whole ordeal has been very positive for our family," says Christine of the years since Riff's birth. "We're doing what we should be doing. Money is not first on our list. We both felt we needed to do something of value, something in addition to a commercial enterprise."

It's a time of great uncertainty, she observes, not only in terms of Riff's health but also the family's finances. The funds they need to make both businesses work while keeping solvent and insured amount to a formidable challenge. "I'm involved in a totally new venture with no security whatsoever, and nobody's written my husband a check yet," says Christine. "But boredom is more uncomfortable."

Indeed, while others might go weak at the knees at the prospect of both husband and wife striking out on their own while their son's health care costs a small fortune, Christine is confident everything will work out. "I know I have a lot of options," she explains, noting that every job she's ever held has been the result of a friend or colleague calling her up with a proposal. "By making these moves, we have some control over our lives. We're shaping the direction we want to go; we're not just being pushed along some path. I have control over the values I want to emphasize. I have control over my time, so I can spend more of it with my kids. Sure, it's scary, but what's the worst case? You fail, you do something else. Things haven't always worked out the way I had planned: There have been wonderful jobs I wanted and didn't get. But, inevitably, going in another direction has ended up being better for me."

Riff's tragedy aside, you might conclude life has been awfully good to Christine. Jobs have come easily, success has always capped hard work, and opportunities continue to snowball as recognition for her abilities grows. That impression registers in part not because she has led a charmed life but rather because where others might see a cloud she sees only its silver lining.

In truth, Christine didn't start out with much advantage. Her parents had little education and no contacts or money to launch the oldest of their three children. She returned home from volunteering in North Africa to teach in a rural black high school in northeast Georgia, where, upon marrying her high school sweetheart, it looked like she'd stay. When he took a job in North Carolina, she followed, working as a director of student activities at a local college.

Her marriage, not her job, proved the dead end, and her divorce prompted her to apply to an Ivy League business school. It was this bold move that vaulted her into the elite circles of media and finance in New York City; it was at B-school, too, that she met her current husband and the classmates whose recognition of her talents has kept her on the fast track.

While she recognizes the need for prestige and financial security, Christine has never been fundamentally motivated by such factors. There's nothing she likes more, she says, than finding a diamond in the rough, something new and intriguing that gives her a challenge and a chance to sow confidence among people who had none to begin with. Her own career has zigzagged from the Peace Corps to Wall Street, from getting a master's in linguistics to getting an M.B.A, from television production to investment banking. Taking time off while Riff was in the hospital had "a negative impact" on her career, she says, but refocused her on the importance of spending time with her family and husband.

Still, despite enormous demands on the home front, Christine has never doubted that her work outside the home is as critical an employ of her gifts—as much a form of self-expression, a source of identity, and a medium for worthwhile sacrifice—as motherhood. Like every working mother, she has known periods of intense resentment toward her job. But she insists that, even in the short run, she is the better parent for it. In the long run, she says, "I don't see how my sons could come out of this household not believing a woman could do the job of a man or a man could be as loving and nurturing as a woman."

Christine's mother, while she herself did not work, champions her daughter in every undertaking and has never even subconsciously urged her to adopt a more traditional lifestyle. "Look around you," Christine recalls her mother saying, "at all these people who grew up with mothers at home in the '50s. Are *they* perfect?"

Perfect Christine is not: There were some deviations in her career path, she admits, that she allowed to compromise her personal values. She feels in retrospect that Wall Street demanded, and took, too much of her time and attention. She worries that she's an "overly self-reliant person," someone who doesn't always know when to stop and say 'Enough.' Work has handicapped her, she says, in that she hasn't always been on hand for her children. She finds herself wishing, when her kids "push buttons no one else knows about," that she were more knowledgeable or better equipped to handle their manipulations. She laments never having enough time, or making enough time, to nurture her own relationships, particularly with her husband. These are all priorities that she acknowledges don't always get priority treatment.

"I feel I have a lot to contribute workwise," she comments, "but I have to find places where I can feel really good about spending time away from my kids. That means getting out of the New-York-Ivy-League-M.B.A. track. I've learned that if you succeed under someone else's parameters, it exacts too high a price. That's why I'm leaving."

Being the corporate "Do-Be," she acknowledges, has enabled her to go out and do what she wants: She learned the ropes, the vocabulary, and the tricks of the trade to the point where she's no longer intimidated when dealing with people in high-stakes business environments. But Christine admits she's always had a lot of confidence—a result, she says, of parents who supported her in every endeavor. "They wanted me to be happy," she recalls. "They wanted me to do the best I could do, not necessarily be better than other people. And they always made me feel totally secure and loved. I'm not afraid to meet new people or try new things."

Meanwhile, the future is looking better for her son. Just when they had given up hope that Riff would ever speak, recalls Christine, "He asked me, 'Can I have a glass of apple juice please?'" Death isn't something anybody dwells on, but its specter keeps her priorities crystal clear. "I think I've ended up being a better mother," she says. "It's forced me not to do what other people think I should do, or what's high-paid or prestigious. It's forced me to focus on what I really want to do.

"Most people will tell you I'm not an obsessive-compulsive person," she continues. "I don't worry about a lot of things: I was probably the only woman in business school who just decided not to study on weekends, and to this day I try very hard not to work on weekends. I get things done that have to get done, not what somebody else wants or what's the appropriate thing to do. I've tried to make good decisions, even though they may not have been popular ones. I believe we do have control over ourselves in that way."

Christine doesn't spend a lot of time worrying about what she doesn't control: her son's health, for example, or the outcome of her new business venture. Growing up with a father in the Navy, she lived in a lot of different places and got used to the ground always shifting under her. As she recalls, she wasn't very happy in many of those places but dreaded moving even more—until it dawned on her that the new situation might just as likely prove light-years better, and not any worse, than the one she was leaving. "That's why I'm willing to make changes," she explains. "I've never been one to set my sights on one thing, one goal I have to get; I'm more opportunistic than that. Life is full of serendipitous events, and I've found it far more rewarding to embrace the detours than fight to stay on the path I set out on.

"I'm always willing to compromise on the means," adds Christine, "but I don't think I've compromised on my original goal, which is to always be challenged—to enjoy my work, enjoy people, and to add value to their lives. I've done a lot of different things, but I've pretty much stuck to that."

CHAPTER FIVE

Imperfect Care, Imperfect Parents

I think I'd die if I had to start looking for a baby-sitter all over again," says Maeve Fegan, the decorator supply rep and mother of two preschoolers whom I introduced in chapter two. She apologizes for sounding "overly dramatic"; it's just that she's been through the wringer trying to find someone she can actually trust, someone suited to her boys, someone she can identify with and feel good about.

"This woman we have now is bright, maybe too bright for what she does," sighs Maeve. "I know I won't have her for the long term. But just thinking about having to replace her I start feeling terribly resentful: I think, if I didn't have to work, I wouldn't have to look."

There isn't a working mother who hasn't wondered if indeed the only solution to the chronic anxiety of having to find, trust, and replace a caregiving arrangement is to quit relying on child care altogether. To entrust one's offspring to a surrogate, even a related one, is to live on a hair trigger. A beloved sitter quits, having gotten "a real job"; a nanny procured at great cost walks out one Friday and never returns the following Monday; the woman in the neighborhood who's been looking after several children in her home announces she's retiring due to health problems. Or worse, the sitter doesn't leave but must be fired for not doing her job; the au pair from Germany proves utterly incompetent and incompatible; the day-care center whose staff was so engaging and effective one month suffers a complete turnover the next. Child care is the rug working mothers expect at any moment to be pulled out from under them, leaving them professionally incapacitated, emotionally vulnerable, and psychically drained.

Living with this knowledge is stressful precisely because none of us has the time, the resources, the energy, or even the will to undertake again what was the first time a needle-in-the-haystack endeavor. "It's the choosing process, not the day care, that I've found most stressful," observes Lori Boyle*, a city planner with a daughter in preschool and a three-month-old baby she occasionally leaves with a sitter. "I've said to myself when it's taken weeks to decide on a nursery program, 'Hey, this is only preschool, not a life-and-death situation.' But I do take it pretty seriously."

As we all should, and as most of us do. But if we find seeking, selecting, adjusting to, and losing our child care a dreadful, daunting, and depressing condition of working, perhaps it's because most of us, like Maeve, don't have the option of quitting work, even if our care situation drove us to consider it in desperation. In fact, it's *having no choice* but to beat the bushes, having no choice but to "settle" on someone or some institution, having no choice but to hand over our child and hope for the best (or, at least, hope to avoid the worst) that gnaws away at even the most unflappable among us: Accustomed to thinking of ourselves as independent and self-determinate, we cannot tolerate the frustration of abject dependence.

Every Mother's Worst Nightmare

Maeve Fegan has more reason than most of us, however, to

dread the inevitable, more reason than most to feel utterly conflicted, desperate, and vulnerable about child care.

Six months ago she came home to find her three-month-old son feverish and whimpering. As the evening wore on, Tylenol notwithstanding, his cries became screams and he broke out into a rash. Yet when she called the doctor there were few symptoms to describe—even the rash had disappeared. Suspecting an ear infection, she took him in to be examined.

Her pediatrician could detect nothing except that the baby seemed to have a sore left leg. Had he fallen? No, said Maeve; the sitter had said he'd slipped out of his bouncy chair, but he hadn't fallen. The doctor postulated a virus and sent her home. Later in the week, when her son showed no signs of improvement, a series of X-rays were taken. And on the third set, there it was: a fractured femur.

"It wasn't until the pediatric specialist asked, 'What about the sitter? Are you sure she's telling you the truth?' that I began to feel as though *I* had done something wrong," Maeve recalls. "I said, 'Look, if I can't walk out the door every day and trust my baby-sitter, how can I go to work? You're questioning my choice in somebody.'"

To this day Maeve does not know exactly what happened to her son—except that something *did* happen: The femur, she was told, is about the hardest bone in the human body to break. And yet for two more months Maeve gave her sitter the benefit of the doubt. Only when she discovered the woman was talking on the phone all day, leaving the baby in his crib, did she let her go.

"For a long time I closed my eyes," Maeve concedes. "Maybe out of guilt: I couldn't believe I had employed someone who wasn't right for my child. Or maybe because I couldn't take time off from work to look for a sitter, or maybe because I felt guilty about how much my work had already suffered, after eight weeks of maternity leave. . . .

"I accepted my sitter's explanations," Maeve struggles to

explain, "because she was such an incredibly open person—because, I guess, I didn't want to know, I didn't want to think. When I asked her about the telephone calls, she claimed she phoned only when he was sleeping. But he was never one to sleep; he'd wake up and cry at the slightest sound, at the sound of my key turning in the lock."

Since Maeve hired a new sitter, however, her son's sleeping habits—and overall behavior—have improved dramatically. "We couldn't get over the change," she adds. "I had just thought he was a difficult baby. My child was difficult because he was a very, very unhappy baby."

Slowly but surely, she says, memory of the ordeal is fading, erased in part by the utterly positive addition of a caregiver who, like herself, is Irish and as capable as her predecessor was incompetent. These days Maeve can talk about what happened; for months she couldn't. "I feel tremendous guilt for what I put my son through," she remarks. "You look at your job, you look at working, you look at the whole dish and wonder, 'Why am I working?' But I know why: I have to work because I couldn't otherwise feed my children. So then you go through the whole guilt exercise. You say, 'If I'd been home, I'd either know what happened or it would never have happened in the first place. And the guilt affects everything: your marriage, the quality of your work, everything. The first six months of this year were really traumatic for me because I was worried about my children. I know I should have let [the sitter] go sooner, but I honestly wondered if getting somebody else would make it any better. I was calling up people in the paper and finding most of them couldn't even speak English."

But because Maeve ultimately did find someone in whom she has absolute confidence, what continues to haunt her are the months when she refused to heed her instincts. "What if I had continued to ignore the situation?" she says. "What if I hadn't done anything?"

The Crisis

Bad child care is the nightmare from which no mother can escape. The professional who can run a business or save a life; the manager who can deal with an absentee receptionist, an office paint job, and a project deadline in the same day; the mother who can organize a community fund-raiser while entertaining two toddlers and nursing a baby—no matter how thoroughly they've investigated a nanny, no matter how carefully they've selected a day-care center, no matter how many years they've known their sitter, all walk out the door haunted by the specter that the sitter or staff member to whom they've entrusted their most precious responsibility is a Hyde masquerading as a Jekyll, or otherwise *not* the woman they thought her to be.

This was literally the case for Rebecca Garner*. For some weeks Rebecca, an elementary school principal, was leaving her three-year-old with a woman who, in addition to her own children, cared for several toddlers in her home. Rebecca felt very comfortable about the arrangement until she noted her daughter continually made the same observation. "I'd ask her, 'What did you do with Marie today?'" Rebecca recalls, "and she'd say, 'Marie was taking a nap.' I thought that was kind of strange, so I went over there and found not only was Marie not taking a nap, she wasn't even in the house. Some girl I'd never met was watching the kids." Rebecca now relies on an in-home nanny.

Yet relying on a single person—one who comes to your house or one who takes children into her own—is problematic for precisely that reason, contends Debra Sucher, a part-time film editor now expecting her second child. "Even if you check all the references, you can only know her so well," she notes. Debra has had her two-year-old daughter in day care since she was three months old and plans to enroll her baby at some point as well. "Good day care is the most secure option," she says, "because there are layers of supervision, with lots of people covering for each other and local and state policies dictating standards."

But day-care centers, mother and math professor Linda Bodini* found, are so prone to staffing problems (low pay and high qualifications often being mutually exclusive) that there's no telling on any given day who's actually watching over your loved one. "Someone with barely a high school education," not the teacher Linda had taken pains to interview, was assigned at the last minute to watch the three-year-olds at her daughter's center. When her daughter starting yelling and acting out at home, Linda recalls, she dropped by the center unannounced one day and found children sitting in the hall crying and the teacher in the classroom screaming. "The kids were in 'time out' all day because the woman didn't have the skills to deal with young children," she explains. Now, with a four-month-old to care for, Linda has cut back to working half days and relies on both a part-time preschool program and a graduate student for child care.

For Carolyn Marth, who taught briefly at a major national day-care franchise, there's only one way to get peace of mind—and that's to stay home, at least during the preschool years. She quit her job and withdrew her two-year-old daughter from day care after observing how kids got "shoved through the day with no structure" because staff members were forced to play "musical classrooms" depending on where the center needed supervisors most on any given day. "In order to make the budget, they'd never have more than the bare minimum of staff on hand," explains Carolyn. "If enrollment was low that day for my class, they'd put me in the room with the most kids—say, the three-year-olds—even though I wouldn't have prepared a day's schedule for three-year-olds. The kids don't know what's going on, and, of course, the parents don't." In her experience, day care has little to recommend it. "It's good having your kids socialized, but they come home and say and do things you'd rather they hadn't learned," she says. "I hate to paint such a grim picture, but in the end, no one takes as good care of your kids as you do."

Of course! we who are working hasten to agree—as though we needed reminding. We're reminded at every turn. The papers are rife with tales of psychopathic sitters, homicidal au pairs, and sexually abusive day-care personnel, ostensibly to keep us on our toes or prod us into constructive outrage, but more transparently to profit off our guilt-ridden psyches. Indeed, for the media child care is the goose that keeps laying golden eggs, an issue tailor-made for selling air time or ad space. We don't want to hear about the nanny who set her infant charge on fire; we don't want to read about the ten-month-old beaten to death by his sitter; we don't want to know about the day-care pornography ring—and yet we can't help but read every lurid detail, can't help but repeat the story at the office or playground, can't help but frighten ourselves senseless by tuning in to the ladies' room gossip.

It would seem we *want* to make ourselves fiercely uncomfortable (as though our circumstances weren't punishing enough already), as though to be constantly reminded of the potential for disaster were somehow going to make us better mothers. Evidence damning child care is like a hair shirt we wear: It makes us miserable, but the anxious mother is the good mother, the one ever poised to commit desperate acts at the slightest wind of doubt. Fear will make us leave a movie for which we've just purchased two tickets and hired a baby-sitter; go AWOL one afternoon from our job, regardless of the consequences; or quit work altogether. This, we persuade ourselves, is acting on maternal instinct, though the instinct is bred purely from guilt and irrational fear. Living anxiously, we have come to believe, is our only defense, child care being what it is.

It's a wonder, sleeping on this bed of nails every night, that any one of us can function on the job day after day—let alone smash through glass ceilings or maternal walls to build a career and make the workplace a kinder, more rewarding place for our daughters. It's a wonder we don't just keel over from the sheer strain of having to work while remaining convinced our children are at any moment likely to be victimized or abandoned by our surrogates.

How can we possibly view ourselves as liberated under such circumstances? How can we possibly hope to blaze new trails for future generations of women when we are afraid to walk out our own door? How can we continue to hope for peace of mind as working mothers when we constantly seethe with anxiety about whether our children are emotionally nurtured, intellectually stimulated, or even physically safe? How many roles can we possibly expect to balance on the head of this pin?

The entire superstructure of the women's movement—equality before the law, equal opportunity in the workplace, equal compensation for equal contribution—is built on the fundamental assumption that others can and will care equally for our children. That the movement doesn't fracture and collapse, given the ever-shifting sands of child care upon which it rests, is testament to the fact that women are incredibly resourceful and indefatigable creatures when it comes to securing what their children need. Yet the resultant jury-rigged system is hardly ideal. It's taking a terrible toll on us and an unknown toll on our offspring; many of us have compromised our expectations, no longer hoping to provide what's best in the way of care, just what we pray is not harmful. For the sake of our children, for the sake of our gender, for the sake of our society, *something must be done* about child care.

But what? And by whom?

Why the System Is the Way It Is

Nobody claims to have accurate statistics on child care, but from data collected by the Bureau of the Census, the picture that emerges is striking for its diversity—a "patchwork quilt" of individual and institutional pieces constituting a blanket of security for some, dangerously thin coverage for others. The bureau estimates that some 20 percent of children under the age of 15 whose parents both work are cared for by their own mother and father, usually in split shifts. Close to another 20 percent are looked after by relatives (grandparents, siblings, extended family members), either in their own home or the relative's home. The majority of children (upwards of 60 percent), however, are cared for by nonrelatives, either in a home ("family day care") or an institutional setting (meaning licensed centers operated by the government or a church, community, employer, or for-profit corporation). Family day-care homes appear to account for nearly 30 percent of the child-care picture, although no one knows for sure just how many such homes exist because anywhere from 60 to 90 percent of them are unlicensed and operating as part of the underground economy. For similar reasons, little is known about the prevalence of in-home sitters and nannies: Current estimates put the figure at 5 percent of all care situations.[1]

Rough as these figures may be, they nonetheless represent a dramatic shift from how children of working parents were cared for merely a generation ago. Parents, grandparents, and other members of the immediate or extended family comprised the clear majority (about 70 percent) of caregivers; centers accounted for less than 5 percent of all care for children under 15.[2] But from the mid-'70s to mid-'80s, the number of day-care centers increased *234 percent*,[3] while relative care eroded as grandmothers and aunts either entered the paid work force, pursued ambitions of their own, or simply became inaccessible, no longer living in the same community or even the same state. In the span of little more than 30 years, child care evolved from a parental duty to a paid job, from a personal relationship with a related adult to a group relationship with a salaried employee, and from a family concern to a social responsibility.

In part because women established themselves in the work force far faster than society was prepared to accept them, surrogate care was from the start a bastard child, the unplanned offspring of the women's movement that we hoped one day to legitimize. In some ways, we have: We do know, having devoted considerable academic research and government funding to the issue, what constitutes *good* child care. We have determined ideal parameters for group size, staff/child ratio, caregiver training, stability of care, daily routine, and organization of space. And we all know, after being bludgeoned almost daily with alarming video footage or tabloid accounts, what constitutes *bad* child care. But the system to which we entrust our children is still illegitimate, undisciplined, and unresponsive to reform because most Americans don't want it around, wish it had never been born, and resent having to take responsibility for it.

To embrace the cause of surrogate care seems to imply turning our backs on the nuclear family and rugged individualism, the two precepts upon which most of us believe a great nation rests. It's not at all clear whether we are prepared to do that, despite overwhelming evidence that we already have. *Redbook* recently polled more than 400 fathers, ages 18 to 79, to determine just how radically the traditional family has changed. From changing diapers (96 percent do) to feeding their kids (80 percent do) to taking them to the doctor's (a startling 86 percent have done so), "today's men conspicuously outperform the last generation"; nearly half (47 percent) insist they're as good at child rearing as their wives, and *two-thirds* say they would like to try looking after their children for a time while their wives work. The fairly obvious explanation: "More couples are sharing economic responsibility these days, so men don't feel pressured to work all the time."[4]

And yet how these men behave in the real world of shared parenting is almost completely at odds with how they think things *should* be in the fantasy world occupied by *their* fathers.

Only 36 percent of those polled have wives home full time, but "by a surprising majority of 72 percent," notes the survey, "men cling to the ideal of a traditional family in which the woman stays home with the children."

How can this be? Says Dr. Ethel Klein, president of the consulting firm that conducted the survey, "Men's roles are in transition."[5]

But according to Donald Hernandez, chief of the marriage and family branch of the Census Bureau, the traditional family deified in popular culture *hasn't ever been* a national tradition: only 41 percent of children born just prior to the 1940 census were born to breadwinner-homemaker first marriages. The figure rose to 45 percent just before 1950 but then began a precipitous decline, to 43 percent in 1960, 37 percent in 1970, 27 percent in 1980, and about 20 percent by 1988. And that's *newborn* children—the number of 17-year-olds who've grown up in Cleaver-type households dropped from 26 percent in 1940 to a mere 10 percent in 1989.[6] In other words, our belief in what constitutes good child rearing is almost completely fantastic—at least compared with how most of us actually raise our children, which is increasingly by proxy and increasingly in response to economic necessity.

And it's not just the men replaying the Ward and June tapes. We, their working wives, suspect that we should be primary caregivers for our own children, a belief reinforced by the Mom we see on television—the one who may now show up at 6 P.M. with a bag of Big Macs for dinner but who is still nonetheless responsible for her family's cholesterol intake, flu treatment, laundry problems, germ exposure, plaque buildup, underwear selection, decorating decisions, and party planning. To assign any or all of these duties to a stand-in is to call into question who we are when stripped of our characteristic tasks. How can we call ourselves mothers when the majority of us entrust our children to strangers and institutions for the bulk of their care, feeding, education, socialization, and nurturing? And yet what kind of mothers are we if we fail to ensure that those strangers and institutions are doing the job we must rely on them to do?

Surrogate care is at once an enslaving dependence and a liberating resource, a despised interloper and a welcome lifesaver, a wellspring of salvation and a fount of doubt. Whereas men's attitude toward child care is "in transition"—implying, at least, movement from the old paradigm to the new—ours is in oscillation, reflective of our perennial conflict. We want to be mothers in every regard, in every sense of the word, in every way our ideal image dictates, but we want, we demand, that our surrogates be capable of safeguarding, loving, educating, and caring for our children as we would were we able to be home.

So is it the crazy-quilt nature of our surrogate system that undermines our commitment to the workplace? Or is it our profound ambivalence toward working motherhood that accounts for our patchy system of child care?

The Ideal

How women answer this chicken-egg question determines on which side of the battle line between full-time and working mothers they stand. In child-care reform there is no middle ground, or so the current raft of literature would indicate: Either you are one who believes that even a good surrogate is no replacement for Mom or you are committed to the Great Society notion that every working mother should be assured of affordable, quality child care (that is, a perfect duplicate of herself who will nonetheless cost less than a fourth of what she herself is paid).

Emblematic of the anti–surrogate care movement is Fredelle Maynard, Radcliffe Ph.D. and mother of two grown daughters, who suggests in *The Child Care Crisis: The Real Costs of Day Care for*

You—and Your Child that even at its best, day care can only be said to not harm a child; the problem with child care isn't so much that it's short on funds and talent but that it can never approximate the role of the child's own mother. "Everything we know about child development, everything research reveals about the effects of substitute care, suggests that those [first] three years—at the very least two—are vitally important to the child's, the whole family's, flourishing," Maynard writes in her preface.[7] In her second chapter, after laying out what little is truly known about the effects of day care, she asks, "Is it appropriate, is it *right* to bring children into the world with the confident expectation that someone else will care for them during the entire period that experts agree is critically important, the first five years of life?"[8]

For Maynard and her apostles, the problem isn't with the current system of child care—the problem *is* child care. Her assessment of the options—from nonprofit community or government-sponsored centers to workplace, family, or nanny care—catalogs all manner of less-than-ideal situations, including staff shortages and high turnover, cramped quarters, inflexible scheduling, excessive competition, inadequate one-on one nurturing, not-so-nutritious meals, occasional injury, neglect, and even death. Maynard then expounds in detail on how the child suffers as a result of this exposure. Intellectual development, she notes, isn't necessarily hampered—but children learn best from those to whom they have an emotional attachment, and "such bonds are rare," she concludes, citing a Vanderbilt University study that found very little evidence of "sensitive responsiveness" even in quality care situations.[9]

Socially, all the evidence Maynard consults suggests day-care kids acquire superior independence and social confidence—but the flip side of these skills, she hastens to point out, is that "day-care children tend to be less tractable, less polite, than children raised at home" and ". . . are more inclined to get what they want by hitting, threatening, kicking, punching, insulting and taking possessions without permission."[10] Emotionally, says Maynard, children subjected to day care too early in life fail to become securely attached to their mothers, although she admits the experts have yet to fully concur with this analysis of the data. And finally, there is the question of moral development: "Parents cannot count on genetic endowment and some judicious 'quality time' to mould this child in accordance with their own value system," she states, observing that "children learn what they live with."[11]

Maynard's indictment of surrogate care hardly ends there. Creativity is hampered in a group setting, language skills aren't properly developed, and health—not just the child's, but that of his parents and his entire community—is constantly endangered with outbreaks of hepatitis A, shigellosis, giardasis, and viral gastroenteritis.[12] So what's a mother to do? "If a mother absolutely must work," concludes Maynard, "then she owes her child the best care possible. If she does have a choice, then I think she owes it to *herself*, as well as to the child, to take two or three years for the most important work she may ever do, nurturing a new life."[13]

Lest she be accused of slighting what she acknowledges to be a growing majority of women who *must* work, Maynard does offer these poor choiceless souls advice on how to ferret out the best possible second-best care. One must first take into consideration the age and stage of the child; his temperament, health, and capacities; one's own situation in terms of job, home, and money; and the attitude of one's spouse. Once the type of care is determined, Maynard then outlines issues of concern and specific questions to pose (of the family caregiver: "Do you have a sand and water table indoors? Is there a place for clay-work? Have you easels for painting? What about finger-painting?"[14]), offering a "Caregiver Observation Form and Scale (COFAS)" for those who would prefer to tabulate the child-rearing value of everything from "using the child's dialect" (+1) to "physically punishing a child" (-100).[15] (I shudder to think how many *mothers* would score in the "non-optimal" range.)

Leading the opposition—those who insist child care is a given, not a choice, for the majority of parents today, and therefore a right, and not a privilege—is Sylvia Ann Hewlett, whom we last heard decrying the hardships and injustices of working motherhood. In *When the Bough Breaks: The Cost of Neglecting Our Children*, she expands her *Lesser Life* thesis to show how ignoring women and family needs in the workplace is ultimately tantamount to ignoring, and condemning, the next generation, the future of American industry and the future of the nation. Hewlett seems to think our lack of initiative in child-care reform stems from our ignorance of the problem, so she devotes two-thirds of her book to the plight of disadvantaged kids; advantaged kids whose parents are never around; victims of divorce; victims of unlicensed, unsafe child care; victims of too little government spending; victims of the federal deficit; premature babies; babies who never get a chance to bond; and babies who will face a lifetime of neglect at both private and public hands. It's a grim picture, in case we hadn't noticed.

On a more positive, if briefer, note, Hewlett then posits what corporate America can do (and in some notable instances *has* done), in the way of family-leave policies, child-care services, part-time/flex-time/job-sharing alternatives, child-care subsidies and special programs aimed at helping kids in school, at home, and in their community. She then outlines a game plan for government that underscores the fundamental role she accords public policymakers—and consequently, their fundamental responsibility for our unconscionably shoddy treatment of our most valuable resource.

"Government should mandate job-protected parenting leave for a period of twenty-four weeks . . . guarantee free access to high-quality prenatal and maternity care . . . vastly improve

access to quality child care . . . significantly increase educational investment . . . provide substantial housing subsidies for
families with children . . . do much more with tax policy to
support families with children . . . shape and complement private sector efforts . . . seek to bring down the rate of divorce
. . . and complement government policy with a new level of
personal commitment," she suggests.[16]

Noting that the Japanese—our economic and educational
superiors—revere the family and dedicate their lives (at least, the
mothers' lives) and disposable income to the nurturance and
education of their offspring, Hewlett laments that we are no
longer a society of mothers who stay home and fathers who stick
around but acknowledges the "contemporary reality" that
women are intent upon working and cannot afford, "with plum-
meting wages and sky-high divorce rates," to stay home. She also
observes that raising children and building families in America is
"a risky, thankless task." Divorce can destroy a lifetime of investment in a family and put a mother on the poverty rolls; public
policy and tax codes as they now stand discriminate against the
pregnant, the married, and the married with children. "The critical task of building strong families can no longer be defined as a
private endeavor, least of all a private female endeavor," Hewlett
stresses. "It is time to demonstrate in our laws and policies that
we, as a nation, honor parents, value families, and treasure our
children."[17]

Taken together, Maynard's contention that the best surrogate
care is none at all during the first three years (or why have children?) and Hewlett's insistence that government and corporate
America shoulder the cost of "investing" in our children represent, in a nutshell, our internal conflict as workers and as
mothers. Part of us knows in our heart of hearts that we should
be taking care of our children, at least while they are very young,
whatever the sacrifice; the other part believes we should be given
the means to keep our hand in our profession—lest we lose our

wage-earning ability and future financial security, our confidence, or even our sense of identity—without penalty to our children or families. Either we shouldn't have to work at all, as Maynard seems to suggest, or we should be able to work at cost neither to ourselves, our families, our careers, nor even the gross national product—the have-it-all, win-win scenario Hewlett advocates. Both are, not coincidentally, *ideal* scenarios, impeccably moral in their underpinnings, laudable from even the most contentious viewpoint.

But both require enormous change in the social, moral, and political fabric, and change of any kind requires total commitment of labor, resources, and public will. If we, the current generation of mothers, could ally ourselves wholeheartedly with one or the other vision, there's no telling what we could accomplish. But, of course, that's why child-care reform remains in a state of suspended animation: We're torn right down the middle. We're pulled in entirely opposite directions, pining, on the one hand, for the blissfully simple concept of parenting as a gender-based division of labor and, on the other, for the blissfully equal and fair shouldering of both work and family burdens by women and men. So polar are these yearnings, so keen is our ambivalence, that we would prefer to remain neutral in this child-care battle rather than risk inadvertently siding with the enemy. We would prefer, frankly, to put our heads in the sand and stumble, on blind faith, through our working day, praying our children will reach school age not too much the worse for surrogate wear.

Understandably, given our divided minds, we are neither any closer to securing the three-year maternity leave Maynard posits as a bare minimum than we are to establishing Hewlett's goal of subsidized, quality day care for all who need it. Indeed, torn in pursuit of two diametrically opposed ideals, we are giving our children arguably the worst of both worlds: guilt-ridden mothering because, in not being home, we're not living up to external expectations, and catch-as-catch-can care because, in failing to provide trained, subsidized surrogates, government and the private sector haven't lived up to our expectations.

The Mommy Track

To be utterly torn between mothering and working, I've endeavored to show, is the *norm* for the current generation of women. It's a conflict we're not likely to be cured of, no matter how many studies are conducted, no matter how many editorials are written, no matter how many feminists or antifeminists try to set us straight. If to reform child care we must take a stand, for or against, all or nothing, then we're in big trouble. But if instead our inner struggle forces a compromise—in which we expect neither ourselves to be exclusive caregivers nor our surrogates to be full-blown parents—then a solution to our current crisis is not only possible, but largely within our power to bring about. Immediately.

Compromisers represent that third side of the coin, the side that presumably doesn't exist but nonetheless accommodates all of us for whom neither staying home nor reneging completely on child care is a reasonable option. Compromisers are women who *won't* sacrifice everything for the sake of a) their children or b) their careers, preferring instead to sacrifice a little across the board, according to their own highly idiosyncratic vision of what it means to be a parent. Naturally, these women would prefer not to have to deny their children or themselves; would prefer child care be made easier to find, afford, and take comfort in; would prefer parenting be made a more exact science so they might know how best to invest their time; would prefer not to be conflicted. But even in the absence of external aid, perfect prescience, and total conviction, these mothers are *acting*. They are making hard decisions, arguably the hardest: what kind of role they want, and need, to play in the lives of their children.

Meet Susan Jones*, mother of 18-month-old and five-year-old daughters, and an attorney. Sort of. Susan is not practicing as she once did, working for a large firm in child litigation. She now job-shares at a major insurance company where she acts as a liaison between the legal and claims departments, analyzing cases, writing memoranda, and telling the lawyers what to do. She quit her full-time job as soon as she got pregnant, anticipating doing some per-diem work out of her home while caring for her daughter. But she didn't like working out of her home, and when her baby was about a year old, Susan took what was initially posted as a temporary, part-time job for retirees with a law background.

"It's a compromise," she says. "If I didn't have children, I definitely wouldn't be doing this; it's not exactly my field." If she hadn't any children, or had more time, Susan would be doing something "more high-powered"—perhaps litigating, which she was trained to do and where her husband, also an attorney, perceives her real skills. "But I know what it would mean, being a trial lawyer," she explains. "The long hours, the working weekends, the constant travel. I'm sure I'll do it at some point, but I just don't know, having little children, at what age they can deal with that.

"It really depends on the type of mother you want to be and the type of children you have," Susan adds, explaining that her oldest daughter, the more sensitive and needy of the two, would most certainly suffer if she worked longer hours—and Susan herself would suffer from the added stress. "My primary motive for taking this kind of job is that I have two kids, and how they're responding, how they feel about me working, how they're thriving on their own—that's the bottom line for me," she says.

Staying home full time, however, was no more an option than working full time. "Working the way I'm working is something I need," says Susan, "and my needs count, too." Her husband understands this: "He knows who I really am, and he knows there's a part of me that won't go away—the fact that I'm a mother hasn't made it go away—and that I'll be happiest doing some kind of work."

On the job three days a week, Susan feels she is striking the right balance for her children and herself. She's home enough to enjoy her kids and give them what they need without being "manic" or "overbearing"; she's working enough to enjoy her job, keep her hand in, and afford a live-in housekeeper—a woman who provides for her children exactly what, in some ways, Susan cannot herself provide. "She's more patient than I am," Susan observes. "And she loves them unconditionally, which is what I want her to do most."

And having full-time help frees Susan and her husband to spend together what little time they do have (her husband feels obliged to put in 70-hour workweeks). All in all, Susan concedes, the "mommy track" she's chosen is the ideal compromise, given her goals as a parent and as a lawyer. She doesn't feel forced, like some women, to prove herself capable of being CEO; nor is she motivated to cut back on her career merely because so many of her male colleagues and stay-at-home female peers find success-ful working mothers threatening. She's at home enough to be her children's primary caregiver, but not so much that she doesn't enjoy parenting. She's working enough to secure her future earning potential, but not so much that she can't enjoy the leisure that money buys her. Her employer couldn't be more accommodating of her needs (she demanded, and got, full ben-efits despite her part-time status), her husband couldn't be more supportive of her priorities, and her caregiver couldn't be more suited to her children.

And yet precisely because Susan chose to compromise—and was not discriminated against or otherwise forced into a mommy track—striking a balance has been anything but easy since she and she alone determines what is "right." Ten years from now, she points out, if she's not happy with how her kids turn out or the career she finally resumes, she has only herself to hold accountable; she can't blame men, or government, for making decisions for her, she can't despise her husband for forcing her into the workplace, she can't bewail a lack of decent child care for forcing her to spend more time at home and less time at the office, she can't resent her employer for taking what she might have given to her children.

"I realize that if I want to be a good mother *and* a good attorney," Susan observes, "I'll never rise to the level of men who can put in more time—and that's not the fault of the corporation, or of men; it's nature. Somebody has to be primarily responsible for the children.

"But I don't resent that I'm the one who is, because I want to be. If I wanted to be partner-track, and work the insane hours my husband does, he'd welcome the chance to be primary caregiver and to be home more and let me do what I wanted to do. We had this discussion, about whose career would be time-intensive, understanding we couldn't both have one. And this was the balance I chose. I just wish it could be less difficult to maintain.

"I was trained as an attorney, did really well in school, made law review, got hired by this big firm—I was totally gung ho," reflects Susan. "Then I had kids. And the conflict was with myself; it was nobody's fault. Some of the things Susan Faludi said [in *Backlash*], I just knew she didn't have kids: My inner conflict revolves around what it is to be a mother, not what it is to be a lawyer."

Child Care, Reformed:
The Parent Track

Susan is no martyr. Having taken the initiative in solving her own crisis, she would welcome more support from the public and private sectors. She would very much like to see women get some help in the way of better maternity leave and more part-time work opportunities ("I was very lucky," she concedes). But most of all, Susan would like the rules changed in regard to the hours *men* are working.

"Men have the same problem we do," Susan insists. "My husband is tortured by the same conflict of roles and guilt that I am. He feels tremendous pressure to be an involved father, not one who sees his kids an hour a day or on an occasional weekend. And he's having a tougher time making changes than I have. He tried to talk to his firm about wanting to spend more time with his family, and they made it clear his priorities have to be at work first.

"Well, we're questioning that," she adds. In fact, her husband is contemplating dropping out of his firm to take a less demanding, less time-consuming, and less high-profile job with a corporation simply because "he doesn't feel it's worth it anymore" to give to his employer what he would rather give to his children.

"Not to sound like Marilyn Quayle," laughs Susan, "but in society in general, how are we going to value the time families spend together? That's not a 'woman's issue.' That's the main issue."

The implications, with regard to child care, of what Susan is suggesting are so obvious as to defy perception: If both men and women are going to work, then both men and women must be regarded in the workplace as parents, obliged to providing primary care to their children and therefore *equally* in need of flexibility to carry out that responsibility. It is not simply up to the woman to structure her commitments to family and firm; it's a joint effort to make equal sacrifices in terms of career—and enjoy, equally, the rewards of joint parenting. What better solution to our overreliance on surrogates than a "parent track," particularly since fathers are as likely to be concerned with the well-being of their offspring while they're at work as are their working wives?

Fredelle Maynard is right to note that surrogate caregivers cannot be regarded as, or expected to be, *replacements* for mothers. Sylvia Ann Hewlett is right to point out that mothers cannot, and should not, be charged with the entire responsibility of shoring up the family and thereby salvaging our future as a nation. And it is unrealistic, we can agree, to predicate child-care reform on either mothers once again providing full-time care or caregivers providing full-time mothering. The "parent track" Susan advocates embraces these seemingly incompatible truths. And it is a solution that requires evolution, not revolution: Instead of fighting to make women equal competitors with men—a fight that requires overlooking the glaring reality that women get pregnant and bear children—the "parent track" urges we merely recognize that men are equally responsible for, and capable of, raising their offspring. Nothing but our conventional attitude must be overcome to secure this kind of equality.

How might it be done? The blueprint has been kicking around for years under the guise of "the mommy track," Felice Schwartz's game plan for corporations seeking to stanch their hemorrhage of female talent. Never once did Schwartz, founder and 31-year president of Catalyst, the research and advocacy organization for working women, use the rather condescending term "mommy track"; the press, grossly misinterpreting her thesis to mean that corporations should "track" employees according to whether they were "career-primary" or "family-primary," put the term in circulation and Schwartz on the feminists' blacklists. But what Schwartz was advocating in that 1988

Harvard Business Review article was essentially a "family-friendly" workplace in which women might be given every conceivable support during their childbearing years, from generous maternity leaves to part-time working arrangements, in order to ensure their loyalty and total commitment to the firm once their children were in school. Confronting maternity as a fact of life, granting female employees the flexibility to heed their maternal instincts, and structuring the workplace to accommodate part-time, flex-time, and job-sharing commitments, corporations would not only keep their best talent but would in all likelihood reap significant rewards in the way of long-term dedication from those women in whom they had invested.

It was a compelling thesis—so compelling that, once the media brouhaha had subsided, Schwartz expanded on it to include men. In her 1992 book, *Breaking With Tradition: Women and Work, The New Facts of Life,* Schwartz breaks first with the literary tradition established by other female writers tackling the work-family crisis: Unlike Susan Wittig Albert, who trotted out *A Work of Her Own: How Women Create Success and Fulfillment Off the Traditional Career Track,* and unlike Judith Posner, who explored *The Feminine Mistake: Women, Work, and Identity, Going Beyond the Myth of "Having It All" and Finding New Paths to Fulfillment,* Schwartz does not propose that women leave the conventional workplace but rather that they foment change within it. First, women need to break "the conspiracy of silence"—pretending that issues of pregnancy, childbirth, and family are utterly irrelevant to their performance—and make clear to their employers what they need in the way of flexibility if they are to continue to contribute in a meaningful way. By *not* speaking out, Schwartz contends, women are contributing to their own oppression by allowing their employers to think having children in no way affects their ability to compete.

"Women are unwilling to acknowledge they may be different from men—that they not only have babies but need to nurture them and may want to spend more time at home—because they're afraid that acknowledgment will be used against them," Schwartz observes. "But you can't address a problem if you can't name it."[18]

Women *would not* lose their jobs or even jeopardize their position by discussing the obvious, she maintains, because companies have every incentive to listen and try to find ways to accommodate, given the sizable investment they stand to lose (upwards of $40,000 per individual, Corning Glass estimated, based on the costs of finding, hiring, training, promoting, and according certain pension and health perks to each employee) should the employee decide to leave.[19]

Indeed, according to Schwartz, the corporate professional community is aggressively seeking ways to stop the costly drain of female talent. "They're not taking giant steps, but it's happening," she reports, having routinely met with CEOs eager to solicit her advice on how to reverse the damage. "By the end of the decade I think we're going to see a lot more leveling of the playing field, and a lot more freedom of opportunity." In part she attributes this change to the Clinton administration—Hillary alone, even—for having demonstrated a commitment to placing women in highly visible positions of power.[20]

But also undeniably in women's favor, Schwartz stresses, is an imminent demographic shift that will give them the leverage they need to demand flexibility and even special treatment: The pool of qualified applicants from which a company may choose is shrinking, not only because baby boomers are having half as many babies but because those children are emerging from high school and college educationally handicapped. Right now companies aren't feeling the pinch—there are still plenty of well-educated men for every qualified woman, and men, who don't have babies, are cheaper to hire and retain. But as the boomers age and their offspring have an average of 1.8 children, the population is undergoing a *halving* trend, according to

Schwartz, and unless something is done about the caliber of both private and public schooling real fast, CEOs will be forced to change their ways in order to attract and keep the few qualified candidates who will exist in the twenty-first century. Only those companies that have shown themselves responsive to the family needs of their employees—men as well as women—will command the competitive edge.[21]

Schwartz makes it clear that she is not advocating we all wait until demographics push the issue. Her argument to CEOs and management is that, in order to recruit women in the crisis years, companies must infiltrate their ranks now to establish a track record for future women to assess. Company leaders with a long-term vision had better seek to correct the "corrosive" corporate environment, perhaps even substituting for the conventional pyramid of power a "jungle gym" that allows lateral, even downward, mobility for employees who require such flexibility in order to attend to their families. In such a hierarchy, employees, not employers, determine the pace and direction of their career, based on their priorities as well as their skills. There is no penalty, no loss of status, no imperative to go find another job should circumstance (such as a new baby or having to care for an elderly relative) dictate a holding pattern. Employees exit and reenter at will, and reenter they shall if no barrier or stigma prevents them, argues Schwartz.[22]

The old paradigm of the pyramid squanders talent, impedes progress, hampers productivity, and throws away its most valuable commodity: dedicated employees. It is predicated on the notion that workers cannot be induced to work without the carrot of advancement perpetually dangled before them, notes Schwartz, when her 30-plus years of experience would indicate that women *and* men respond more favorably to the prospect of ever-increasing levels of autonomy. Productivity, not hours logged in the office, might be the new measure of worthiness in such a scheme. And then the playing field might be truly leveled, no longer penalizing women for heeding their biological clock, no longer encouraging men to succeed at the expense of their spouse and children.

"Flexibility is a tough nut," Schwartz concedes, "but with the compression of the pyramid in recent years, companies are forced to look for alternative rewards to keep their talent, and flexibility is not only the best but also the cheapest of those alternatives. It will take only a couple of companies to launch a revolution."[23]

In terms of allowing women to have both an active parenting role and a meaningful career, Schwartz concludes that the ideal situation "will be when men share in parenting and companies come to realize that the single most effective thing they can do to enhance the productivity of women is *to legitimize and facilitate the role that men increasingly want to take in family life*" (emphasis mine).[24] Employers aren't quite ready to respond to fathers' needs, she concedes, but what they do for mothers in providing flexibility will prove model policy for what they might ultimately provide fathers.

The Role of the Individual

What Schwartz envisions and what Hewlett is lobbying for are really not all that different: Both would like to see the family emerge strengthened and triumphant, for the sake of the children, the parents, and society at large. But they differ markedly in what role they accord the individual. In Hewlett's brave new world, government and the major corporations must take the initiative to revamp public policy and the workplace in order to foster family values; as Schwartz sees it, women themselves must lead the way, asserting what they want and what they need, confident that their priorities ultimately deserve to reshape the workplace, instead of the workplace dictating what role they play as parents. After spending two-thirds of her book addressing what employers can do to capitalize on, rather than lose money to, the recruitment and retainment of mothers, Schwartz addresses the responsibility women themselves bear in changing the status quo: They must become self-determinate, choosing, consciously, to "adopt, modify, or reject the norms" according to what they know to be right for themselves and their families.

"Becoming self-determinate," she clarifies, "means not allowing oneself simply to drift with the current but to be proactive in creating the conditions of work and family that will be personally fulfilling." It means asking perhaps the most profound question of all: "What does parenting mean to me, and what does work mean to me?"[25]

And becoming self-determinate has to start with the recognition that we cannot have it all, no matter how responsive companies become to working mothers, no matter how many obstacles are removed for women who aspire to the highest levels, no matter how much child care fathers assume. A 1993 study of senior women executives sponsored by Korn/Ferry International, the executive search firm, indicates that women have indeed attained positions accorded more money and more status than they might have held ten years ago, but at a price— an emotional, physical, psychological price great enough to prompt 75 percent of them to say they want to get off the fast track before retirement.[26]

Carol Scott, the U.C.L.A. marketing professor who conducted the study, observes that while these executives enjoy greater financial success (having doubled the average salary of a decade ago to $187,000) than their predecessors, they also tend to be married with children—as senior women executives were *not* ten years ago—and hence feel burned out from juggling work with a "disproportionate" load of family obligations. One might conclude that their burnout reflects the current *inflexibility* of the workplace, but a Catalyst study of 70 companies in a wide range of industries shows significant progress on the flexibility front: Whereas in 1989 less than a third of those companies polled had offered nontraditional (part-time, shared, or compressed-work-week) arrangements for at least five years, *three-fifths* had such alternative policies in place in 1993.[27]

"There will always be a delicate balance of what accommodations employers will make in order to retain good people," writes Schwartz, "and what individuals must sacrifice to achieve their goals. The central question we will always have to ask of ourselves will not go away: 'What do I want most, and what am I willing to trade off to get it?' It is only to the extent that we search out the answers within ourselves that we can hope to pursue our goals with minimal energy and psychic drain and with a maximum sense of fulfillment."[28]

In exhorting the individual to be self-determinate, Schwartz is, of course, addressing both women *and* men, but it is women, she believes, who will lead the way to the shared parenting that could resolve our most painful conflict, as mothers who cannot be full-time mothers. Men already have the inclination to play a critical role in their children's lives, and society is highly approving; Schwartz recommends that women ask men not simply to share in the domestic responsibilities but to agree to redistribute total responsibilities according to what each wants most to do and what each does best. That may mean the woman is acknowledged to be the primary breadwinner and the man the primary caregiver, or a more traditional arrangement—but personal choice, and not simply gender, should dictate the roles in the partnership.[29]

And toward this end Schwartz sees real progress. "It matters not what men and women would choose to do if they were indeed free to choose; I just want them to have that opportunity, and one of the first steps toward ensuring they do is to face the fact that women have babies and parents need time to parent. I like to think that in fighting for flexibility in the workplace,

women are making real gains on improving the quality of life—
and the range of opportunities—for *both sexes.*"[30]

The Crisis Revisited

So back to the question I posed earlier: Is it the patchwork
nature of our surrogate system that undermines our commitment to the workplace, or is it our profound ambivalence toward
working motherhood—our uncertainty as to what we want, what
we deserve, and how we're going to get it—that accounts for the
failure of both private and public sectors to give us reliable,
affordable surrogate care?

Or to ask the question a little differently: Is bad child care
something we endure as victims, yet another manifestation of
our oppression and overall beleaguered status as mothers? Or is
it a problem we're in a position to do something about?

I have to agree with Schwartz that our primary concern
shouldn't be the failure of private industry or government to
provide decent child care but our failure to define our role as
parents and demand more recognition of it. I believe public policy cannot initiate social change but can only respond to it; I
believe a capitalist economy is motivated to do not what is right
but only what makes good business sense. Therefore it is up to
us, as individuals, to chart a moral course, to speak our minds
and vote with our feet, to demand the flexibility we need to be
good parents with the understanding we will give back our very
best as employees.

To repeat: Both public and private sectors can and must take
steps to vouchsafe the well-being of our children when we are
not in a position to do so ourselves; no one would dispute the
importance, the necessity, of their participation. But to expect
anyone or anything to relieve us of our parental duty, to offer us
guarantees that might assuage all doubts about surrogates assum-

ing our job, to make painless our inner conflict by making easy the rearing of our children—these are not only unrealistic expectations but irresponsible ones. Good child care is neither cheap nor easy, whether government or business provides it. For all that we know about early development and the emotional maturation process, no one has yet hit upon a care formula on which every baby can thrive. Assessing the needs of a child and responding to them adequately is a challenge most parents, as keenly motivated by love as they are, find difficult and costly in terms of time and money.

Even if the subtleties of child rearing could be quantified and institutionalized, what it would cost to provide in full, nation-wide, would make health care look like a freebie. Monies already allocated to child care are estimated to total $48 billion per year by 1995. Yet if we were to spend what current standards of quality dictate on every child (an estimated $4,000 per pre-school-aged child and $2,000 for school-aged children), child care in the United States would total $126 billion per year.[31]

And even if we could afford such a staggering cost, could we expect money to buy us peace of mind? If we charge the private sector with the creation and maintenance of a child-care system, we can anticipate quality to be determined strictly on the basis of a cost-benefit analysis; if we look to federal and state entities to expand on the social services they already provide, we can expect a system where a lack of cost accountability would create a bureaucracy most adept at perpetuating itself, as our public education, welfare, and health programs already demonstrate. Either way, if we will not address the issue of child care first as *parents*, as mothers and fathers equally committed to assuming primary responsibility for their children, however that "parent track" compromises or alters our career ambitions—then we can expect, and will deserve, to have compromises chosen for us and our children, compromises utterly indifferent to individual choice and utterly unresponsive to individual need.

On this last and critical point let me be perfectly clear: When I speak of parents assuming primary responsibility for their children, I do *not* necessarily mean either or both parents becoming primary caregivers. Mothers may be career-intensive while fathers take a greater role at home; fathers may be career-intensive, allowing mothers either to work part time or not at all; both parents may work but give the bulk of their energies to child rearing; or both parents may work and choose to play a role secondary to that of hired surrogates in their children's lives. All of these combinations can translate into a healthy upbringing for the offspring *provided* the parents are committed to making it work for their children, and that means a) actively deciding on their level of personal involvement rather than passively assuming a parental role according to what employment or child-care circumstances dictate; b) assessing, and accepting, the trade-offs inherent in any decision; and c) paying the associated costs, because in terms of either time spent as an involved parent or money spent on the best of surrogates, raising children well is, and deserves to be, an extremely costly endeavor. It is our responsibility as parents to determine our role, compromise our lifestyle, and invest our time and money in our children. To expect society to relieve us of any or all of this "burden" is to forget we ourselves *chose* to have children.

CHAPTER SIX

Good Enough Mothers, Good Enough Surrogates

T here is no perfect solution," Debra Sucher responds when I ask her how the question of child care might be answered. "No one standard system can be perfect for everyone, given our individual styles of parenting and the individual needs of our children. Everyone should be entitled to a minimum level of support in terms of care; to keep their sanity, parents need to have a safe place to take their child while they work and to be able to respond to emergency needs without fear of losing their job.

"But even in a society where government and industry bent over backwards," notes Debra, "we'd still walk around with tremendous ambivalence, because there's not a choice you can make where for one second you can absolve yourself of your responsibility as a parent for your child."

To work and be a mother is to suffer tremendous ambivalence toward work because we're not spending every waking hour devoted to our children—and being devoted, on hand to answer every need, is what we were raised to believe mothering is all about. Why bring children into the world if we're not prepared or able to do that? Even if we were to concede that, given our temperaments, our talents, or our economic needs, staying home is not ideal for *us*, we don't question for a moment that it constitutes the ideal for our children.

Thus from the get-go having to rely on child care is a damning proposition, a compromise we impose on our children, who if they could choose would no doubt choose us. To mitigate our guilt for denying them (they didn't ask to be born—we asked to be parents), we want whatever surrogate arrangement we can find and afford to be *perfect*. Our children deserve nothing less.

This is a pretty tall order for us and for our surrogates to fill. In fact, we are doomed to fail, doomed to feel like *bad* mothers. Because if perfect child care existed and we could secure it, then, comparatively speaking, we would by definition assume second-best status. And if, as is likely, we choose care that's just average, or are economically forced to accept care that's even less than average, we have no choice but to conclude we're lousy mothers for not only reneging on our primary role but also for failing in our secondary role—failing, that is, to appoint a superior replacement. Surrogates need to be at least as good as mothers, and mothers, as we all know, are perfect: No harm ever comes to a child in the care of his mother, or so we torment ourselves into believing.

Given our profound bias that good mothers stay home and that stay-at-home mothers are infallible, it's hardly surprising we want someone or something else to wave a magic wand and make child care come with a money-back guarantee. Only then can our guilt about not being primary caregiver be assuaged. Forced to rely on an imperfect system, we are unbearably vulnerable, because if the system "fails" our children in any way, we look like monsters for using it in the first place (never mind all the myriad ways in which full-time mothers can fail their offspring: The standard against which all institutional care is measured is *perfection*). We'd like some overarching body to assure us our children will be protected from our own fallibility, our imperfection as mothers (because we are not home), our imperfection as employers of imperfect surrogates.

Someone once explained to me that the reason finding good child care is so frightfully difficult is that we are looking for a duplicate of ourselves—ergo, we are embarking on an impossible quest, because anybody who is just like us would, like us, be working at a better paid and more prestigious job and *she*, if she were also a mother, would be looking for someone to take care of *her* kids.

Well, in fact, that's not the underlying problem. What makes our quest so impossible and frustrating is that we are looking not for ourselves but someone patterned after our ideal image of ourselves, someone *better* than we are as mothers, someone as perfect as we keep trying to be, someone who won't make any mistakes. (Susan Jones, the mommy-track lawyer introduced in the previous chapter, says what impressed her most, upon becoming a mother, was not that she needed to be perfect but that she could no longer afford to screw up, now that it wasn't just her but a totally innocent life her actions or inactions might hurt.) It's having to work, we assure ourselves, that accounts for why *we* have fallen short of our ideal, but we're not going to compromise in whom we hire for our children.

In short, the difficulty in finding decent care isn't so much the system we're dealing with, but *our expectations of it.* We've merely externalized our highly futile internal exercise. The problem isn't simply that child care isn't good enough: We're not good enough.

Our Surrogates, Ourselves

Lest you think I'm blaming the victim, let me give you an example of how unrealistic expectations of ourselves translate into problematic care.

Maeve Fegan, you'll recall from the previous chapter, made a mistake in whom she hired to watch over her infant son. A fairly trusting, easygoing person herself, Maeve was snowed by the sitter's openness, her competent attitude, her ready explanations. Maeve, after all, is only human.

But for two excruciating months, Maeve refused to accept the idea that she might have chosen poorly, might have made the error that ultimately had severe ramifications for her child. Already guilty about leaving her baby to go back to work, already condemned, in her own eyes, for not being his primary caregiver, Maeve couldn't bear any further indictment of her mothering skills or her judgment. That she had hired an incompetent—what would that say about her? Who could forgive her such a lapse in judgment? Who wouldn't question her fitness as a mother? Who wouldn't conclude that maybe she did not deserve to be a mother?

So Maeve shut her eyes, unwilling, unable to confront her sitter's flaws because she couldn't bear to confront her own. And to this day, that's what haunts her—not what happened to her son but that she ignored it, afraid of being implicated for her role in hiring the woman in the first place.

Of course, the most vigilant, the most exacting of mothers have chosen poor sitters. My friend Gail tells of coming home one evening to find that the girl to whom she had entrusted her infant and two toddlers had been entertaining a boyfriend; my mother, at various times in her child-rearing career, hired a closet drinker, a petty thief, and a woman who routinely dozed off on the job. We've all suffered from imperfect judgment. But the consequences our children suffer as a result of our judgment vary widely depending on how quickly the problem comes to our attention and how quickly we act on our discovery. And, unfortunately, guilt—the guilt of being a working mother, the insecurity of being inadequate to the task of motherhood—can blind us to inadequacies in our surrogate arrangement and then paralyze us from doing anything about them. In our caregivers we hope to see ourselves reflected, but if we suspect the reflection is one of imperfection, we just won't look. And then we cannot act.

I know whereof I speak. For a few months prior to the birth of my second child, I had endured a sitter two days a week whom I had ample reason to suspect was not looking after my son in the ways she described. Since she was the beloved and trusted employee of one of my dearest friends, I gave her the benefit of the doubt until the evidence was simply not to be ignored, and then let her go. In my efforts to replace her I swore I would not tolerate second best; I would comb the county, if need be, demand extensive references, brook no compromise in my wish list. I would hand-pick this candidate based on *my* exacting standards.

I must have fielded 50 calls for the ad I ran; I must have interviewed 15 women, calling all references, checking all claims, even, in some instances, hiring them for the afternoon to see how well they did in practice. And I found what I wanted: a mother of four grown children, a licensed nurse with 20-plus years of experience, a religious woman but no fanatic, a loving but firm hand with my children, a caregiver keen on cooking hot, nutritious meals, taking the kids to the park, reading to them, and eschewing the VCR. She came with the highest praise from the head of pediatrics at our county hospital. She was perfect.

Or so I believed until my husband pulled out for a guest his stock of single malt scotch and found all three bottles (one of them previously unopened) drained to their last ounce. I confronted Mrs. Ford and dismissed her the following morning, but that wasn't fast enough to avert a terminal case of guilt. I had a brand new baby in the house whom, on occasion, I had left with her for an hour or two (never more; Kathryn absolutely refused to take a bottle). My son, an impressionable and sensitive toddler, was spending three days a week in her exclusive care. How could I have overlooked her drinking, I who worked in my home! Why had I brushed off my husband's observation that she sounded somewhat slurry on the telephone? Why hadn't I 177heeded my own doubts, when in the course of our frequent conversations I sensed she was not hearing me? Hindsight engulfed me with countless instances when I suspected something—but what?—wasn't quite right, instances when I had inevitably rationalized her behavior in order to maintain my illusion that I had chosen perfectly. I had loved her. I had trusted her. And I had defended her, zealously, when a friend had so much as intimated she was "odd."

The sense of betrayal, of violation, made me, like Maeve, want to quit work for the foreseeable future, to be spared the agony of having ever again to trust a stranger, to spare my children all that I envisioned might have happened in my absence. But like Maeve, I felt I was in no position to throw in the towel; no sooner did Mrs. Ford leave than my husband lost his job. I spent a bleak Christmas bewailing my lack of options, angry at Mrs. Ford, angry at my husband's circumstances, angry at a system that failed to provide me with reliable, affordable, convenient care, angry at myself for failing to secure the quality my children deserved. Because ultimately I had to come to terms with the fact that, whatever Mrs. Ford's failings, *I was responsible* for my children's well-being. It wasn't working that made me an imperfect mother; it was guilt about working and insecurity about what kind of mother I was. It wasn't my failure to initially *perceive* her flaw that was reprehensible; it was my failure, for three months, to *acknowledge* my doubts and address her flaw.

Any kind of child-care crisis puts all working mothers, potentially, in a despicable bind: Either we're damned for the imperfect choice we made or we're damned for not acknowledging we made it. Short of government or industry miraculously revamping the system and offering us foolproof child care, the only way a working mother's going to avoid being made to look like a bad mother is to stop working and stop relying on child care. And yet, undeniably, that's not an option for most of us. So how, given the perennially imperfect nature of surrogate care, are we going to do right by our children?

The Child-Care Equation

We can start by lowering our expectations.

Yes. Because our expectations of our surrogates are right up there with all the other unattainable goals we set for ourselves as mothers. We cannot be perfect, even if we could stay home; indeed, our imperfections would only glare more intolerably if we were home because we'd no longer be able to blame our shortcomings on having to work. To hold our surrogates to a standard not even the most devoted, committed mother can uphold is to doom ourselves to disappointment, frustration, and anger.

The key to getting good enough care out of an imperfect system is, in fact, to candidly assess ourselves as mothers, recognizing our strengths, accepting our flaws. Based on that assessment we can then determine what role we want to play as parent, according to our strengths; and likewise, based on that assessment, determine what role we want our caregiver to play, in compensation for our weaknesses. A caregiver can be good enough when she is not expected to be ideal in all capacities but simply in those where the parent needs help most. A caregiver, we should remember, is *not* ideally our replacement but our *complement.*

"To try to create a second parent isn't the answer," says Debra Sucher, noting that "even parents for whom money is no object" haven't come up with the ideal solution to taking care of their children. Debra clarifies that money wasn't the determining factor in her choice of day care: What she likes about the center is that the staff takes care of her daughter in "a manner complementary to ours as parents." She and her husband have made professional decisions according to the role they feel they must play, and want to play, in their children's lives. "There's no substitute for parents," Debra asserts.

To expect a surrogate to be a substitute is to concede we're not doing our job. But what *is* our job? What role should parents play? What role do they want to play? What role *can* they play?

If this were an easy question to answer, we wouldn't be wringing our hands over society's failure to look after our children. It is most certainly difficult to find, in the child care available to us, what we *want*—but it is arguably much more of a challenge to determine what we really *need*, what our children must have because we are not in a position to provide it ourselves. It is next to impossible to find a surrogate who can do it all and do it all well—but we would rather try than look within ourselves and come to terms with our own shortcomings.

Difficult and challenging as it is, however, to really know ourselves, it behooves us to try, because only when we know what we can truly give to our children can we determine the remainder of the child-care equation: what "x," in the way of surrogate care, equals. Too many of us feel robbed of choice in terms of child care because *we*, the parents, are the unknown quantity. We let what's available in terms of day care or nanny care determine what role we play, instead of actively choosing our role and looking to surrogates to fill in in ways we cannot. We allow circumstance and other people to decide for us what's most important—and understandably bridle when the outcome doesn't reflect our innermost desires. Having to depend on surrogates, we feel denied choice, denied control—when in truth we have abdicated our responsibility.

Mary Brittingham, an immigration attorney and mother of a five-year-old girl and eight-year-old boy, is a good example. Mary has, to all appearances, an ideal situation, a mommy track of her own design: She works part time, a decision made after her daughter was born and one that allows her the emotional resources to enjoy her kids without denying her the professional identity she recognizes she needs. "I think I've figured out the balance for them and me," she says. "I have the benefit of seeing my children very happy. I don't feel guilty."

But neither is she at peace. "I have great fear and trembling about what the future holds," Mary admits. "What's going to happen when I'm 45? Because I realize what I'm doing professionally, I'm off the track. I fear I've given up my chances for making a real contribution workwise. There's really only a decade and a half left in which I can make that contribution. So I question the timing of all this, whether I've chosen wisely, being home more now as opposed to when they were first born. I tend to think children have more and more need of you as an adult in their lives—not less—as they get older. But is there time for me to get back in [to the professional competition]?"

Mary will concede she didn't exactly choose this timing. She worked full time after her son was born because she "wasn't secure enough professionally, or ready" to leave a field in which she had only a year's experience, but went part time after her daughter's birth because she was even less secure about the sitter who was then looking after her son. "Child care has been a real problem," says Mary, whose solution has been simply to rely on it as little as possible. "Imperfect assistance" has more or less determined her current mommy track.

Hence her current midlife crisis: At 41, Mary says, she is frantically trying to decide whether to have one more child, because in so doing she would answer, once and for all, the nagging question about her career. "One way or the other I have to confront my professional ambitions," Mary remarks. But she's not going to. Regarding the possible baby, she says, "I can let time and my husband decide."

Noting that "there are days when I feel I'm not a good enough lawyer, not a good enough parent, that I'm shortchanging everybody all around," Mary observes that her generation's sense of inadequacy stems largely from the fact that "so many of us *chose* to have children. Children have taken on incredible significance and importance, have become the focus of so much more attention and obsession than ever before, because the whole act of having children is laden with choice."

Think of it: How much less guilt might we feel if children were, as they used to be, an inevitability, a duty to which we responded rather than a luxury we elected? How much less responsibility we might bear for our decisions concerning work and child care if we were merely reacting to fate rather than masterminding our destiny and that of our children! But, of course, we do choose to have children. We choose to get pregnant or to stay pregnant. Having made this single choice, we are committed to a lifetime of actively deciding what is right, for our children and for ourselves.

And yet we persist, like Mary, in "making decisions out of indecision," in *responding* to pregnancy, parenthood, and working motherhood rather than acknowledging our autonomy. Throughout the millenia women have proved themselves singularly resourceful, incredibly tenacious, and fiercely protective of their families in response to circumstances beyond their control, childbearing chief among those circumstances. Our flexibility, our tendency to roll with the punches, our ability to adapt—all are skills born of having to accommodate what we were in no position to change. In that much of life remains to this day out of our control, these are skills that will serve us well, that may even grant us the competitive edge should we find ourselves the object of gender discrimination.

But in having the power to choose to bear children, we grant ourselves the awesome privilege of becoming self-determinate. Motherhood, for perhaps the first time in history, does not entail abject dependency. We do not renounce choice in choosing to have children. If anything, determining the kind of parent we want to be, need to be, and can be for our children is obligatory, our chief responsibility. There is not a right choice or a wrong choice. There is only our choice.

Electing to be Secondary

Carla Straeten, to many of her peers, is a career woman—ambitious, successful, and anything but a mommy-tracker. She is not the kind of parent celebrated in *Ladies' Home Journal;* she is not the kind of mother women 30 years ago could have ever imagined. But in that she is the kind of parent to her six-year-old daughter that she chooses to be, based on who she knows herself to be, she is good enough.

As vice president of fixed-income marketing at a major brokerage house, Carla enjoys considerable career satisfaction and "excessive" financial remuneration. She has the professional incentive and the money to keep herself physically fit and well attired. She can afford and has retained the very best child care money can buy; her daughter attends a $13,000-a-year kindergarten and an exclusive summer camp. She has been married for 12 years to a man who has been her "coach," who takes pride in all that she has accomplished. She has what she wants. She has, she believes, what most other women want.

"I feel confident," says Carla, "that if I were to go up and down my block and say to the mothers, 'This is my job, these are my responsibilities, these are my privileges—would you want it?' they'd take it. I think many of them gave it up because they didn't realize they could get this far."

It has not been easy. "I was raised to think that this was normal and natural, having a career and a family—that there wouldn't be any obstacles," Carla explains. "Now I know better." Most of her male colleagues, she says, have nonworking spouses tending to the home front so that they can devote themselves to their career. These men can afford to make a big fuss over their children at the office; she feels she cannot, that to speak of her 'other' commitment would create the impression that she wasn't wholly devoted to her firm. At home, despite enjoying her husband's satisfaction in her higher level of achievement, she does not enjoy his equal participation: "He's overly reliant on me to make all the arrangements, to play a more traditional role," notes Carla.

And there have most certainly been trade-offs. "The cost has been that I have only one child," she points out. "I've always been frustrated having just one, but then I think, it's hard enough on the one, let alone two or three." Not that she thinks her lifestyle is compromising her daughter; on the contrary, Carla is very pleased at Stephanie's independence, her creativity. "She's unlimited in finding alternatives to dealing with a problem," says Carla, "and that does come from having a mom who does a lot of different things. Her environment has allowed for much more flexibility in terms of her thinking. And she's miles ahead socially."

Carla will concede that she doesn't know "the long-term ramifications of having help" to raise her daughter; she's read all the research showing how children left in nonmaternal care from the age of six weeks on suffer emotional problems later and finds she's not "entirely comfortable breaking new ground in this area." Yet Carla asserts she would not have had a child if she couldn't stand on her own two feet financially. In light of "the few husbands who truly can provide for their families and who will be around for the next 40 years," she notes, working is "an appropriate mandate for women in the twentieth century."

Indeed, as a mother, Carla sees her primary role as doing "pioneer" work for women, opening doors, "making a difference for females coming down the pike"—including her own daughter. "I have, in fact, made some strides for females," Carla says. "Not major changes, but I think men are beginning to see a woman is at least comparable to, maybe even better than, a man in certain respects. I think they're also starting to enjoy being married to someone who's more intelligent."

Stephanie, Carla notes with pride, has been exposed to a lot. She's seen her mom in charge, being something beyond a wife and mother. She's seen that both parents can nurture and both contribute to the family's economic strength. She's seen how a man and a woman can get along as equals. "I think I'm giving her more options than I had," Carla says. "I was pushed as a child to achieve economic parity, to compete in a male world. My parents weren't trying to deny me; they were trying to open up horizons. But they didn't tell me how to cope as a working mother; they couldn't.

"I've had to learn the hard way," she continues. "By the time Stephanie's old enough to choose, I hope I'll have the appropriate advice to give her, to show her that she can have a balanced life: career and children, just children, or just a career."

Needing to be Primary

"It was my choice, yes," Jean Stauffer Schoenleber says of her recent uprooting from a community she loved, a job that couldn't have suited her better, and a network of colleagues and friends she has yet to replace. Her husband was miserable in his job, so when a better opportunity came up in another state, she agreed to move. And by so doing, she has become a full-time mother to her two-and-a-half-year-old son.

"I could have said no," she reflects. "I left an ideal situation in terms of my career: I was working maybe 15, 20 hours a week in private practice, and it was very lucrative." She misses, in fact, having her own income. "It certainly changes the dynamic in a male-female relationship," she observes. "Now I control all the finances, but there's always that unspoken argument about whose money it really is."

But Jean said yes to the move, and no to her career, both for her husband and for herself. "I really enjoy being home," she says. "I really enjoy my child. I know that for some women that's hard. I'd love to find something part time here in Connecticut like I had in Illinois, but the part-time opportunities I see here just don't pay that well, and after paying for child care I'd be making nothing, so why do it? I'm not one of those people who enjoys working or has to work for the sake of working; I really love being a mother. If I'm not paid well, I can't justify not being home."

Not that her transition from 13 years as a respected child psychologist (12 of those years spent working on a hospital staff) to full-time motherhood has been painless. Like so many mothers who've left a profession, Jean has known the identity crisis of wanting to blurt out who she "used to be," the sudden vacuum of self-esteem and confidence. "A former colleague of mine called me here because she wanted my professional advice on a case," recalls Jean, "and I actually started crying on the phone because someone still valued my opinion!"

Still, she recognizes that what she really resents is not being home but being home in a new town. "I'm not one of these women who can keep moving around," she explains. "I hate it. I hate starting over because it takes so long to develop really good friendships, and I get my strokes, my support, from other women—not from my husband. Many of these mothers I'm socializing with now, I fear our friendship is sort of shallow, because I'm not sure, if we didn't have kids, that we'd be friends. But then I think the same could have been said of my colleagues, many of whom I became friends with merely because we shared an interest in the profession.

"It's just that it takes so long to really get to know one another," sighs Jean, who's joined support groups of similarly disposed ex-professionals to try to jump start the process. "In truth, I can't be all that unhappy about not working or I would have done something about it. I want to be home. I want my son to see a self-confident person who really enjoys being with him. That's the most important thing for me to be right now."

The Part-Time Solution

In the spectrum of parenting options, Jean Stauffer Schoenleber and Carla Straeten represent the two extremes, mothers for whom being good enough means two very different things, mothers for whom surrogate care plays either a primary role or no role in the rearing of their child. But overwhelmingly, mothers who've examined the options tend to feel they give their children the best of all possible worlds by working part of the week and staying home the rest.

"I don't think seeing your kids 24 hours a day, seven days a week is good: That's an overbearing parent," says part-timer-at-peace Susan Jones, whom I profiled in the previous chapter. "On the other hand, I think 60-hour workweeks tip the scales too much in the other direction. My feeling is, nothing horrendous can happen to either your kids or your career if you strike a balance right down the middle."

Marcie Bradley, who works on a per-diem basis for a local hospice, has always been very clear about what kind of role she wants to play as a mother. "Children were our choice," she says of her three-year-old and 18-month-old daughters. "I would never work full time, or in a really structured job, because we never wanted day care or sitters or [our] parents to raise them." Indeed, after the birth of her first child, Marcie—who had been very career-oriented, with a master's in social work and a supervisory position with a lot of responsibility—stayed home full time.

"I had intended to go back, but once she was born, I thought, no way, this is too important."

And it was great being home, says Marcie. But when a coordinator at the community medical center approached her about taking on the hospice job a couple of days a week, she jumped at the opportunity: After all, she could set her own hours, determine her own pace, keep adult contact in a field she enjoyed, earn a little money, and continue to be her daughter's primary caregiver. She established a small network of sitters to call on and relied on her parents, who live only a mile away, to cover for last-minute commitments.

"The first few times I was away from my daughter six or seven hours I felt almost guilty," Marcie recalls. "But it didn't take long to pass." For one thing, she says, doing something for herself makes her a more patient parent. "And I think it's helped in my relationship with my husband: I can remember when Mark would come home and ask me, 'What did you do today?' and I'd say, 'I changed seven diapers.' Now I bring something to the conversation." Additionally, Marcie notes, going back to work has taken some of the pressure off her husband as the family's sole support.

But money has little to do with her enjoyment of her job and her satisfaction as a mother. "I'd do volunteer work if I couldn't get paid," says Marcie. "It's a lot being home with the kids and taking care of the house, but I need a little more, something people-oriented." To that end, Marcie has found the perfect job: She counsels terminally ill patients, most of whom have prognoses of less than six months; she tends to their emotional and physical comfort, keeps tabs on how their families are coping, helps everybody at the funeral, and follows up with the families for a year to see that they're grieving normally. Far from undermining her priorities at home, says Marcie, her work reaffirms them. "The nature of my work makes me appreciate my family even more," she says. "It makes me examine mortality: I don't take my family or my value to them for granted."

Reveling in Who We're Not: What Caregivers Can Give

Resolving the critical question of who we are to our children is by far the biggest step we can take to attain peace of mind about our child care: After all, if you're everything you feel you need to be, and can be, as a parent, then whatever else your child gets or fails to get from other caregivers—provided safety isn't an issue—is probably good enough.

Those who feel they're good enough parents almost inevitably regard the role played by their surrogates as a decided boon, both to their children and to themselves. The caregiver isn't the enemy, the competition, or the stopgap measure; she is the safety valve, the extra set of hands, the extra source of love, the additional exposure every child needs, the additional perspective every parent could use.

"Mothers are human," observes Susan Jones. "We're not cut out of the mold of what every child needs. Maybe there's something I can't give, and my daughter gets it from her caregiver. Is that the end of the world?

"I know my housekeeper fills in some important gaps," Susan continues. "She's more patient than I am. And one thing I've noticed: She really accepts my children for who they are. She's not their parent, so she doesn't feel the need to mold behavior or impose her own values, whereas I come home and I have a certain agenda. I think a child learns how to be a person, how to approach the world, from her parents, but I think a child should be exposed to other ideas, to other ways of doing things. And I think it's an important life lesson to learn that people other than

Mommy and Daddy can love you, that the world can be a safe and friendly place."

"My daughter's preschool does a great job," says Linda Bodini (introduced in chapter five), a university professor who has always found it very difficult "to sit down and play" with her young children. "The two teachers there are not only her friends but they've helped me with her biting, working with her and with me. She gets the one-on-one attention with an adult that I can't always give her here at home, with the baby."

"I'm certain alternative care is good for my four-year-old," notes Lori Boyle (also introduced in the previous chapter), who is her infant's primary caregiver. But Lori can appreciate the value of good day care because that's where she spent her own preschool years. "It's not an unpleasant recollection," she notes. "I may have been better off there, because my mom and dad were really young and didn't know what to do with little kids. I'm of the firm belief that if a parent is uncomfortable parenting, probably her kids should be in day care."

"I think my children are better off because I *do* work," asserts principal Rebecca Garner (from chapter five as well). "Other people can be better caregivers than I can. Christopher's nanny is a real baby person, and we have it set up so that she focuses on him. He'd never get as much attention from me if I were home because I'd be trying to do a million things. The one-on-one contact she gives him is something I can't provide." Rebecca, to be sure, has not always had caregivers who were better than she in every way: Her six-year-old daughter is testing below average in language skills, and Rebecca feels the problem probably reflects a shortcoming on the part of her caregiver. "But I don't fault myself for not staying home," Rebecca clarifies. "I fault myself for not hiring the right person, and for not coming to grips with the problem sooner."

One bad sitter, that is, is one bad sitter for these women—not an indictment of child care, not an indictment of working motherhood. Invariably, mothers who feel good about the effects of surrogate care on their children feel even better about the indirect effects on themselves as parents and as wives. "If I thought leaving my daughter with a sitter three afternoons and evenings a week was somehow hurting her," says Catherine Beekman, whom I quoted in chapter four, "I'd quit. But instead I see how much fun we're able to have when I'm not working because I can be with her one hundred percent. I'm not on the phone, or cleaning, or trying to do a bunch of things. So the laundry doesn't get done. So a lot of things slide. I can pay someone to do that stuff: Being with her is just more important. Having a sitter part of the week focuses me on being totally a parent the rest."

Having a housekeeper full time, Susan Jones believes, makes her marriage work—unquestionably a vital consideration for her kids' well-being and her own. If she didn't work, Susan reasons, she couldn't afford or justify having help, so when her husband was around she wouldn't be able to devote herself to the relationship. As it is now, "we have better time together because neither one of us has to do any cleaning."

In short, having to rely on hired help can mean bringing in reinforcements that, coupled with one's own efforts, add up to a whole that's *greater* than the sum of its parts—greater, certainly, than one full-time mother alone could bring to the job. "I never feel inferior having to lean on my sitter," says Lori Boyle. "If anything, I feel I'm liable to provide inferior care if I *don't* get that break."

Putting a Value on Caregiving

If working mothers find themselves repeatedly taken to task for handing their kids over to surrogates, it's because in hiring someone or paying tuition to a center we are putting a price on what has historically been considered priceless. "I want my child to have the benefit of my background, not that of a caregiver to whom child rearing is a four-dollar-an-hour job," says one of the full-time mothers introduced in chapter three, expressing the widespread sentiment that caring for a child is so much more than "a job" that any wage paid for it cheapens the act. Surrogates are likened to mercenaries, hired by women too craven "to serve" in active duty themselves. Child care thus becomes a moral issue—a choice that ethically minded, honor-bound, decent women would never make.

This is an interesting attitude, in light of the fact that historically motherhood has been consistently undervalued, underappreciated, undersupported, underprivileged, and undermined by society precisely because it carries absolutely no economic value. The enormous productivity of those who are home rearing children and running households isn't factored into the gross national product; it literally doesn't count. Homemaking does not accrue health benefits, social security, or any kind of pension for those who make a career of it. Those who shoulder its burden take on the reverence accorded saints. Given the wages of saints and martyrs, it's easy to see why there's such a hue and cry to return mothers to the home.

The opposite argument—that putting a price on child care *elevates* our respect for the job—might just as easily be made.

Consider the case of Bonnie Ferro. Home full time, raising her own two children, Bonnie is that rare mother who enjoys not only the satisfaction of doing the job well but the respect and appreciation of those for whom she does it. Her husband, who works at home, frequently tells her what a great job she's doing and helps with much of the cooking and cleaning. Her children take care of their own rooms and do their homework without prodding. Her friends see her as a woman who has something to contribute, not someone to sit quietly in a corner, invisible. "Mommy is usually the one to get stuck holding all the bags at the ball game," notes Bonnie. "Mom is the family doormat. But I'm not here to be walked on."

What accounts for this enviable level of self-esteem? Bonnie is *paid* to be a mother. She is a "professional," academically accredited and licensed by the state to care for as many as five children in her home daily. She is the last person on earth to undervalue the job of child care, having quit her job as a purchasing agent for a large corporation to get her degree in child development and go through the licensing process; indeed, so strongly does she feel the need to elevate the status of caregiving, she teaches a course to other mothers on how to professionalize. Make the mistake of referring to Bonnie as a baby-sitter and she will correct you.

Not that she regards herself as an expert: "I listen to my clients and do for their children what they want me to do," says Bonnie. "I consider them my friends and equals, and I'm just as likely to call them regarding difficulties I'm having with my children as they are to call me about theirs." Yet having the academic and state certifications helps ensure that she sees herself, and others see her, as a professional, to be valued, appreciated, respected, and paid as such.

And as a professional caregiver she feels entirely fulfilled. "People remember me and remember me well," notes Bonnie with pride. Even her tiny clients manage to give her strokes: "Just today I had the two babies out for a walk to the A&P," she reflects, "and when I looked down and saw them giggling together, I thought, I'm giving these children a *lot*. It made me feel wonderful. I thought, it can't be better than this; I can't ask for more."

Looking back on the brief period before she professionalized, when her son was just a baby, Bonnie says she felt "trapped," without the financial wherewithal to do what she wanted to do with him. Today, she says, "I feel pretty self-determinate. I'll accept choices my husband makes, or my son makes, but I'm also in a position to determine what's going to happen in my own life.

"For right now," Bonnie continues, "this is my ambition. I wanted to prove I could get out there and have my own niche, and I'm proud of the one I have now. I'm helping to raise children who are going to grow up and respect other people. And that makes me *very* proud."

Given Bonnie's shining example, I'm of a mind that Connie Lezenby (of chapter one) is right: If we really want to accord motherhood the respect and support it deserves, we should pay mothers to rear their own children—not so *they* value the job, but so *society* does. Short of that estimable goal, however, I'm all for paying surrogates as much as we can possibly afford out of our individual or collective pockets. Yvonne Kearney, the headhunter with two toddlers whom I introduced in chapter two, pays a Brazilian woman "an astronomical sum," but because she appreciates what the woman is doing for her and her children, and because the nanny, also a working mother, appreciates what Yvonne is trying to do, the nanny's salary needs to be commensurate with the respect they accord one another. "It's anything but menial, what she does," remarks Yvonne. "I wish I could afford to pay her more."

I am deeply distressed to see how many women *don't* hold this view, women who have demanded their due in the workplace, women who have fought for equal advancement opportunity and equal pay for themselves only to turn around and exploit their caregiver or begrudge every dime they spend on day care. Can we expect to gain liberation as a gender when we enslave one another? Do we expect our freedom to be free of charge? Out of one side of our mouths we decry the overall sub-par caliber of child care, a level of quality reflective of the low wages paid to child-care workers; out of the other side, we rail against having to pay a good percentage of our income to child care, insisting it should be "affordable." We cannot have it both ways:

Quality costs, and while those who cannot afford to secure quality for their children should have it anyway, the rest of us must then be willing to shoulder the cost. So what if it takes *all* of our disposable income—what else might we possibly buy that could approximate the importance, the inherent value, of our investment in child care?

Because what we pay in child care ultimately reflects not merely how much we value the job but how much we value ourselves. Having assigned a high economic value to caregiving, I have become keenly conscious of the value of *my* time. Say I pay a sitter eight dollars an hour to watch my kids. I'm not going to fritter away that hour doing some pointless, low-priority task *or* slaving away at some meaningless salaried job, because it is costing me not only money but also time—time with my kids. Together, the cost of the sitter and the cost to my relationship with my kids impels me to do something I accord *top priority*, to justify paying such a high tab for the opportunity. And I have all the more reason to value, and make the most of, the time I do have with my children, paying, as I do, to be away from them.

At Peace With Our Imperfection, At Peace With Our Surrogates

Perfect Mothers *can* do it all; the rest of us (everybody I've ever met) need help. Simple as it sounds, it's not an admission we make readily. Even if we're working and unarguably must rely on others to help with the child rearing, we feel guilty. It's a count against us. And if we should be so unlucky as to rely on *bad* help, why, it's a criminal indictment.

But the fact remains, we must have child care, and however many pitfalls await us in the current system, we must choose well because ultimately we are responsible, every second of every day, for our children's well-being. Government and private industry may yet make our job easier, but we are in no position to hold out for guarantees. The burden of getting good care remains ours.

Yet if we can assess ourselves honestly and, for all our short-comings, believe we are *good enough* mothers, then our attitude toward caregivers is likely to change—from resentment (because they must supersede us) to gratitude (because they are providing merely what we cannot or choose not to)—and, consequently, the difficulty of our search is likely to ease. And the caliber of our care will arguably improve, because we will be determining what is "good" care not according to some arbitrary societal code but according to what we and our children need most. In acknowledging that we are not perfect, we relieve ourselves of the burden of having to find perfection to stand in for us. And in readily perceiving our own flaws we stand a much better chance of perceiving what is wrong with our child care—and acting to correct it.

Nonmaternal care, far from making us look like bad mothers, can qualitatively make us better mothers. Factoring child care into the parental equation can add up to a whole that, with regard to our children, is greater than the sum of its parts. But there is no getting around our obligation, as mothers, to determine our contribution to the equation; we cannot let child care, however bad or good, decide that for us.

A Workaholic Who Kicked the Habit

With motherhood, Elizabeth Woodman has finally learned how to say no. At 40, she has limited her focus to her boys, now six and eight; her marriage; and her job, managing a production team of 15 for the couple's publishing company. Every one of these priorities could no doubt benefit, she says, from more of her energy and attention, but she's finally comfortable with the balance she's struck. She would like to be more involved in her community, she would like to address the day-care and child-advocacy issues that beset every woman she knows or employs, and she would like to make sure the workplace accommodates more women at the highest levels. But she concedes she's had to compromise on her wish list—and that's okay.

"I've done a complete reversal," Elizabeth explains. "Ten years ago, if I were to describe myself as a compromiser, I would've considered myself a cop-out. Now, I think of it almost as a religion, a way to keep me spiritually and emotionally sane."

Recently, when members of her church approached her to do a monthly newsletter, she turned them down. "Realistically, I don't have enough hours," she says, noting with some anger that the church didn't approach any fathers with the request. "It was going to take four to six hours out of our home life, and I'm not prepared to give that. Sheer exhaustion would be the price."

And she has cut back at work, with her husband's support. In order to have more time at home with the boys, she doesn't travel as much as the business demands. That means their company doesn't grow, but she and her husband have agreed that's an acceptable trade-off for more time with their family. "I don't feel the least bit apologetic for not being a complete workaholic," comments Elizabeth. "I find it incredibly difficult to say no, but the more I'm able to do it, the more balance I achieve."

This is a relatively new attitude for Elizabeth. Conditioned as a little girl, she says, to be polite and helpful, to take care of her four younger siblings and help out both parents, she never felt "no" was an option. The women's movement during the mid-'70s "was instrumental in making me the person I am today," she observes, "because it really helped me stand up for what I wanted, to become more assertive and take more responsibility for decisions in my life."

Yet the confidence to make those decisions was slow to come, not merely because she hadn't been encouraged at home but because the society in which she was educated reinforced the belief that women, like children, needed decisions made for them. "Looking back, it's amazing to me how unfocused my schooling was," Elizabeth recalls. "Nobody ever talked to me about life after college; it was assumed I'd get married. So when I did get out, I realized I had no skills, nothing to prepare me for a role in the work force."

With so little practice making choices when she was growing up, she made a lot of "wrong" choices, she says, as a young adult. Making poor choices eroded what little confidence she had. And, understandably, it ultimately became easier to mask her indecision by not deciding, or choosing, at all. As a result, in her 15 years as an editor there were plenty of 3 and 4 A.M. workathons, self-imposed out of a constant fear that she might "fail" to do everything. But after the birth of her second child, when she and her husband launched their own venture, Elizabeth started to notice all sorts of symptoms—irritable bowel syndrome, outbreaks of hives, terrible headaches, strange tensions—and recognized that, for herself and her children, she was going to have to start letting go. Control had become a compulsion.

"In many ways, control is addicting," she says. "The more you have, the more you think you must have, until it's a kind of tyranny. I was treating life like a marionette show, making everybody miserable and myself exhausted."

Ironically, it was motherhood that both pushed her to the edge and rescued her from the brink. Forced to acknowledge she was losing control, she decided to give it up. "I've become a much better delegator," Elizabeth remarks. "Pressures at work that used to keep me up until two in the morning I can now distribute better. With two children I just couldn't get away with doing everything myself."

She's also found that having to hone her communications skills in order to be utterly understood by her children has paid off professionally. "I always had a tendency to assume too much," she notes. "When I'd be working on a project with other people, I'd assume they already knew what I expected of them—and then was disappointed when I didn't get back from them what I hoped to get back. The boys taught me the importance of being very thorough, and very clear, in expressing whole expectations; it's made for a much happier home life and better working relationships."

Perhaps most notably, motherhood has made her a more "nurturing" employer. "It wouldn't have occurred to me to give as much feedback to people as I do now," she muses. "I see how much it means to the boys, and to me, and I've brought that to work; I'm not as quick to react negatively. What I *don't* lose control of is my temper. I've learned the importance of really cooling down and addressing difficult situations rationally. I can't allow pressures of the business to affect how I relate to my staff, and the same is true with my boys: I can't let upsetting news that has nothing to do with the family affect them."

And work, in turn, has made her a better mother by giving her a new set of skills from which she derives considerable satisfaction and confidence. But there have been plenty of moments when she has weighed the rewards against the sacrifices and wondered if her job wasn't subtracting from the quality of her life. She recalls all too vividly the panic and distress she felt when her children were "day-care nomads," going from one situation that didn't work out to another. As swiftly as she acted, these caregiver upheavals inevitably affected her schedule, and she fell behind at work. Her husband absorbed some of that time, but everybody, she says, felt the ramifications.

"There were times when our child care was so precarious, I thought maybe it wasn't worth it," Elizabeth recalls. "I thought maybe I should just stay home until the kids reached a certain age. There were moments of real soul-searching, when I wondered, 'What the hell am I doing?'"

Hence when her older son was diagnosed with an attention deficit disorder, Elizabeth's first response was to feel responsible. "I thought maybe I didn't spend as much time with him when he was a little boy as I should have," she recalls. "Maybe I hadn't been a good enough mother."

But after a battery of tests and hours of consultation with teachers and therapists, the Woodmans learned their child's difficulties stemmed from delays in fine motor skills, from physical frustration rather than from any neurological or emotional disorder. Elizabeth was able to quell the guilt and silence her personal demons because so many professionals in the community went "out of their way" to make it clear the couple's parenting had nothing to do with the problem. Her instinct, said

Elizabeth, told her this. Her ongoing struggle is having the confidence to tune into that voice.

"I think I'm doing a fine job raising my boys," she asserts, "and I enjoy it a lot. But confidence still doesn't come easily in the rest of my life. As a child, choices were always made for me, from what kind of shoes I had to wear to which college I would apply to. One thing I try to do is allow my children to make choices now, so that they'll be much more decisive and confident as adults."

It's been painful, says Elizabeth, to watch some of her sons' choices—from what they elect to wear to what they favor as playthings. She had been, she laughs, the "non-war-toy dictator," steadfast in her insistence that no guns would be permitted in the house. But she yielded her stance upon realizing that the boys were making them out of sticks and using them in pretend play.

"Guns are going to be a big part of their lives," she explains, "and while I'm not thrilled about it, I can't do anything but try to educate them better about them. They should be making some of these choices for themselves. I want them to have the confidence I was denied. Without it, you can't let go, you can't loosen up, you can't slow down enough to enjoy anything."

This realization has in part prompted Elizabeth to make a lot more effort to keep up correspondence and social initiatives with her friends. "I used to think they understood how busy I was with the kids and the business, that when I had time later I'd spend it with them. But then you go back and say 'Here I am!' and they say 'Who are you?'" Elizabeth is also making a point of setting aside one-on-one time with her husband ("that's the relationship that suffers most whenever I feel there's not enough of me to go around") and saying no to pressures or requests that eat into her time with her boys.

"I'm really disheartened when I hear about some poll that says teenagers today wouldn't want to raise their kids as they'd been raised," she says. "They say they hated growing up feeling constantly rushed. I know what they're saying; I know as a working parent I've been guilty of rushing my kids. I'm trying very hard to slow down, both for myself and for my children."

Single, Selfish, &
Self-Sacrificing

"I t's true," sighs Wendy Lindman, a single mother of a three-year-old. "I don't have a lot of options. But on the whole, I feel incredibly lucky."

When I met Wendy, she was five months pregnant and looking eight. I was seven months along and prided myself on looking five—as though by staying small I could almost detain the arrival of this baby, almost deny its inevitability. Wendy, on the other hand, was reveling in her fecundity. At 41, she had beaten all the odds and conceived through a sperm bank. She was aglow with anticipation. I was ashamed of my ambivalence.

In the tumultuous year following my son's birth, I found myself often thinking of Wendy—a woman I barely knew, had no contact with whatsoever, would never, in all likelihood, meet again (my husband was friends with her ex-sister-in-law's new husband.) The first two weeks postpartum, when I doubted I would ever be able to manage parenthood without my mother or my husband on hand, I imagined Wendy pacing her Chicago apartment, alone with an inconsolable infant. I can remember driving Chase for the first time out of Manhattan to visit friends of mine and encountering a hurricane on the New Jersey Turnpike: Did Wendy ever feel this vulnerable, I wondered? Didn't she ever feel it was all just too much for one person to

handle? I found just getting out the door in those days tantamount to Operation Desert Storm, what with amassing the
stroller and Snugli and diaper and bottle paraphernalia requisite
to the simplest of outings and timing it so as to be between feed-
ings, changings, and naps. How did she do it?

More incredibly to me, then home full time: How did Wendy
possibly run a business when she, like I, was probably up all
night? And how could she handle the crushing responsibility of
being the sole support, the lone prop, the one thing between
her child and catastrophe? When I wanted to throw in the towel,
I could at least entertain the notion, knowing my child had a
father. Wendy surely could not. Throughout those formative first
months of motherhood, through Chase's bouts of fever and
bronchitis, bumps on the head, diarrhea and diaper rash, I often
coped with my incipient panic merely by conjuring up the image
of this braver lone woman.

When Chase was ten months old, Wendy and I finally compared notes. I was writing an article on "Why Mothers Compete"
and wanted the perspective of a single mother. Her daughter,
Elizabeth, was then eight months old, and Wendy harbored a
host of new-mother concerns that pretty much paralleled my
own list of neuroses, except that I was two months closer to
recovering from them. She hadn't gotten the hang of nursing
right away and inadvertently failed to give Elizabeth enough
nourishment. She pined for more time with her child and worried that she also wasn't giving her enough stimulation. She
wondered if Elizabeth should be crawling more, eating more,
gaining more weight. And she felt other mothers weren't supportive so much as out to prove their children were crawling
sooner, growing faster, and otherwise validating their parents'
skills.

In the course of our conversation I kept forgetting that Wendy
was single, so much did she sound like all the other new mothers
I'd interviewed. "In what ways do you miss having a mate?" I

asked her, certain there must be *some* handicap inherent in solo parenting.

"In the most practical, obvious ways," she laughed. "Someone to help me park the car. Someone to cover for me when I have to run out and do an errand. Someone to watch her so I can just try on a dress!"

Three years later, Wendy is still lamenting having no one to cover for her, although otherwise "everything's going a lot better than it was at the beginning." She has managed to keep her small advertising business afloat despite the economy; she hasn't yet found the right guy but is dating; and Elizabeth, by all accounts, is physically and emotionally thriving. But motherhood has profoundly affected Wendy's outlook and circumstances in ways she never anticipated. "A lot of things change when a child becomes a reality," she sighs.

What she never anticipated, she says, was feeling that Elizabeth really needs a father. "While I was pregnant I didn't think about the future, didn't question any long-term problems," she recalls. "I just wanted this child, and my options were running out. I chose the way right for me—I'd been married, and I didn't want to take that step with someone I didn't love just to get a baby out of it. People thought I was tremendously courageous, going it alone. But it was a selfish thing for me to do, really."

Wendy says she no longer makes public the circumstances of Elizabeth's conception. She doesn't lie; she's just not entertaining perfect strangers with the details of her pregnancy, as she did when I met her. "Growing up is difficult enough these days," she explains, "no matter how traditional or perfect your parents. I don't want her to be ashamed of what I did; I'm certainly not. But I don't want to have to get into a full-blown explanation before I absolutely have to."

Long before Elizabeth asks questions that demand the truth, Wendy hopes to provide her with a father. Not that there are behavioral problems a father would solve: On the contrary, Elizabeth is "very easygoing, very easy to raise, happy, and totally affectionate," says Wendy. But on weekends, when they go to gymnastics and music class together, she notes that a majority of the other little girls come with their dads. "I can see that's a relationship that's very special," she admits. "Elizabeth doesn't know what that's like, to have a doting father. She gets all her affection from women."

Wendy is doing her best to remedy the situation. She tries to expose Elizabeth to other fathers, to male friends, to her ex-sister-in-law Jennifer's new husband. She's also trying to date—not to provide a father for the sake of a father, but to find companionship for herself as well. Single parenting can be relentlessly lonely. "One guy said to me there wasn't room in my life for a man," says Wendy. "And yes, it's true that Elizabeth is the most important person to me. But that doesn't mean I don't need the love of a man."

Dating, however, has proved tremendously "awkward." She's not sure how Jennifer managed to get remarried after divorcing Wendy's brother, what with four kids, the youngest in diapers. But then, she muses, Jennifer wasn't working, so she wasn't as protective of her time in the evening and had no conflict being separated from her children, plus her kids had each other to turn to when their mother turned her attentions toward another adult. "When I come home," Wendy explains, "if somebody comes over, I'm really torn over paying attention to him as opposed to Elizabeth. Plus we have our bedtime bath and story, and that routine can run as long as an hour. I have to say to my guest, 'Hey, you're on your own for an hour!'"

Still, Wendy concedes, the reality of single parenthood is harshest for Elizabeth—an injustice she regrets, something she feels she should have foreseen. "If I've had a really bad day," she continues, "Elizabeth bears the brunt of it. There's nobody I can ask to cover for me, no one I can turn to and say, "Look dear, I'm not feeling well, you take over.'"

And single parenthood's final rude shock: Wendy's business is suffering. When she was single and "forced," after losing a job at a large agency, to make one for herself, she put in tremendous hours: 12-hour days, weekends, work at home. It was her business, her lifeline, and, at the time, her only option. She insisted on maintaining a hand in all aspects of the creative process, "obsessively" watching every detail. She did everything, and her labors were rewarded: The agency flourished. It was at first a relief and eventually even rewarding, says Wendy. But it was not enough.

"I was never one of those people who could love a business, who could make it her life," she explains. "But because I was single and had my own company, others tended to categorize me as a power woman. Well, when you don't have anything else, you'll expand your business to fill up the time. I always knew having a child entailed much greater reward than running a business; that's why I had a child. But it changed the whole focus of my life. And so my business is slipping—slipping big time."

There simply aren't enough hours in the day, she's finding, to be the best mother she can possibly be *and* run an ad agency. She's putting in at most about six hours a day at the office, what with taking Elizabeth to school and picking her up, doctor appointments, school functions, and an infinite array of other things she never counted on. Her staff has dwindled to two. "I'm sure I could address the slippage," says Wendy, "but I'd rather devote those hours to Elizabeth. Working for yourself is sort of a catch-22: It's because I have my own business that I can spend as much time as I do with my child, but because I spend that time, I'm in jeopardy of losing the business.

"In a nutshell," she summarizes, "I've come to see you can't have it all. I've chosen to make my child my priority, and I've sacrificed my business to do it. I know lots of working mothers who don't do that—my neighbor certainly hasn't changed her 12-hour daily routine for her kids—but that's not how I want to parent my daughter. I'm not letting my business go down the tubes: I don't feel I have *that* choice, short of winning the lottery. But the trade-off is, I'm never completely secure. There's always this specter of financial disaster hanging over me."

Wendy is neither stoic nor cavalier about her lack of options, her limited resources. "I guess what it boils down to," she reflects, "is that you do whatever you need to do. If all I have to rely on is me, then that's tough but not impossible. Yes, I chose this, I chose to be a single mother. But other single mothers *also* chose to have children; it's really easy to forget that, easy to fall into that trap—and I do—where you say, 'Oh, gosh, this is really hard—how can one person possibly deal with it all?' The one undeniable, culminating fact is that I have Elizabeth, against all the odds. I got a miracle: I got a wonderful little girl. That fact pretty much overshadows everything else. How many people don't ever have that, married or not?"

There was a time, Wendy recalls, when she used to physically ache to hold someone, a feeling that haunted her before she had Elizabeth but that now serves to remind her how much of her fulfillment is purely physical—the hugging, kissing, and cuddling—and how much she loves it. "Nothing comes close to the rewards and satisfaction of being a mother," she continues. "What I've gained is truly remarkable; what I've lost I don't even think of as trade-offs. I haven't read a book since Elizabeth was born, but I'd much rather curl up with her than a novel."

For that very reason, Wendy's a little envious of full-time mothers: Parting every morning only gets harder, not easier, and there are days when she counts how many hours her sitter spends with Elizabeth and resents that her own tally falls short. "But I wouldn't want to make my child my whole life, either," she reflects. "I think that's an unfair thing to do to a child. I also think it makes you not a very good role model, someone not of interest to her as she gets older."

As for her business, Wendy says having Elizabeth as a clear priority has forced her to deal with issues that should have been addressed years ago. "I always prided myself on being able to do everything," she explains, "and so I did. That wasn't a handicap when I had the time, although I always knew it was a dangerous position to be in. You reach the point where you can't go out and work on any new business because you're too busy keeping current accounts going. I'm delegating more now.

"The other good thing is I no longer think everything at work is of monumental importance; before Elizabeth, I used to get panic-stricken if I lost a client or an art director. Now I realize the world isn't coming to an end. I haven't always been this pragmatic, but my experience as a mother is that there's almost always a solution, whatever the problem. If you take a deep breath and stop responding emotionally to the situation, you can almost always find a way."

For all of the hurdles, seen or unforeseen, that Wendy has yet to confront, she says she no longer anguishes about the future. She can remember fretting about so many little things, like whether Elizabeth would crawl or walk or talk on schedule—things that were not only out of her control but that were "such a waste of energy." If she doesn't get married, well, she says, that's okay; it's not ideal, but it's hardly catastrophic. She chooses to look at the bright side, noting that her married friends contend with a burden she does not: conflicting opinions on how to raise their child. There have been times when she could have used a second opinion, moments of doubt when another parent might have validated her instincts. But overall, Wendy doesn't feel any more or less concerned—or more or less able to cope—with what lies ahead than her married peers.

"I'm trying not to lose sight of the big picture," she explains. "It's all too easy to obsess over what you don't have, but I look at

Elizabeth and I see a happy, responsive human being. We have such a wonderful relationship. I keep going back to that."

Just watching her daughter interact with other children at school—the way she handles herself, the way she heeds the teacher—gives Wendy a great deal of joy. At the last monthly meeting with the school psychologist, Wendy says she sat there with her mouth agape as she listened to parents discussing problems they're having with their children, because she's not been confronted with any of them. She's delighted at how easygoing Elizabeth is. And she's surprised at herself, surprised to find how much self-esteem motherhood has bestowed upon her.

"Self-esteem wasn't part of my upbringing," says Wendy. "If I had any sense of worth, it was because I met certain criteria, like being attractive or accomplished. So I've always wanted to raise my child to be confident, to feel good about herself just because she's Elizabeth, not because she's pretty or smart or plays tennis well.

"And in that, I think I'm successful," Wendy concedes. "I think I'm a wonderful mother. I think I'm better at mothering than anything else. I'm one of those people who believes we're here for a purpose, to make a difference. And if you can raise a child to be a loving, giving human being, then you've made a huge difference."

PART THREE

Resolving Key Relationships: Arriving at Compromise

CHAPTER SEVEN

The Gender Gap: Husbands & Wives

Jody Norris*, 30, is an artist and sculptor; Alex Norris*, 40, is a professor of literature and writing at a local college. Self-employed and home with flexible hours, Jody takes care of their adopted three-year-old, Kyle. Both assume responsibility for household chores, but of late the question of *who does what* in terms of housework (Who shops? Who makes out the list? Whose turn is it to clean the bathroom? Who is in a better position to cook dinner?) and child care (Who's going to give Kyle his bath? Who should take him to the pediatrician's? Whose turn is it to get up in the middle of the night?) has begun to erode what was, pre-child, a passionate and decidedly egalitarian relationship.

For starters, the couple is no longer "equal" in terms of career commitment. Child-care duties have eclipsed Jody's creative endeavors; teaching takes far more time than the hours Alex actually spends in the classroom. Arguments over parental obligations have compelled the Norrises to put Kyle in full-time day care, but now they argue about money because it is in such short supply. Because, in fact, there's "never enough time, never enough money," the two are still negotiating everything, from the moment Kyle wakes up (Who's going to take him to the sitter's today?) to the moment he falls asleep (Who's going to go upstairs and comfort him?). "Both of us feel like we're doing more than our share," Alex observes.

Having moved every two years for Alex's job, the couple is also without emotional and practical support in the way of family or friends; Alex started at the college only two months ago, and friendships among colleagues are too germinal to lean on as yet. Hiring additional baby-sitters is financially out of the question. Hence the Norrises have little, if any, time together to work out the tensions of their overloaded partnership. "Even if we were to get a little breather," comments Jody, "we wouldn't spend it together. We're too angry."

From a pollster's perspective, the Norrises are the dual-career couple with children we imagine to be archetypical of marriage, '90s style. They recognize the importance of one another's careers; neither entered the relationship on the assumption one would quit once children entered the picture. They acknowledge the value of an egalitarian relationship, not simply on ideological grounds but because it seems the most pragmatic approach given the fact that both put in a full day outside, or beyond, the home. They wholeheartedly support the notion of co-parenting—again, not merely because it's the 'right' thing to do for their child, but because they have little choice and few resources. Theirs is the kind of marriage, *in theory*, to which most women now working aspire. And yet, perversely, the Norrises enjoy none of its perceived benefits. Indeed, they're on the brink of divorce—and Kyle, given up first by his natural mother, is about to lose one of his adoptive parents.

Dual Careers and Disintegrating Families

Half of all marriages now end in divorce; a million children each year go through the divorce or separation of their parents, and almost as many more are born out of wedlock. "Family disruption is at its peak," reports Barbara DaFoe Whitehead, a research associate at the nonpartisan Institute for American Values.[1] In a highly provocative article assessing the real costs of divorce to children and society, Whitehead traces the phenomenon to the mid-1960s, when the search for personal fulfillment eclipsed more civic-minded goals[2] and women and minorities started asserting their rights. At the height of the women's movement, in 1979, the divorce rate peaked at 23 per 1,000 marriages, up from fewer than 10 during the 1950s and early '60s.[3] In the context of the times, Whitehead observes, divorce was viewed rather positively, certainly by the feminists: Greater financial autonomy among women meant that they could afford to be mothers without also being wives. "For many, economic independence was a stepping-stone toward freedom from both men and marriage," she writes. "As women began to earn their own money, they were less dependent on men or marriage, and marriage diminished in importance."[4]

Whitehead is by no means trying to ascribe blame or determine causation for divorce; rather, she seeks to prove what most of us—who have, after all, come of age in the Age of Divorce—already suspected: that broken homes are bad for the children, however the parents may benefit. And, indeed, poll after poll shows Americans are deeply concerned that society is coming apart at the seams because marriages aren't holding together. According to a 1993 *Wall Street Journal*/NBC News poll, "there appears to be a growing belief across the political spectrum that social values are eroding and that the decline of the family is at the heart of the problem."[5]

Yet Americans are divided as to what accounts for the decline of the family. Almost exactly half those surveyed—the younger, more liberal, typically Democratic half—believe couples like the Norrises are foundering on the treacherous shoals of a weak economy. Both parents must work merely to ensure the basics of middle-class life, and without access to decent child care, without the safety net once provided by an extended family, and without *real* flexibility in terms of *paid* parental leave, it is little wonder the families fail to survive intact. "A lot of it is that both parents have to work," says Sharon Nutbrown, a Pennsylvania mother of two, in the *Journal* story.

The other half—those who tend to be more conservative, Republican, and childless or retired—contend that the family is plagued by an overall decline in moral values. Narcissism, hedonism, materialism, and, ultimately, the primacy of the individual have collectively destroyed the family unit by devaluing motherhood and undermining paternal authority. Economics, according to one Oklahoma father polled, is "merely an excuse."

In short, Americans not only agree that society is in a state of decay and that the dissolution of the family is to blame *but also* that having both mothers and fathers work outside the home *for whatever reason* is what's behind the breakup of the family. The Democrats would argue that economic necessity accounts for the dual-career phenomenon; the Republicans that ego gratification and materialism are driving forces. The Democrats see women staying in the work force but the effects on marriage and children mitigated by governmental solutions such as mandated parental leave and quality day-care programs; the Republicans insist that motherhood needs to be revalued (through tax incentives, for example) in order to induce women to return to the home, and abortion must be prohibited.

But both liberals and conservatives perceive that having both spouses working outside the home puts marriages under terrific strain and leaves children with the short end of the stick. According to a poll conducted for MCI Communications, in fact, while 80 percent of those surveyed said they accepted the practice of women holding paying jobs while raising children, *50 percent* said the trend toward both parents working has had "a negative effect on families."[6]

Psychologist Arlie Hochschild, author of *The Second Shift: Working Parents and the Revolution at Home,* notes that as more and more women have gone out to work, divorce has indeed risen almost in lockstep with their infiltration of the workplace. "But people who conclude that it is women's work that causes divorce look only at what the *women,* one-half of the couples, are doing," she writes.[7] Examining the lives of 50 dual-career couples, 10 of them quite intimately, Hochschild had ample opportunity to examine what the *men* were doing—or, rather, not doing. Alluding to a study of 600 couples applying for divorce, she points out "the second most common reason women cited for wanting divorce—after 'mental cruelty'—was 'neglect of home or children.' Women mentioned this reason more often than financial problems, physical abuse, drinking, or infidelity."[8] Women are the agents of divorce, Hochschild observes, but their unsupportive husbands are the cause. A distinct minority of mates (18 percent of Hochschild's sample) in dual-career households work the "the second shift" (child care and housework), a shift that is tantamount to an entire extra *month* of work every year. "Men's resistance to sharing the extra month a year is by no means the only cause of divorce," writes Hochschild, "but it is often an underacknowledged source of tension which underlies the others."[9]

Hochschild found, conversely, that sharing the second shift benefited families in that a) wives were happier, which made for happier marriages, b) children were better off, having fathers directly involved in their care and nurturance, and c) the family unit was economically stronger because the wife was freed up to maintain and enhance her earning ability. Hochschild describes the vicious cycle set in motion when the man refuses to assign equal importance to his wife's employment: When his work time is worth more than hers, usually literally, it allows him to more easily justify the importance of his leisure—so that he might refuel enough to work longer hours and get promoted and paid even more and thus deserve even less to have to swab the toilet bowl. Meanwhile, the woman, whose work comes second, carries more of the second shift in order to support her husband's work. Her ambitions, earnings, and opportunity contract as she provides more and more of this "backstage support," so that ultimately "the extra month a year that she works contributes not only to her husband's success but to the expanding wage gap between them, and keeps the cycle spinning.

"In general," concludes Hochschild, "the more important a man's job, the more backstage support he receives, and the less backstage support for her job a woman receives, the less important her job becomes."[10]

Portrait of Modern Marriage

This is pretty much what's going on in the Norris household, but for one interesting twist—Alex, the breadwinner and elder of the two (by ten years), is the *wife*.

Marriage is about power; power is usually measured in money; and Alex, however she tries to downplay the fact, wields the power because she makes the money. She is very proud of Jody's profession and keenly aware, as a writer herself, of the tortuous career path artistic talent of any kind describes. But the financial pressures introduced by having a child have run roughshod over this understanding: The family needs money, and Jody is not earning it—or at least not enough to justify, in Alex's mind, hiring full-time day care so that he might pursue his craft. Bearing most of the financial responsibility, Alex fumes at how little relief she gets in exchange for keeping them afloat; she feels Jody is in no position to make demands right now, to put his career ahead of caring for Kyle and burden their already strained finances. Too, she believes Kyle should have a parent caring for him; his adoption was morally justified because his own mother could not look after him. Alex would like to put more hours in at home, but she cannot afford to jeopardize her job. Jody can be available, and in that his vocation is not yet a viable source of income, she feels he should be.

Jody, at the very dawn of his career when he married at 25, is likewise resentful of Alex for saddling him with a child before he ever had a chance to establish himself as an artist. The oldest of five children, he knew far better than she what rearing a baby entailed, knew what tremendous demands it would make on both of them. He knew he wasn't ready. But he wanted badly to give Alex what she wanted most: a child. Particularly after she was forced to abort their own baby at five months because its organs hadn't developed properly, Jody wanted to be supportive, to fight along with her to adopt when it appeared she could not again conceive.

So he had gone along with the plan to stay home and care for Kyle. But he chafed daily at his impotence—his inability to father his own child, to pursue his art, to earn a living, to compete among his peers, to maintain equal standing with his wife, to ease the constant tension over money, to shore up his own self-esteem. He is more than willing to do his share, but as Kyle's primary caregiver he felt denied the opportunity to contribute as he wanted to: as a wage earner. Imprisoned by the demands of an infant, he couldn't build his art into a living. Even now, freed up by a surrogate caregiver, he feels trapped.

In short, the Norris marriage is an equal partnership only nominally; the balance of power has been radically altered by the presence of a child. A new set of financial obligations, a new set of priorities, and a new drain on the time Jody and Alex once spent with each other have conspired to destroy that which they worked so hard to create: a family. Like many couples making the leap into parenthood, the Norrises were operating on assumptions that would prove totally unrealistic once their child was a fact of life. And like many couples, they were ill-prepared to come up with a means of communicating needs, desires, and mutual goals once the time for having such discussions became a rare luxury. Compounding the difficulties of becoming parents were, for Jody and Alex, the difficulties of privately adopting a newborn; the difficulties of moving, adjusting to a new town, and starting over in a new job; the difficulties of having no friends or family to turn to; and, perhaps most of all, the difficulties of having no money. Money buys time, and time is what the Norrises could sorely use.

Striking an Imbalance of Power

There's nothing terribly new, of course, about the Norrises' travails. A child arrives and suddenly neither parent knows what the other is thinking, appreciates what the other is doing, understands what the other needs. Communication in many dual-career relationships is arguably what it has always been in homemaker-breadwinner partnerships: a vital link between separate spheres, but the first thing to go in times of duress and, too often, the last resort of those who need it most.

And aside from the gender switch, there's nothing terribly new about the imbalance of power in the Norrises' relationship: Whoever has the higher-paid job is entitled to call the shots, make the decisions, determine the sacrifices, and renege on certain duties he or she finds onerous. Because men still make about 25 cents more for every dollar women earn,[11] men would seem likely to command, still, a disproportionate amount of the power in any relationship, whether the wife works or is home full time. And so long as he holds the upper hand, the cycle

Hochschild so eloquently describes—the man "deserving," and getting, "backstage support"—is likely to guarantee he retains it.

In fact, a number of studies paint a rather bleak picture of modern marriage, one completely at odds with the media's rosy portrait of "the new man" and "the new egalitarianism." Hochschild found 80 percent of her male subjects resistant to a 50-50 division of the second shift;[12] a Boston University School of Social Work study of 651 employees of an unnamed company found that women work twice as many hours at homemaking and child care as men, *even if the woman's income is greater,* making the working mother's week 85 hours long compared to the working father's 65-hour week.[13] In a 1990 opinion poll conducted by the Roper Organization and Virginia Slims, 52 percent of the wives said they resented their mate for not helping more at home; 46 percent resented the way child-care duties were shared; and 70 percent said they could balance children, marriage, and work far more easily if they got some help on the home front.[14]

In the most recent study to date (1993), Joseph Pleck, project director at the Wellesley College Center for Research on Women, finds that men's participation in the second shift is considerably greater than Hochschild documents—34 percent, or almost double her figure of 18 percent—and on the rise.[15] But he concedes the evidence does not yet support the widely publicized image of the 50-50 household.

Men are particularly resistant when it comes to sharing in the *housework.* In that "time spent on housework is a measure of power relations in the home," notes Letty Cottin Pogrebin, quoting National Research Council staffer Heidi Hartmann, "perhaps more than any other issue of family politics . . . housework is that 'intimate frontier' on which love and power are equally coercive."[16] Anita Shreve, author of *Remaking Motherhood,* also points to the division of domestic chores as an example of men's reluctance to forgo power: "Housework has always been a servant task

. . . and it has so long been associated with the powerless that to invest in it may suggest a relinquishing of one's own power within the family."[17]

But what's received far too little press is how women (or secondary wage earners) are dealing with this imbalance. Because with the vast numbers of women working, with the begrudging acceptance they have won in the workplace, with every sign pointing to their continued (if not increased) participation, there seems no question that husbands, while obviously in role transition now, must *eventually* get the message that their wives need help.

And they will—provided that's the message wives *unequivocally* send.

Blaming the Victim

"The presence of the working mother has been a powerful force in the American family," writes Shreve, "but she cannot, by her presence alone, command an egalitarian partnership. The time-honored traditional division of labor and the residue of deep-seated fears about the androgynizing of the male hinder progress toward shared responsibilities in the home and in the workplace."[18]

Society, men, tradition—the usual conspirators—are keeping women in backstage support roles. Such is our first impression upon noting how few working mothers seem to be really enjoying the fruits of their many labors. But there is considerable evidence to suggest that *women themselves* are preserving the status quo. Men may be resistant to change, but women *allow, tolerate,* or even *embrace* this resistance even as they vociferously denounce or mutely resent their husbands for it.

Hochschild documents no less than five "strategies" that women who would prefer an egalitarian relationship adopt so as not to have to confront their husbands on this volatile issue. "Supermoming," not surprisingly, headed the list: A woman who does it all never gives her mate occasion to complain, keeping the domestic peace at the rather enormous sacrifice of her personal needs. Other women simply cut back—on their jobs, primarily—but also on housework, on time spent with their spouse, on time spent on themselves, and, lamentably, even on time spent with their children. Where money was in ample supply, women contracted out their second shift to cleaning ladies and caregivers so as not to have to "make demands" of their mates.

Then there were those women, the traditionally minded working mothers, who felt the home and the children in it comprised their turf, or who felt they had passed a certain appropriate 'power' mark (by earning, say, as much as or even more than their husbands) and needed to restore tranquility by taking themselves down a notch and becoming dedicated hausfraus. One woman in Hochschild's study even claimed her husband deserved to be exempt from child care and housework because "he was smarter and had more to contribute to the world" (yes, such a woman existed as late as 1989!). Some didn't "make room" for their spouse at home, playing expert regarding the baby, the dinner, and the social schedule, effectively edging out their spouse so as to claim credit for doing it all.[19]

Joseph Pleck insists that Hochschild's data were out of date in that her survey was conducted over a ten-year period starting in the late '70s.[20] Yet in my own interviews with some 70 wives (and ex-wives) between 1992 and 1993, fully two-thirds said they were largely, or entirely, responsible for the house and the kids. As might be expected, those who were full-time mothers chose this traditional division of labor as "part of the deal" they struck with their husbands. But among the working mothers—who outnumbered full-time moms six to one—I found a disturbing trend: It was the rare woman who *demanded*, and won, her husband's support on the home front. Much more common were the strategies Hochschild describes. And supermoming prevailed.

"I'm not doing anything for myself," notes Helen Rice, the magazine editor introduced in chapter four. "I get so taken up with satisfying everybody else's demands, whether it's my husband, child, boss, or editor, that the only time I have to myself is in the shower every morning. It's kind of good for me, in a strange way: To see that you have this strength to do all these things is very ego-gratifying." But then Helen reflects a moment. "It's also sort of *sick*," she adds. "You shouldn't need to do all this to feel good about yourself."

"Maybe I'm in the mode of trying to be a Superperson," speculates Morgan Weston*, an accountant with a preschooler, who admits her definition of a good wife is very traditional. "My husband says he'd rather we spent Saturday and Sunday as a threesome instead of me cleaning, him doing his thing, and the baby doing his. He says I'm eating into our time together, that there are other ways to get things done." His solution is not for her to stay home—he doesn't want to be sole breadwinner, and he doesn't want her brain to go to mush, says Morgan. But she won't get a cleaning lady, even though right now she could really use some help because her husband is currently working out of state and she's more or less a single mom. "I can deal with this," she says, noting that some people might not be comfortable with all the things she's had to give up: softball, visits with her girlfriends, and other "personal" needs. "As long as I have a routine, it's workable."

Nancy Belser, a pediatrician with kids five and two years old, is married to a physician; throughout her residency, he filled in at home with their daughter, and with his help she has accomplished, professionally, the goals she had set for herself six years ago. But now, working a part-time schedule in a group practice, Nancy finds "things have fallen back in my lap." Sometimes their relationship approaches 60-40, she says, but usually it's more like

70-30 because "technically speaking, I have more time to prepare dinner, do the wash, clean the house, go to the store, get dinner, get the kids fed, and get them into bed. All of a sudden more domestic things have to get done, and the children want to play with me, so I've requested more participation from my husband. And his response is, 'Well, but you're home two days.' He's working five, so I should be able to do all that stuff. He expects me to pick up the loose ends. He was raised in a house with a traditional mom; her husband never ironed anything in his life.

"So that's what we argue about," Nancy continues. "And we'll argue in front of the kids. He doesn't think that's appropriate, but I don't like to hide my anger, because then it will brew up. If I had time to pick up the loose ends, we wouldn't have these arguments, but if Paul weren't so busy, I'd have more time."

Diane Turner (introduced in chapter four), a dermatologist with kids five and two, is also married to a doctor and also works part time. She says she is "the typical stressed-out woman for all the traditional reasons in addition to the career" but excuses her husband because "it's harder for him"—he works six days a week, and she works *outside the home* only four.

She has not a spare minute. "In terms of the children, my head is always spinning. Even though I have help, I still have to be the one to run things, to make doctor's appointments, sign up for school, buy their clothes. I'm a very efficient person, fortunately. I have a Filofax brain, and I'm very good at organizing things." But it's a burden having to be exclusively responsible for the home front, and sometimes she resents her husband because "being home with the children is harder work." Still, she doesn't ask to change the current division of labor. Pretty soon, she notes, her older child will be in school. And besides, in terms of running the house and rearing the kids, women "are best at it. If my husband were to do it, I'd always be checking up on him."

"I'd have to say our roles fall along pretty traditional lines," agrees Lori Boyle, the city planner from chapter five who gave up her job rather than live apart from her husband, a research mathematician, or ask him to relocate. "I have more talent juggling kids and household and work; if our roles were reversed, he would have to have more time to work." Lori bought him a book on speed cleaning, which has helped, she says, but "he's not domestically talented, and it's hard for him to learn because he doesn't *notice* dirt. His mother, who was home full time, never asked him to do anything, so he has an extreme lack of awareness of his environment. He can calculate pi to 21 figures but not know where the pots go in the kitchen cabinets."

Mary Brittingham, the part-time immigration lawyer from chapter six, got fed up with the imbalance on the home front and hired help. "I just made the decision to get a housekeeper in addition to the sitter," she explains, "because we fought too much about it. I felt like I did everything. He did some things, but it was never adequate. So I decided this was the way to resolve it."

Resolution, inevitably, comes at a cost. Linda Bodini (introduced in chapter five) and her husband, both university math professors, have come to an understanding. He does a lot of the picking up around the house, since his tolerance for disorder is lower than hers; he does the shopping and half the meal preparation, and at night helps her get the two kids bathed, read to, and into bed. She handles the bulk of the child care, makes out the shopping list, and does the laundry ("I don't want to risk his messing up my clothes"). They have hired help for the lawn and the housecleaning. Change came about, says Linda, when she started asking herself, 'What's in this marriage for me?' and initiated "a big discussion." And yet she finds it hard to remain confident in her choice to continue as a mathematician "because I'm not as good as he is; I'm not going to win the Nobel Prize, because my strengths are in teaching, not research." She has stuck it out because she didn't want her decision to be based on an external judgment of how good she was at her profession.

"But I can't help but imagine him thinking, 'If you're not good enough, then stay home and get these children off my back!'"

So while Linda's efforts are presumably halved in terms of child care and housework, she's working overtime to try to prove his sacrifices are justified. "I'm trying to perform well enough at my job," says Linda, "to be, in his eyes, worthy of all the effort that's going into our both working and parenting."

Even among the stay-at-home mothers, resentment hides behind assertions that they chose the second shift and think it's "fair." "Anything he does I appreciate," says mother of two Carey Furillo (from chapter three) of her husband, who's starting up his own business. "But the other night I was doing the dishes, trying to get the baby's bottles ready, and the older one needed to be put to bed, and I just wanted to ask him, 'Did it ever cross your mind to help me?' Because clearly it never crosses his mind."

But rather than speak up or seek to renegotiate their pact, these women, too, find a hundred rationalizations. "He should probably do more," Carey notes, "but with a start-up situation, I feel I've got to cut him a little slack to make the business viable. I don't want to be the cause of this thing *not* working; I don't want him saying it failed because I made him do housework. Since homemaking is my so-called profession, I've got to give him a break." Carey sees her sacrifice as a limited-time-only offer, however. "Of course, it's all going to have to change once he gets this thing going," she says, "and I should be preparing him for that."

Jean Stauffer Schoenleber (introduced in chapter six), now home with her preschooler after 13 years in a profession, claims her husband is "a very involved father." From the beginning, she says, she's insisted he take on at least one child-care duty per night, whether it's dinner or the bath-bed ritual, and he pretty much has ("although tonight," she admits, "he didn't because he was really pooped and I'd had a good night's sleep"). "Our relationship probably should be more androgynous," she says, "but I don't mind the differentiation of roles. I don't have any expectations he's not meeting."

And yet apparently he has expectations of her, now that she's home, that *she's* not meeting. "I do get from him the sense that, now that I'm not earning any money, what am I doing all day?" muses Jean. "I get the sense I should be doing more, getting more done. I was never one to obsess about a clean house, but when I was working it was easier to excuse the mess. Now I know he wonders what I do that I can't get more done around the house."

Some of these mothers look forward to the day when they can get more involved outside the home—typically, when their children are in school—precisely because of the effects of the imbalance of power. Carey anticipates putting more of her considerable education to use, even as a volunteer, because then her husband would know that a couple of nights a week he'd be responsible for some family chores, such as putting the kids to bed. "I'd feel our time was valued more equally," she says. Right now, however, she's working on her boys—the three-year-old, anyway. "My sons will be better," she claims. "I'm exposing them to responsibility, teaching them how to do certain things my husband was never taught because his mother never expected it of him. You can teach new dogs, not old ones."

Indeed, the most telling evidence of my interviewees' dissatisfaction is how adamantly they insist their sons "will be different." Beth Miller, a formerly full-time mother of two boys, six and one, and a single working mom since her husband walked out, is desperately keen to bring up her boys to be partners and caretakers. "I don't want to produce another generation of men who expect to be treated like kings," she says. "It's a big question for me: How am I going to guide them? I hope my sons will see me struggling to make a better life and understand why I'm not at home like the other mothers. I'm really struggling to be my own person and not someone's dart board."

But Beth, who used to be as tirelessly accommodating as all the other stay-at-home moms in her working-class neighborhood, doesn't blame men so much for being childish as she blames women—for making them that way as mothers and putting up with it as wives. "We're our own biggest problem," she says. "I look at the women on my block, and even those married to men who have lost their jobs don't get any help from them at home; the women do everything. They don't stand up to them, probably because they have no self-confidence. Women tend to blame men, but women have to take control and say, 'This is what I want, and if you don't want it, fine'—and have the confidence that they can leave and make it on their own."

If not for themselves, says Beth, they should do it for their children. She cites the example of a woman on her street who works as a day-care provider—a very strong, capable woman, says Beth, who is nonetheless oppressed by a husband "who gets his orders from God." She stays with him, she tells Beth, because he's not an alcoholic (and she's the daughter of one) and because he doesn't fool around. "But I have to wonder," remarks Beth, "how her children see this relationship, how they interpret it. They're bound to carry it around as I have, and it will color their relationship as it has mine. This cycle has to be terminated.

"I've come to the conclusion that women are definitely stronger than men," says Beth—speaking, no doubt, from her own experience as mother of a baby who weighed two pounds at birth and now, 14 months later, weighs 23 pounds. "It's women who raise children, and so it's women who in essence bring about change."

One-Paycheck Thinking

"Women bend over backward to fulfill all their roles without inconveniencing men. In fact, they think their jobs cause far more inconvenience than *men* do," writes Letty Cottin Pogrebin in *Family Politics*. "Sex role strain is alive and well because so many women are still overdosing on the feminine mystique, still confusing their personal identity with a clean house, still fearing male disapproval and doing penance for stepping out of the domestic sphere. For all her new earning power, the nontraditional woman remains trapped by tradition: She does not want to feel that her husband is deprived of advantages he would have obtained if he had married a 'true woman.'"[21]

Such is the phenomenon Shirley Sloan Fader explores in her book, *Wait a Minute, You Can Have It All: How Working Wives Can Stop Feeling Overwhelmed and Start Enjoying Life*. Fader notes that, in 20 years of interviewing working wives, she has found that even women earning high incomes—$60,000, $80,000, $100,000—come home to launder and iron husbands' shirts, scrub kitchens and bathrooms, and do the rest of the housework. They could well afford cleaning help, and yet they resist, programmed to believe that, job or no job, a decent woman and a good wife takes care of the home and the kids and does it perfectly. They also labor under the notion that their work *costs* their man, that he's losing status and power within the family and a whole host of wifely services. Some are so conscious of how their work makes their husband look like "a failure" for not being the exclusive breadwinner that they try to pretend he is making their living—even though they may be earning more. "Unfortunately, when women refuse to take credit for their earning power, they automatically accept the continual overload of doing most or all of the housework and child care," Fader writes. "They give up their bargaining chip—the truth."[22]

Advising working wives to take "a good hard look" at their home life, Fader shows how husbands clearly benefit (far more than wives) from two paychecks. Gone is the stress and anxiety of being sole breadwinner; men may even find added security knowing that if they're laid off, the family won't be in jeopardy, and if they want to change jobs or even fields, go back to school or start a business, they have the financial buffer to do so. Men with working wives also have more choice about the conditions of work, meaning they can say no to overtime and heavy travel and thus enjoy greater quality of life.[23]

They're also more likely to enjoy greater intimacy with their wives. Fader points out that in any household, having more money usually means less stress and less resentment all around. But gone are the days when a husband would drag himself home, looking for peace, and have his house-bound wife extort conversation and interaction: Now that wives "understand the pressures, anxieties, and triumphs of the workplace," says Fader, conversation about either his work or hers is likely to be far more engaging and effortless. A better relationship is, of course, better for the kids. And by working Mom forces Dad to get more involved in their care and nurturance.[24]

Finally, study after study shows that with the wife's extra income, men buy themselves leisure time, while the wife usually keeps struggling with her endless to-do list of job/home/child care. Fader makes this point by showing how professional lawn care has become a *two-billion-dollar* business as more men contract out their chores to free themselves up for televised sports or time with their kids, while women still shampoo their own rugs because commercial cleaning services are too costly. "Based on all that your job is doing for him," Fader urges, "it's time for you to feel entitled to have him make it up to *you* by working out a fairer division of the family's entire work load.

"Men have never had to choose between job and family," she concludes. "They expect to have it all—spouse, children, paid employment. Since he's entitled to enjoy all three, so are you."[25]

A Question of Gender

So what are we waiting for? Why are we bending over backward, clinging to a tradition that serves neither our husbands' best interests nor our own? What are we afraid of?

To be sure, asserting oneself in a relationship with an "old dog" (a man raised with the mindset that his needs, as primary wage earner, come first)—to claim one deserves equal status for equally important (if not always equally compensated) work—is to rock the marital boat. The greater the actual disparity in income, the more difficult it would seem to justify one's own demands. And admittedly, many men do not react well: Either they "just don't get it" or they get it and don't like it one bit. If a woman believes she is jeopardizing her relationship to the point of divorce, and children are involved, she's more than likely to back off, particularly since mothers with custody of the children stand a much greater chance of winding up impoverished after divorce than their ex-husbands. Plus, many women who are resentful don't believe their resentment is equal to or greater than the love they bear their spouse. Better to bend, yield, and accommodate, and justify the sacrifice in the name of the children—whom they vow to raise to be better partners.

I am intimately acquainted with these arguments, as are most of my friends. We are not likely to lead a revolution, given that our beliefs regarding egalitarian marriage so rarely translate into action on our own behalf. And yet I believe there is something else holding us back, something the feminists have yet to identify, or regard, as a significant roadblock to our liberation: our gender. By gender I mean that identity which is not programmed by culture, media, and economic realities; that 'essence' which is *not* interchangeable, however many roles we interchange; that concept of ourselves which we do not readily trade in for an androgynous image.

Much has been written about *men's* reluctance to give up their essential natures. Power, strength, and the protective instinct, once virtues women prized in their mates, seem almost barbaric notions of masculinity today. We pooh-pooh a man's insistence on being the breadwinner, having discovered ourselves perfectly capable (if not equally regarded) in the workplace. We no longer esteem physical strength, now that our survival depends so little upon it. We rail against dominance, having found the price we pay for passivity too high to endure. We are insulted by those who suggest we need protecting; we can take care of ourselves, given an equal opportunity to do so.

But what of *our* reluctance to give up the trappings of femininity? I say trappings because so many of us don't really know what or who we are when stripped of our familiar roles, any more than men know what or who they are when stripped of the mantle of being in charge. What is it to be a wife when we no longer perform a wife's characteristic duties or even a mother if our husbands can literally take over immediately after we give birth? What is our contribution to the egalitarian relationship *as a woman?* What does a father bring to parenthood that is distinct and unique from what a mother gives? Surely women need not be second-class citizens in order to feel feminine, any more than men should be domineering in order to feel male. But in a dual-career marriage with children, must male and female be rendered androgynous in order to be equal? And if so, is it any wonder we are ambivalent in our pursuit of the 50-50 marriage?

Gender and Equality

Alex Norris is, arguably, a product of the kind of change Beth Miller hopes to make in the next generation. Alex's mother, an esteemed and published psychologist, imbued in her by example the importance of, and the rewards associated with, being professionally competent; Alex, having also earned a doctorate, feels respected and admired by her peers, and she has traveled enough, experienced enough, and seen and done enough in the world to have the confidence Beth finds lacking in so many of her oppressed neighbors.

And yet, having the confidence, having the means to make it on her own, having the *power* to stand up and make demands of her husband, and having the mindset of a liberated woman, Alex has not enjoyed her role in the relationship. Gender roles, she has come to believe, are not nearly so fungible as women think, and not simply because men feel "emasculated" by a wife who brings home the bacon: Women can feel "defeminized."

"If you have the entire financial responsibility and you're not getting any help—no financial relief, no emotional accessibility, no time out—it's not a real exciting situation in the bedroom," Alex explains. "It makes me feel more manly, less feminine. I just don't feel very desirable."

Alex had always recognized that she and Jody suffered a lot of interpersonal problems over his sense of inadequacy as a conventional male: "For men, being economically successful is intrinsic to their identity," she observes. What came as a surprise, however, was the importance she placed on her sense of inadequacy as a female, as a woman desirable to other men. Indeed, what pulled Alex out of her doldrums (and into seeking help from a marriage counselor) was "an affair of the heart" that sprang up between herself and one of her students. "He took an interest in me and I in him, because no one had inquired about my emotional life. He made me feel like a desirable woman again. It was like a new spring. I thought, I can have a life, I deserve to have a life. Then the problem was how to bring this home to my husband—how could I see Jody as a lover? I wanted us to be a family, but we were both dead inside. We hated each other."

The feminist in me positively cringes at this confession. But as a woman, I'm more than sympathetic: I don't want equality at the price of my sexuality. I persist in believing gender can be acknowledged without being exploited, that none of us want to be "just like men" simply to guarantee that we be accorded men's respect. Still, my sensibilities clash upon hearing Martha Eden, the financial analyst introduced in chapter four, claim she could be "hell on wheels" but appreciated that there was something in her "that wants to be dominated."

Sure, Martha says, it'd be great if it traded back and forth, but everywhere she looks in nature (she and her husband live on a ranch) there's domination—and it's usually exercised by the male of the species. Not that females are at a disadvantage: On the contrary, watching the fillies graze and the colts fight 24 hours a day, Martha's convinced "women are far stronger than men will ever be." She's not at all ashamed of exemplifying the more "feminine" virtues—"someone has to give," she remarks— but is sorely distressed that the world doesn't value these virtues more. She looks back rather wistfully to the pioneer days, when men and women were truly equal partners because each understood that without the other's labors they literally could not get bread on the table. "It's hard to translate that kind of partnership to today's life," she notes.

So Martha and her husband operate on the understanding that his sphere of influence is the ranch, and his income goes toward supporting it, and her sphere is the house and kids, and her income goes toward supporting them. "It's worked out real well," says Martha. "I would recommend it."

Equal but Separate

At no time do the "essential natures" of men and women become more apparent—and more of a stumbling block—than when couples become parents. The biological fact of women carrying, birthing, and nursing offspring cannot be massaged away but neither can the psychological facts: Men and women not only care for children dissimilarly (not better, not worse, but *dissimilarly*), but they *feel* differently about their child-rearing roles—or at least so found psychologist Diane Ehrensaft in her study of 40 couples sharing parenting 50-50. In a chapter of her book, *Parenting Together*, titled "Day-to-Day Sharing: Easier Said than Done," Ehrensaft applies the term "separate but equal" to what she observed as "clearly gender-based" modes of parenting: Women tend to be particular about how a child is dressed, for example, while men think it's totally frivolous; women tend to be worriers, while men can distance themselves; and women are the ones who oversee the larger picture of what needs to be done and whether it is done—organizing, making lists, checking follow-through—whereas men defer to women or remain oblivious.[26]

All three areas of parenting (dressing the children, worrying, and "psychological management"), Ehrensaft finds, are carried out by men and women dissimilarly because, dedicated as the fathers were to child rearing, they were likely to be more *distanced* than the mothers. They did not perceive their children as extensions of themselves, whereas mothers did (hence, for instance, the concern among mothers as to what their children wear: mismatched clothing is a reflection on them personally). Ehrensaft concludes that women "are" mothers while men "do" mothering: "It seems obvious that the contrast between the feminine 'connected' self and the masculine 'separate' self coincides with the mother who worries more and sees her child as an extension of herself vs. the father who leaves his parenting worries at home and experiences his child's appearance as constituting no reflection on him."[27]

Ehrensaft devotes a whole chapter to showing how such differences are inculcated by upbringing, socialization, and internalization of early family relationships—to prove, in short, that gender differences are not innate but acquired. By making this point she clearly hopes to comfort those of us struggling with co-parenting: Our problems can be pinned on our early gender programming. Eliminate the programming—as she seems to think we shall, in future generations—and mother and father will no longer be *dissimilar*, but utterly equal in their parenting. Eliminate what we now perceive as "separate but equal" mindsets in fathers and mothers and we will close the gender gap troubling so many dual-career households today. The ideal she describes is within our grasp, she insists: Among her couples, she does observe that fathers develop an intense emotional involvement with the child that approaches the "relational" experience women have always known. "By reclaiming those early capacities (to create intimacy) . . . they come closer to what has been the women's legacy, the 'being' of parenthood," she asserts.[28]

As further evidence of this ultimate feminization of men, Ehrensaft quotes the psychoanalyst D. W. Winnicott on the differences between female and male experience. As an infant, a child experiences his parent as one with himself; the child does not perceive himself as distinct from his mother. Winnicott calls this state of nonseparateness "feminine." Later, when an infant recognizes the parent is "not me," he can act independently on his environment—the "masculine" phase. Winnicott writes, "The male element *does* while the female element (in both males and females) *is*."[29] Because Winnicott finds both male and female elements in well-adjusted men and women, Ehrensaft concludes that men can and *should* "mother," even to the degree that the child becomes an extension of the father, because then parents can truly share parenting equally.

Her underlying assumption, of course, is that "separate but equal" is a sorry state of affairs, a gender gap that must be closed. This assumption is so axiomatic of the current antigender (anti*difference*) political agenda that no correct-thinking adult would even question it. In order to eliminate *sexism* (a worthy goal, I think we can all concur), we have adopted a dangerously simplistic solution: Eliminate disparities and dissimilarities in the sexes.

On the face of it, our gender differences *are* a nuisance, baggage that clutters our relationship, burdens we pass on to our unsuspecting children. Our mission as parents today, according to Ehrensaft, is to stop the cycle; to the degree that we neutralize differences of gender, believes Anita Shreve, we are succeeding. "The population of androgynous role models for boys continues to grow," she notes optimistically. "They in turn can be expected to model androgynous behavior for their sons and to have this behavior infiltrate the culture at large."[30]

But among the women I interviewed, those in marriages where gender distinctions were recognized were far more likely to have arrived at an egalitarian partnership. Equal, no, in that each spouse brought entirely different skills to bear on the tasks of child rearing and running a household. Separate but equal, most definitely. It was in relationships such as the Norrises', where gender was *not* acknowledged to be a significant factor but studiously ignored in the name of androgyny, that role confusion and gross disparities in perceived contribution arose.

A Stop (Gender) Gap Measure: Compromised Equality

By no means do I want to suggest that women are a certain way and men are a certain way and therefore egalitarian partnership succeeds only upon recognition of those sexist traits. Quite the contrary: In my research, gender switches as radical as the Norrises' crop up repeatedly among those who enjoy a balance of power. The difference, in these happy marriages, is that child care and housework are not divvied up 50-50 arbitrarily but according to gender-specific strengths. In other words, rather than pretend men and women are not fundamentally dissimilar but perfectly interchangeable, these couples recognize—and capitalize on—their differences. Their contributions may be distinctly different, but they are accorded equal merit.

Rebecca Garner (introduced in chapter five) and her husband offer a remarkable example. Rebecca is the driven one: At 36, having successfully switched careers from music teacher to school principal the year before, she got married; at 37, six months after the birth of her daughter, she enrolled in a doctoral program at a university an hour and a half from her home while continuing her full-time job as elementary school principal *and* pumping breast milk for her child. Eighteen months later she finished her doctorate in education administration. Today, at 43, she is still a principal and now mother to a son, nearly a year old.

But she is the first to admit her husband deserves half the credit for her accomplishments. She is no superwoman—at least not anymore. "My biggest stretch has been relying on others," she admits. "I've always been self-sufficent, and parenthood—especially on top of a full-time job and night school—demands a team approach. I'm learning to be much more dependent on my husband and family. I could never have done this without their support." And Rebecca is not talking merely *emotional* support but day-to-day child care and housework support. Her husband, her caregiver, and her parents admittedly don't do things exactly as Rebecca would like them to be done. But rather than drive herself and everyone around her crazy trying to meet her standards, she has elected to compromise—because the rewards of holding her many roles far outweigh the trade-offs on more traditional fronts. "I truly enjoy everything I do," she says. "I really enjoy my job for the people interaction, and when I get home I welcome the change in focus to my children. Likewise, they refresh me for the challenges I face at work."

If anyone's overwhelmed, she says, it's probably her husband—but "he recognizes I thrive on this schedule; he's happy because I'm happy." And there are weeks when his job will take him out of town, and then she pulls more than her share of the weight as a single mom. "I think what our children see is a team," she concludes. "We both do everything, although I'm the delegator; I'm a great one for saying, 'I'm going to work now, and this is what needs to be done.' But I bear the burden of being the schedule keeper: I keep track of what day is ballet day, what day is snack-at-school day, what party my daughter has to go to—the minute I wake up I'm rehearsing everybody's schedule."

Housework, which the Garners used to hire help for, is now theirs to share because they bought a house and support a bigger mortgage. Rebecca does the laundry; her husband does the cleaning. It's her job, however, to notice when tensions are building up and housework is taking far more resources than it warrants; when her husband starts complaining that everywhere he looks something needs doing, she calls time out and everybody takes a walk. In many ways, however, their domestic chores fall along traditional lines: Rebecca likes to cook, and he cleans up. He cares a lot about yard work, and she likes to have her house looking nice because she likes to entertain. But Rebecca has a clear sense of her priorities, and drapes, for example, do not figure high on the list. Last Christmas she entertained her entire faculty at the house, as she had the year before, and only after the party was over did it occur to her that the dining room light fixture that had been missing the first Christmas was still missing a year later. "People must have thought it very strange," laughs Rebecca.

She's much more conscious of what other mothers think of her when she's trying to confer with them, as part of her job, about their children; many are full-time mothers who know she's a working mother, and Rebecca must continually ply her diplomacy skills lest she appear judgmental about their choice to stay home. She's also much more attuned to how her husband is managing—how his emotional health is faring, how she might give him a break. And she's highly conscious of how her daughter perceives her. Because however "androgynized" Rebecca's role might appear, she's highly "relational"; being able to empathize, intuit, and anticipate are skills that have rewarded her in her job, her marriage, and her relationship with her kids. Because she does not undervalue these skills, neither do her boss and her husband. As for her kids, Rebecca hopes they will perceive their parents' contributions as equal, however different, and that they will feel free to choose their own roles.

But it's tricky, she says. Her daughter betrays a distinctly different set of values than her own, along decidedly traditional gender lines (with her son, it's still too soon to tell). "It's scary when you don't see yourself in your own child," says Rebecca. "My biggest nightmare is that she's going to grow up to be a cheerleader. The other day she told me, 'I'm not going to drive. My boyfriend will drive.'

"People keep telling her she's beautiful, that she's such a *nice* girl," Rebecca sighs. "I don't dwell on that, because I don't want her to have an inflated impression of how far that's going to take her. I want her to be confident and capable, so that whatever she's presented with, her attitude will be 'I can do this.' I wouldn't want her to feel stymied by perceived sex roles. But on the other hand, I don't want to overdo my zeal that she turn out otherwise. I hope I can understand her so that I can see what's good for her and encourage it instead of thwart it."

More Separate, More Equal

The Garners' approach to partnership is 50-50 not so much because each does exactly as much child care or housework as the other but because Rebecca's skills as a delegator are recognized as carrying equal weight with her husband's skills as an executor, and her contribution as a "people person"—her contribution as a woman—is never perceived as frivolous. In the Neimans' partnership, however, the husband, and not the wife, is the "relational" spouse, and so their division of labor reflects this particular gender reversal. Jan (whom we met in the introduction), a photographer, consented to having her first child because Paul, who is ten years older, threatened to leave if she didn't, so from their son Julian's infancy on, Paul has assumed the bulk of the child care.

"We never had any of those child-adjusting problems," says Jan, eight months pregnant with her second child. "Paul doesn't have to be by himself; he always wants to be with me or Julian, whereas I'll tell Paul to go away, take the baby, I need to read a book. Ours is sort of the reverse stereotype: I don't cook, and he shops more than 50 percent of the time.

"But I run the house," Jan expounds, "because I like to. If I asked him, he'd do anything, but I like doing the laundry, and I'm anal-compulsive about cleaning—attention to detail is what makes me a good photographer, and I have very exacting standards. There have been times when I've been working a lot and haven't done my obsessiveness around the house, and he'll say, 'What happened here?,' but I don't feel underappreciated. I think he just doesn't understand what it takes to make the house look like it usually does, and that's because I'm not willing to let him help."

The division works for them, says Jan, because her husband takes great pride in her talent as a photographer; when she cut back her work to spend more time with their son, Paul was actually upset, fearful she was losing the professional identity he so admired. "We had a long talk, and I think he understands that who I am isn't going to disappear simply because I also happen to be a mother. My take on it is, he thinks it's very sexy that I'm a photographer."

Maeve Fegan (last mentioned in chapter five) is of a mind that neither gender makes a particularly unique contribution in terms of child care—the roles really are interchangeable, she feels, if women give their spouses half a chance. Her work schedule necessitates that her husband be the one, frequently, to go home and get the kids fed, bathed, and put to bed. "I couldn't do what I'm doing if he didn't do what he does," says Maeve, noting proudly that the other night one of the kids was sick and her husband not only bathed him again and changed the sheets but took it all in stride. "Women have a tendency to think they do it better," she says, "but a spouse does a perfectly good job."

However, Maeve notes, she and her husband are on an even keel now *because* she was for so long the family breadwinner. "If I gave up work completely, we'd be back to square one," she observes. If she did not work, that is, gender would play a distinct role in making their relationship *unequal.*

Indeed, not one of the women I interviewed fingered her job as the source of marital discord—anything but. Without their work role, in fact, they entertained no hope of maintaining the egalitarian relationship they either enjoyed or were working toward. To quit work to shore up a marriage was decidedly a step back, in their eyes. Many feared their husbands might revert to a Neanderthal code of behavior once the incentive to pitch in was removed and the assumption was that whoever was home more would do more at home. "I've always had a sneaking suspicion that being dependent on a spouse would be damaging to the relationship," says Yvonne Kearney (introduced in chapter two). "A weird streak comes out in guys when they know they have you there."

As it stands now, says Yvonne, she *is* dependent on her husband with respect to the happiness of her children: "I wouldn't want to give them a blueprint without two dimensions," she says. "He nurtures them in different ways, and I'm definitely dependent on that. Also, it's great feeling there's someone there when things aren't good—career, finances, health. It's great to know someone is there who understands a lot about you. That's a really pleasant dependency."

Others suspected *they themselves* might revert to patterns of "the good wife," and in so doing feather their nest with nails. Catherine Beekman, the "semi-single" mom of chapter four, admits she's "grateful" her musician husband is away as much as he is because "I'd be the kind of wife whose life revolved around his, doting on him, trying to be the perfect wife. This way I have to keep my own life, even when he comes home—I can't just drop everything, and that's good. He doesn't expect me to; he wouldn't want me to be that kind of wife. It's me who expects me to. He's really proud of who I am, and I'm who I really want to be, so it's good it's worked out this way."

Communication, Communication, Communication

"The presence of the working mother in the majority of households has necessitated the appearance of the new working father," writes Anita Shreve. "He exists because she exists."[31]

To the extent that he does exist, "the new father" is, I would agree, a direct consequence of wives and mothers working. There is no question in the minds of the women I interviewed that work is the marital glue insofar as work has necessitated, or catalyzed, the participation of their husbands in the second shift. Yet as we have seen with the Norrises, two careers and equal participation in the domestic sphere are not enough to guarantee a happy marriage. Good communication—a mutual understanding of what each spouse has to contribute, what each wants to contribute, what each resents contributing—is essential. Without it, the most like-minded couples can drift apart; with it, the most gender-reversed, disparately driven couples can endure.

Children, clearly, can throw a wrench in the works. The Norrises are hardly singular in finding themselves overwhelmed by parental obligations and pressures. Jill Mallory (of chapter one), looking back on her daughter's infancy, admits that she was utterly consumed with the demands of her new role on top of her new job, but her husband was "absolutely silent—he withheld an incredible amount of feelings because he was afraid to express bad ones," she postulates. Jill feels there's a "conspiracy of silence" regarding the reality of having babies, particularly the tremendous strain it puts on relationships. Husbands have a tendency to feel left out, wives have a tendency to be overwhelmed and hormonally imbalanced, and babies have a tendency to be utterly self-absorbed and needy. "If you don't have a system for resolving disputes," notes Jill, "that's not the time to get one. I wish we had had an understanding from the get-go that this was going to be stressful, even awful, but that it would be worth it and we would come through it. By the time we did reach an understanding of what was going on, he'd gone too far [in his relationship with another woman]."

But children, too, can be the catalyst for what may have been long overdue anyway. Connie Lezenby (of chapter one) and her husband, Scott, found that they themselves didn't have such great communication when they started working on their relationship with their kids. "Teaching your children teaches you a lot," says Connie. "We were trying to teach our kids to be better listeners by being better listeners ourselves, and both Scott and I realized we didn't know how. We'd never been listened to as children."

She and her husband likewise found they both had a real need to be appreciated. "We'd both been kids who'd done everything for our families growing up, who felt we did more than our fair share, but nobody ever made us feel recognized for all that we did. It's been the same in our marriage. So we're making a point of telling each other when we appreciate something the other has done. It's helped a lot, because you start seeing what a mutual effort parenting really is."

The relationship a couple has going into marriage is critical, asserts Susan Asher, a corporate video producer who works part time while raising her daughters, ages two and three. "I think we have an excellent relationship," she says. "My husband probably expects me to make more money, but he's very supportive as far as the kids and the house are concerned. Ninety percent of the time he knows what needs to be done. And I don't usually have to ask him for help because I try not to take on more than I can really handle. But then, we've always been equal. I wouldn't have married someone who wouldn't help me."

Yet Susan stresses that what really has made all the difference is not so much the equality they enjoyed before having kids but the level of communication they have managed to maintain, despite the considerable stress of not only working but having two children very close in age. "At this point, given the girls' ages, we have no life of our own," says Susan. "But we make a point of letting each other know that we're trying to accommodate each other as much as humanly possible. Our understanding has always been, if you give the other person a break, you'll be rewarded."

It is true that dual-career marriages are especially reliant on good communication; there are more moving parts, and working out the nitty-gritty of who does what requires communication, however well each spouse thinks he or she knows the other. It is also true that because time is at a premium in such marriages, constructive dialogue all too often gets a low priority. But according to Dr. Jacqueline Olds, a psychiatrist at Harvard Medical School's McLean Hospital, two-career marriages are more stable than one-career marriages over the long haul because of the communication engendered by sharing child-care responsibilities. In the 30 couples she and her colleagues studied, Olds found that the most estranged mates came from traditional unions in which the wives had become child-rearing experts while the husbands threw themselves into their work. As a result, she says, couples came to lead nearly separate lives. "The sense of connection that comes from needing each other to complete a mutual task such as raising children got lost as each parent became more and more self-sufficient."[32]

Olds is not the first to note that while the opportunity for meaningful conversation may be greater in those marriages where only the man works outside the home, there is less to talk about. Certainly there's less negotiating, since the whole idea of a traditional partnership is to eliminate confusion over who does what: The housewife runs the house and rears the children, and the breadwinner makes house, children, and marriage economically possible. But when duties don't overlap, the gender gap between men and women can yawn to a chasm. A lack of understanding of the challenges each spouse faces can lead to a lack of appreciation for the talents each applies to meeting those challenges. A lack of appreciation leads to resentment. And resentment, in any marriage, is the precursor to divorce.

Toward Mutual Understanding— and Greater Appreciation

Good communication may be logistically more difficult in dual-career households, but in that its rewards are proportionally greater, it is perhaps not so surprising that so many couples rely, at some point, on marriage counselors to "decode" their communication. Through therapy, Alex and Jody Norris have come to a new—and highly constructive—understanding. Alex is more cognizant of the second-rung status she has assigned Jody based purely on his income; now that she's more supportive, he's doing better in his work, and he's more confident and less angry.

Jody is more aware of his wife's need for emotional nurturing, and to make time for that they have worked out a schedule in detail in which every household and child-care duty is delegated. Now Friday afternoons are set aside for walks or time together without Kyle, and each enjoys one night a week to do as he or she pleases (both tend to do work). On weekends they alternate spending time with Kyle. The fact that their son is easier—and a lot more fun—to take care of now that he's a preschooler has also made a big difference in how they view parenthood.

But perhaps the biggest breakthrough, for both of them, was coming to understand the nature of their commitment as parents. Whereas for some time they had seen only the limitations imposed by that commitment, now, says Alex, they are beginning to see the constraints of parenthood as a catalyst for infinite spiritual growth. "My role is still pretty rigid," notes Alex. "I must work, I must mother, and I want us to be a family. Those conditions still define my existence, and it's hard not to see them as entrapping. I think I've lived most of my life with a sense of unlimited possibility—I've always been able to reinvent myself through multiple jobs, multiple relationships, travel, and all kinds of experiences. So it came as a great surprise to find myself in a situation I couldn't leave. I'd never met up with that because I'd never had a child before.

"It freaked both of us out," Alex continues. "I was confused because I had always wanted a child. For 20 years, since an abortion at 18, I had idealized it, worked toward it, pined for it. Jody said, 'You don't know what you're getting yourself into,' but he knew I had to have one. And adopting—that's a heavy kind of pronouncement. You're saying to a mother, 'We're ready to parent. Give us your child.' It's double the responsibility and doubly conflicting.

"There was no question we would get through it," she asserts, "but there were times when I felt what made me vital was the infinite possibility in my life, and to accept the life I had would mean a slow dying of my multiplied self. In fact, what I used to equate with infinite possibility was sexual freedom. It has always been easier to chuck what I've got and envision a new beginning in a new relationship.

"But I've just turned 41, and I have to face the fact that if I want a relationship to last, I'm going to have to work at it. And what I'm finding out is that I can rediscover that vital self through other avenues, through what I've got in terms of my marriage, my job, and my responsibilities to Kyle. The necessity of wanting to remain a family has been, for me, the mother of invention: Without those limitations, I would never have had to invent ways to deal with them and never have reached the next spiritual rung. I see motherhood and marriage acting like the limitations that result in a better creative product—as the discipline of a deadline helps my writing, as the sonnet form makes for the art of poetry.

"And I find I want to go through this rediscovery with Jody. My relationship with Jody is *the* relationship. Kyle needs both of us together. Parenting loses so much meaning when you lose a spouse. I realize I could do it alone, but I don't want to—and what an unfortunate thing to do to Kyle.

"It's so *exciting* to face this and feel like we'll make it," gushes Alex. "And you know what? Just now that we've made this commitment to each other, now that we find we can handle parenting and really enjoy it—now I want another child!"

Reaping the Rewards of Long-Term Commitment

Verna Tweddale is an emergency-room nurse at a major metropolitan hospital. For the past five years, since the birth of her third child, she has worked evenings, 3 P.M. until midnight, but with her youngest going into school and her oldest going off to college next year, she has opted to work days to have more time with her husband and children.

Actually spending that time with her family, however, is a struggle for Verna—despite the fact that her husband cooks and a woman comes in every two weeks to help clean. Bills beckon to be paid, laundry must be folded, dishes demand to be washed—an endless array of "scut work" must nonetheless be attended to. By 9 P.M. she's managed to read Ben, her third child, his bedtime story before tumbling into bed herself so that she can get up at 5:30 and start the cycle all over again. The stack of books by her bedside remains unread; the piano in her living room, too often silent.

Yet this is a life Verna insists she has, to a large degree, chosen for herself—despite the fact that working is not a choice. Her family relies on her income. She has little flexibility as a staff nurse, not enough clout to call the shots on when or how much she'll work. Part of her, she admits, would like *not* to have to show up at the hospital day after day, holidays notwithstanding; part of her wishes she were living back a generation or two and could "settle in and do crewel stitch." Like most working women, she says seeing other mothers in their sweats in the middle of the work day can make her skin crawl with envy.

"But there's another part of me," says Verna, "that knows when I'm at work I have a real talent there. I get a lot of satisfaction from my days off, but I wouldn't want to be just at home. If I'm to be real honest, I never want to be that dependent. I don't want to feel that vulnerable. I just want the time out, not to suddenly sell Tupperware."

Her greatest challenge is giving herself moments for pure reflection. On her days off, she says, there's little question of what the day will hold: "I'll hit the housework hard, get all the drudgery out of the way so that I can look forward to some renewal time later." But later never comes, Verna admits. Some task is always pulling at her, forever postponing the promised down time. Short of doing everything that needs doing, she feels she must "earn" a break and then give herself permission to take it. Of late, Verna's learned that permission isn't even enough: she must leave the house. "I have to go for a five-mile walk," she laughs. "If I'm here, I'm morally bound to be participating, whereas my husband comes home and gets his rest by just . . . taking it!"

It's not that her husband doesn't help, or that she can't get the cooperation of her children. Her midwestern work ethic, she says, is mostly to blame. Where she grew up, women derived their self-esteem from and judged others according to the tasks they tirelessly performed. Everybody worked hard; nobody with any self-respect or social consciousness slacked off. Verna has only this year made her peace with having someone come in to clean. "Given a free moment," she says, "I wouldn't read, I wouldn't play the piano—I'd go do the floor. So I decided I can get help: It's not a personal comment about my energy or lack of organization that someone else mops my floors."

Still, productivity is the yardstick by which Verna measures herself. "I guess it's a question of self-worth," she observes. "Women have to believe in the fundamental worth of what they're doing. I'm always asking myself, 'Is my time spent packing a smiley-face cookie that I decorated in Ben's lunch important enough to earn me the right to leave the house and all its obligations? And can I give myself permission to feel unaccountable should the system break down while I'm gone?'"

Staying busy and being productive is at once enslaving and liberating for a high-energy person like Verna, for when she's utterly consumed by an important task, she is freed from the onus of having to weigh the worth of her actions. What she likes most about the E.R., she says, is its high intensity, its unpredictability; she doesn't think so much as she acts, or reacts. She must do "ten things at once in a split second," solving problems on her feet instead of pondering the possibilities behind a desk. "I want to help fix it, and then I don't want to hear about it," she says.

Rarely does she look up a patient she treated to see how he's doing, and rarely does she think about work outside of her eight-hour shift. In the E.R. she lives in the present moment, crisis to crisis. There's no time for second thoughts, for self-doubt. There's never an opportunity to torment herself with thoughts of what she might, or could, or should be doing: What, indeed, could be more important than saving lives? In the chaos and hyperactivity of the E.R., Verna is, ironically, at peace.

It's when she comes home that she finds herself agonizing over how to spend the hours. Productively? Leisurely? Picking up the living room? Practicing her music, her singing? Verna recalls the pleasure of anticipation she used to feel when she could get her two children to nap simultaneously, only to find herself so eager to "do something" with the opportunity that she sat paralyzed, unsure of how to use her freedom to greatest advantage. "I was relieved when they woke up," she chuckles, "because then it was clear to me what I should be doing."

But the same skills that make work so rewarding grant her little in the way of satisfaction at home, where she laments not having more to show for her efforts as facilitator. "I wind up spending my free time making sure everyone else's free time pays off. If my husband says he can wallpaper the bathroom one day next week, I try to pave the way and get everything in readiness so that when he comes home he can get started. Then, for one reason or another, something comes up and the bathroom doesn't get finished.

"At work I save lives," Verna observes wryly, "whereas at home I wait around for the forces in the universe to come together just to get a simple project done!"

Something can always use her attention; something will always use up her few hours at home if she allows it to. But Verna is starting to cut herself some slack. She is gradually giving herself permission. Because while the treadmill affords her ample distraction and fleeting fulfillment, she has begun to perceive that it will deny her the long-term contentment she wants "so that when I'm 95 and alone in a hospital bed, it'll be okay."

Verna says that she stays busy in part to spare herself the pain of confronting life's inevitable losses: Her oldest son will be going off to college; her youngest entering school full time. Yet the strategy that enables her to avoid the inevitable is at the same time robbing her of the reflective moments that constitute her fondest memories, fuel her most important relationships, and clarify her spiritual goals. Motoring at high speed makes her feel ten years younger, but it does not reverse the maturing of her children; it only prevents her from enjoying them while she has them.

"It seems you've got to go through a whole string of little

deaths," she reflects, "before you realize it's up to you to make a rebirth."

Six years ago, Verna suffered a series of "little deaths" before giving birth, nearly 11 years after her second child, to Ben. She was living in Indiana, surrounded by family and friends, working at a job she adored, raising her son and daughter—and contemplating a divorce. "It was sort of a restless time in our marriage," she recalls. "We'd gotten to that point where you have your kids, you've done your career, so now what?" And then her husband was offered a new position in Pennsylvania. Now what indeed, thought Verna. Suddenly she had options she hadn't considered.

"I loved Indiana," she reveals. "It was as close as I thought we could come to living like the Waltons. But I knew for my husband, this wasn't where he was going anywhere. I had to decide, do I watch him wither on the vine and keep my nice life or risk it all for him and move? Intuitively I knew I had to do this, and yet it made no sense to me in terms of my own needs and goals and wishes. I couldn't help but think if it doesn't work, I've lost everything dear to me, and if it does I don't know what I'm gaining."

For Verna, college had culminated in marriage, marriage in children, children in the all-American dream. She had no experience in initiating transition; her life had demanded reaction, and she had responded. She feared she lacked the requisite pioneer spirit to make an unprompted step. She was also afraid to put her marriage to the test, afraid circumstance might prove there was no "mettle" to the relationship. "But I finally saw the choice," she recalls. "I said to myself, 'Am I going to go through the motions here and pretend to live this life or roll up my sleeves and see if there's anything in this for me?' And I decided, if we knew nobody in Pennsylvania, then it would be sink or swim: We'd find each other or give up the marriage."

So Verna came East, played solitaire, and got pregnant. There were more little deaths: Much as she cherished the notion of becoming the close-knit family she fantasized her mother's to have been, she realized she could never reverse the long-term effects of seeing her parents split when she was ten, could never undo the damage to her sense of trust. "It's my profound regret I don't have a higher tolerance for intimacy," Verna sighs. "That's part of the damage from my childhood. After my parents split up, the only way I felt I could survive was never to trust or open myself fully to anyone again. I can't sit in a cocoonlike setting and just 'be' with someone else; I'm too much a high-energy person, and I need my personal space. Perhaps my children are more independent for it—they're very capable kids. What they get from me is like what I give at work, where I open my soul in very short, very intense bursts and then step back and see another patient.

"But they get the message, so I guess I can accept that's just part of who I am," she says. "I know I'm not Livvy Walton and that I can't have the prolonged kinds of contact she did, but I know I have my own style and that the intentions and spirit are the same.

"Besides," Verna adds, "it's not 1940 anymore, and none of us would organize our lives that way even if we had the choice."

She is, however, making a more conscious effort to just "be" with her children. She's trying to allow for those moments that "make life worth living," trying to stop whirling in anticipation of tomorrow's pitfalls so that she can simply revel in the blessings of the present. "Just the other night," she recounts, "the kids and I were all sitting on the stair landing, all of us in our jammies, just having a talk. It was no big deal, but we were all physically there, the sort of thing I'll remember when I'm 75. Such moments carry me a long way.

"I think that's the greatest thing children do for us, forcing us to live in this instant," Verna continues. "We're always living in the future, so we rarely enjoy the moment. No matter what we're doing, we feel like we should be doing something else, so we're never wholeheartedly in anything we do. If we give ourselves a respite, we spoil it by feeling guilty, thinking what we *might* be doing or accomplishing instead."

Women are particularly prone to the treadmill, she speculates, because they tend to equate satisfaction or fulfillment with total mastery or completion—all the while realizing that nothing will ever be finished or perfect or *static.* By way of example she cites her efforts to be "more thorough" than her mother, who, she has no doubt, struggled to improve on *her* mother, ad infinitum through the generations. "No one's gotten any closer to the ideal," she says. "It's the same old struggle, with the same old questions and the same sense of dissatisfaction."

If fulfillment remains elusive, Verna adds, it's because women are taught that the answer is outside them, that they can't possibly discover it on their own; they need, for example, the help of a man. "So we embark on this heroic journey, thinking if we can just marry the right guy, have enough money, have wonderful children, that we'll become the person we were born to be. Then we wake up at 40 and wonder, 'Is this all there is?'

"I've come to realize there's no such thing as 'enough' in human nature," Verna observes. "I'm never going to be satisfied. The house will never be clean enough or big enough. I'm never going to 'have arrived.' I know this treadmill: You never get anywhere; you just exhaust yourself trying. And you can never slow down enough to enjoy what you've already got."

But she's come to believe that "the universe gives us the very vehicle necessary to accomplish our goals, if we can only make ourselves open to the opportunity." Recently Verna took off for a minivacation with her daughter, spending a weekend doing what she loves best: singing with a choral group. She'd never allowed herself such an adventure before, but she told herself her daughter was 16 and their time together was running out. "The bottom line is, I did it for me, and that's okay," says Verna. "Only when our needs are met as mothers can we meet others' or teach them to meet their own. I knew I had to get away. I had to go sing. Now it's one of my most cherished memories."

If we often miss the opportunities for rebirth, Verna muses, it's probably because we're so *afraid* of the losses, the little deaths. We concentrate so heavily on what we're *not* that we can't see how much we *are.* "As women," she elaborates, "we should feel victorious for rising to just about any occasion, for proving ourselves tremendously resourceful when circumstance is against us. Yet we talk like victims, act like victims, get stuck in this gender thing where we say, 'Poor little me, I have so much to do!' Let's face it, the human race would come to a screeching halt if women were to quit. So let's pride ourselves on being able to ride the wave; let's make it a plus instead of being mad all the time."

Verna's long-term ambition these days is to become "a grand old lady," the kind who recognizes she's come through the fires and derives great satisfaction from it. "I see them in the E.R., I talk to them, I pay them attention," laughs Verna, "hoping by osmosis to adopt their outlook." And it seems to be working: Verna says she's much more comfortable in her skin, much less inclined to have to prove herself, much more confident that she could if she had to. "I'm spending less time wondering if what I'm doing is noble enough or worthwhile enough," says Verna. "I'm figuring out when to rest, how to play more."

Her whole life, says Verna, she's been looking for a place where she can relax, "a nice warm lap to crawl up in and feel at home." Having tried all the avenues, she had almost concluded it didn't exist. Now, she says, she's of a mind that the lap is her own.

"It's our privilege and curse, as women, to figure that out," she observes. "Home has been there all along: We just need to give ourselves permission to rest in it."

Forging a Legacy Out of Her Heritage

T ina Lloyd has always had a strong sense of self. She's always had a clear vision of what she was good at and what she wanted out of life. The eldest of three children born to a prominent black Southern family, she was raised to appreciate classical music and the ballet, to marry a doctor or lawyer, to have children, and to pursue a "respectable" career in community service as her mother, a schoolteacher, had before her. But Tina, "a bit of a prodigy" in the theater arts, had her heart set on being an actress. She wanted to command the stage; it wasn't her destiny, she felt, to play a bit part. "It was a difficult rebellion for everyone around me," she recalls. "But I felt this was where I was needed, where my gifts might serve a higher purpose."

Opportunity came sooner than anyone anticipated. As a senior at the University of Alabama, Tina seized the national spotlight when she was made homecoming queen—an honor for which no black woman in the state's history had ever been considered before.

"I didn't even want to be up for it," Tina recalls. "I told the African-American organization on campus to nominate someone else. 'No, no,' they said, 'you have the best chance of winning, and that'll mean an opportunity to bring about some real change.' *That* got me interested; then I got involved. I've always been one to enjoy the process, the work itself—whether I get rave reviews or no attention whatsoever. Well, I got a lot of attention. George Wallace campaigned against me. People threatened to kill me if I rode the float. They brought in the FBI, and I can remember watching myself on all three networks. I couldn't help but feel I was part of something important."

Tina no longer courts that kind of limelight. But she still feels called to serve a higher purpose, more so now, as a mother, than ever before. And she has a project before her in which she sees the potential to bring about real change, or at least affect the way people see themselves. In researching her family's roots she stumbled upon the story of her great-grandmother, a Cherokee born 15 years after the Trail of Tears, a woman who survived a siege in the mountain caves of North Carolina and slavery in Alabama to eventually buy the land that gave her grandchildren the freedom to become whom they chose to be. "I think of what she accomplished in the time she lived, regardless of odds—and I'm in awe," says Tina. "I feel now I have to live up to my own mission, whatever that is; find my inner voice so I can demonstrate achievement through that."

The medium, she feels sure, is film, a medium she's been schooled in and trained for as an actress. Now her role, she says, is likely to be as writer and/or director, somewhat behind the scenes but more in control of the outcome. "I feel I'm the only person in the world who can take on this challenge," she comments, "because I bring a unique perspective to the subject."

And her instincts tell her the timing is right. She would have liked to have already tackled a project of this dimension; having gone back to school and then had a baby when she did, she realizes, has made her a latecomer to the industry. But she feels her son, far from holding her back, is now her primary reason for plowing ahead, whatever the obstacles. "I want him to have the best, to expose him to a world of opportunity," she says, reason-

ing that if the film comes off she might finally establish the financial security for him that she threw away for herself.

But it is more than money, more than fame, more than having
the final say that drives Tina to tackle the challenge. "I have to
get the notes out or I will burst," she explains. "If I don't get this
screenplay written, if I don't finish one of these larger projects, I
won't be able to live with myself: I'll have to question who I really
am, at least professionally."

What has stymied Tina in realizing her creative ambitions, of
course, is motherhood. She can no longer turn off the phones,
stay up all night, and "just knock this thing out" the way she
might have before Malcolm was born. She can't find the time or
even the place: Her three-year-old is so covetous of her attention
that she cannot work in her house, even if her husband covers
for her. And going out to her car—a haven she discovered one
night when she was desperately trying to finish an article assignment—isn't feasible for a hundred-page endeavor. "It's so
frustrating," says Tina. "Some days I feel my professional goals
are getting further and further away from me." Her short-term
solution: to take Malcolm back home to Alabama, where she
hopes his cousins and aunts and uncles and grandparents will
distract him long enough that she can make some headway on
her screenplay.

It is Tina's gift, as an artist, to be able to envision a project and
then dedicate 100 percent of her ability, concentration, and will
toward its successful completion; it is her curse to be equally
compelled, as a mother, to throw herself into parenting.
Compromise doesn't come easily, not when, as an actress, she
has trained for each part by becoming that character in every
gesture, thought, and movement, to block out all competing or
distracting roles. An actress may play many parts over the course
of her career, but critical acclaim is reserved for those who keep
those parts separate and distinct.

Tina had no intention of keeping family and career separate

and distinct. Her mother had always done both; she had always imagined herself doing both. But a problematic pregnancy had her first too sick to work and then bedridden. "When they learned I was in danger of losing the baby, I gave in completely," she says. "I said to myself, 'Nothing else matters—I won't try to write, won't stretch my mind, won't do anything that will make me want to get out of this bed.'" She promised herself that once the baby was born, she'd get around again. She hadn't given up her life, just taken a sabbatical. "When people told me, 'Oh, it'll be at least three years before you'll be back at full speed,' I didn't believe them," Tina recalls. "I thought, I've met so many challenges, why not this one?

"I didn't realize," says Tina, "that without family to turn to for baby-sitting I wouldn't be getting out at all, what with my husband trying to keep us on our financial feet. I had no help for the first year, so I couldn't work, and my whole social life was wrapped up in work. I felt like a nonperson. By Malcolm's second year, I was ready for therapy."

And for a career "reevaluation." Acting was out of the question. With a child, she could no longer be available at the slightest notice; her agent had already dropped her because she repeatedly turned down opportunities. ("I realize," says Tina, "I didn't think through the nursing thing at all.") For the first time she reckoned with the possibility that she might never see her acting ambition realized—that she might not ever make the big screen. So she enrolled Malcolm in a KinderKare program at the local YMCA and hired herself a manager, determined to concentrate her talents in directing and producing.

"It was my choice," she insists. "Acting just isn't one of those areas I can work in and still have close time with the baby. Unless you're a bankable movie star, you have very little control over when you work or how. So I chose to reestablish myself as a writer or director because I can design that career: I can determine when the work is done, or whether the baby will be able to go on the set, or how I'll structure my time and child care.

"And the truth is, I don't feel forced from something I loved," Tina continues. "I learned very early on that when you're thrust into the limelight, you end up being a conduit for everybody else's goals and ambitions: They make of you what they want out of it." Indeed, while she was acting in the soaps, she found out just how compromised an actress's life could be. Total strangers accosted her in public, responding not to her but the character she played; she felt forced to go "under cover," even, for a while (in the wake of John Lennon's shooting) to carry a gun. "It was very frightening," she recalls. "I've come to prefer the low-key, behind-the-scenes environment."

Now Tina's of a mind that her "sacrifice" in terms of spending time exclusively with her son has more than paid off, both for Malcolm and for her career. "I think I'm more patient as a director," she reflects. "I'm not as cut-and-dried as usual; I look for other ways to communicate. I can see I bring a certain fullness— a word I never thought I'd use!—to my work since I became a mother."

She finds directing, in fact, in many ways kindred to mothering: She talks of "birthing" her productions and then learning to gradually "let go" her control so that they might stand on their own merits. She likes the collaboration and teamwork aspect, likes orchestrating something that inevitably turns out to be much more than a sum of its parts: "What one body can do, as an actress," she notes, "seems small to me now." As a director, and as a mother, Tina enjoys having her vision realized in ways larger and more wonderful than she alone could have accomplished.

Equilibrium often eludes her. On a typical day she'll be rushing all over town keeping tabs on her theater productions, working with the actors, fine-tuning her direction, doing interviews for an article she's writing, or working on a script. When she gets home, her son insists on "getting whatever hours of the day I didn't give him," meaning several hours of her total attention. Tina says she and her husband "mumble a few words to make sure all gears will mesh the next day" and then go to bed to wake up and do it all over again.

"I'm not half of what I was," she says with a sigh, noting that for all her running about, she's not really getting anywhere. Malcolm is throwing more tantrums, she reports, showing less patience with her for fear she'll be dashing out the door any minute. She's showing less patience with her actors, so distracted is she with Malcolm. Recently an actress she'd never worked with before ignored her direction, and Tina nearly blew a gasket. Only later did she recognize that she simply hadn't spent the time making this woman aware of what she expected from her. Her husband, Tina admits, is also getting the short end; he's been "on the back burner," she says, since Malcolm's birth, along with her family and friends.

"The problem is, the nature of my work is so irregular," Tina sighs. "Each project has different demands, and I don't know what they'll be ahead of time. There'll be periods when I can really put things aside and give Malcolm my full attention, and times when I'm not here at all."

Nonetheless, she is confident she will find equilibrium, confident things will work out. "They'll have to," she stresses, "because this is my life." The pendulum may be swinging away from her family right now, but she doesn't feel guilty about it, doesn't see it as anything but the counterswing to her intensely domestic period following Malcolm's birth. "My husband may complain I've been away too much, but he doesn't realize how few women can work and have their baby with them a good part of the day, sometimes all day," Tina says. "I feel very privileged, working at what I love."

She is grateful, too, for the example her own mother provided, working as a schoolteacher and being a pillar of the community while raising three children. "She always managed to do what she loved, in one way or another," Tina muses. Part of what made that possible was having both maternal and paternal grandmothers on hand to help with her children—a familial backbone Tina misses both for herself and for her son. More than her own parents, this extended family raised her, imbued her with the strength and the self-esteem to be the "trailblazer" her father perceives her to be. Tina's maternal grandmother, "so full of peace she was Christlike," helped smooth the rough edges of her adolescence; her father's "feisty" mother supported her when she chose to pursue a career in acting over the more traditional expectations of her parents. "If I could be a blend of the two of them," Tina laughs, "I'd feel really good. I'd know when to kick, but I'd also have inner peace."

Tina was given the freedom to discover, and pursue, whatever talents she might possess, and that's what she hopes most to give Malcolm—the freedom to be self-determinate. Exercising that freedom, Tina concedes, may entail some sobering costs: Her own rebellion forced her to leave her hometown and make her way in a large city, and she misses, with a child, the communal embrace and support of her relatives. That rebellion also ensured her a boom-or-bust financial roller coaster, a ride Tina thrilled at initially but has since grown weary of as a parent looking to secure her own son's future. And while working in the theater proved more color-blind than most professions, it was rife, says Tina, with sexism and sexual harassment.

Hard work and honest talent, that is, haven't always met with commensurate reward. "Every day is full of compromise," Tina observes. But she insists she hasn't compromised her ultimate goals or "the soul of what I am." The screenplay will get done; Malcolm will become a more independent child. And the pendulum will right itself, she has no doubt.

"I think balance is possible," says Tina, who maintains she sees few distinctions between her work in and outside the home. "I've just got to make sure I don't take on too many small projects so that I'm too busy and too stressed to make time for what's really important. I've just got to stay focused and keep my belief system in order."

Tina's philosophy is founded upon the belief that each of us is responsible for our own environment in that we create it with our thoughts and words. She's working through her anger, she says, lest she create an angry environment: "Whether I'm bitter because my agent didn't take me back after the baby, or because Malcolm won't do what I want him to, or because my husband loaded the dishwasher wrong, it's a waste of energy and time; I've learned you've got to move beyond that, to channel your energy where it can make a difference.

"I've always been a fearless person," Tina elaborates, "but what attracted me to this philosophy is that what you hold in your mind is what you attract. My mother was of an era where a worrying, fearful parent was a good parent. Her thinking was, 'It won't happen if you worry enough, if you hold it in your heart.' I believe just the opposite: that if you harbor fear, then you will attract what you fear into your life."

She has never been one to dwell on setback, even though as a black woman she has, she says, known plenty of it. "We're not talking fictional harassment," says Tina, alluding to the cross burnings that made her a reclusive adolescent, the sexual advances that threatened to derail her career.

"But I've always believed if I don't carry that banner—the one that says 'I'm black and I'm a woman'—then people won't see me in limited terms," she continues. "A lot of our limits are self-imposed; if I can break through them, I can break through anybody else's. It's helped me get control of my life, realizing how much the future depends simply on how I perceive myself. I can make changes; I can effect change. It's my responsibility. I've been dealt this hand, so I'm going to play it."

CHAPTER EIGHT

The Generation Gap: Mothers & Daughters

One recent summer's evening, waiting to meet my husband's train, my kids and I were joined on the station platform first by a sixtyish woman with her grandson and then by a man about my age, in sandals and shorts, wheeling a toddler in a double stroller and carrying a baby on his hip.

The train was late; every 60 seconds or so my three-year-old, Chase, would announce rather convincingly, "It's coming. I can hear it." After a few minutes the grandmother turned to Chase. "Is that Daddy's train?" she asked. "What a nice surprise for Daddy, after a long day at the office, to get off the train and see you!" Then she turned to me, as I stood there looking for all the world like a full-time mother in my T-shirt and leggings, and smiled a knowing smile.

"We're waiting for Mommy's train," the man suddenly piped up. "Isn't that right?" he asked his older child, who now stood clutching his father's hand. The little boy nodded solemnly.

I forgot about the train, so curious was I about this family. "What are your boys—about 15 months apart?" I opened.

"Fourteen months," he corrected me. "I grew up in a family of four born in five years, and we were all very close, so I'm glad to have convinced my wife this was a good idea."

Yes, I agreed, there were many benefits—only during the first four months did I find difficult.

"Really?" he asked in genuine amazement. "We had a bit of an adjustment to make during the second four, but probably because my wife returned to work and I didn't have that extra set of hands to count on."

The Generation Gap

I know I'm not supposed to even blink anymore at the sight of this newly evolved species of man. If I were a stalwart feminist instead of a conflicted one, I wouldn't want him to think he was the least bit unusual or special—just a father doing what a good father does, caring for his children without apology or explanation. But in truth I am amazed. He exists; he is no media fabrication. Just seeing him fills me with hope and optimism: hope that the wrenching changes of the past 30 years have resulted in something positive; optimism that the worst trade-offs of women's quest for equality are behind us and that the rewards are at hand.

But what do I know? I am 31 years old; the woman on that platform with twice my years and experience might well have regarded this man as a symbol of all that is wrong with the American family today. Where I saw an involved father, she perhaps saw an absentee mother. Whereas I came away feeling encouraged about the fate of the next generation, she might well have concluded that society is headed for extinction. She is entitled to her opinion; I may one day share it. Indeed, it is my greatest fear that in later life I will come to regret my chosen course, regret the convictions that steered me to it, regret that I so outspokenly championed mothers who chose to remain in the work force, at least partially, while their children were young. In anticipation of this future self-betrayal, almost daily I recite for myself a little mantra to the effect that however age colors my perspective on these years, I *am* enjoying them, I *do* believe in the balance I have struck, and I *will not* torture myself, 30 years hence, with coulda-shoulda-woulda scenarios because memory, I well realize, can make decisions that were made utterly consciously at the time look hasty, ill-thought-out, or, worse, not made at all.

Therein lies the crux of the working-mother conflict: However our voice of instinct may reassure us that our choice to balance multiple roles is a good one—for our children, for our marriages, and for ourselves—another voice (the voice of generations past) whispers that the stakes are far too high to trust merely our instinct. We should consult those who have always known best. We should ask our mothers.

And what we hear from them, or *believe* we hear from them, is not encouraging. Virtually every one of my peers with whom I spoke identifies her mother as the ideological source of her conflict. Not that the working thirtysomethings accuse their mothers of being unsupportive; they just suspect the older generation does not *approve* of the choices they're making.

"Oh, my mother's proud of me," says Nancy Belser, the pediatrician introduced in chapter four. "But she doesn't dwell on the fact that I'm a doctor. She'll ask, 'Now how is that day-care situation working out?', and reading between the lines, I know she thinks a child should be home with its mom. Bottom line, she thinks *I* should be home."

"I think my mother realizes it's beneficial for me to work and that it's an economic reality," says Susan Asher, the video producer introduced in chapter seven, "but I think she would like to see me quit my job and live next door. She's a controlling kind of person."

"I know my mother thinks I'm some sort of breeder," photographer Jan Neiman (first mentioned in the introduction) told me. "'Why have another child if you're not going to be home to take care of it?' That's my sense of how she feels." When I asked if I might speak to her mother to find out for myself, Jan hastened to add, "She won't be honest. She'll tell you what she thinks you want to hear."

I understand all too well these women's paranoia. My own mother has made perfectly clear how she feels about full-time motherhood, and a good deal of her positive influence on her children lies in the strength of her conviction that mothers should be dedicated to child rearing. And yet I know, too, that having gone back to school to be professionally certified as a landscape architect, my mother appreciates what it means to have a career, to have a focus outside of the home, to have a sphere of influence beyond one's own children—to have a life and an identity that is separate from, but complementary to, her identity as mother and wife. She has articulated her support for me; more importantly, she has given it, traveling two hours to bail me out of a crisis, putting in time on the phone networking for me, taking the kids when I saw no other way to respond to the demands of my job. But like Jan and Susan and Nancy, I torment myself second-guessing what she *really* thinks. And I am certain I will never know, because my own doubts will not allow me to trust what she tells me.

However, on the assumption that *other* grandmothers would have no reason to be anything less than candid with me, I solicited opinions from 15 of them regarding us, the current generation of working mothers. All, as I suspected, had lots of opinions to share, as all had grandchildren age six or under to be concerned about. Their responses to my questions—the questions that frame the contents of this book—confirmed some of my assumptions, challenged others, and flatly dismissed a few. But the sheer diversity of their experiences, even after I narrowed my sample to the nine most representative, defied any attempt on my behalf to discern one clear path, one direct route to fulfillment on a road map crisscrossed with possibilities.

To be sure, my interviewees were in almost universal accord (as I presumed they would be) that mothers should stay home to rear their children, at least until the children were in school full time. This was, they agreed, the *right* thing to do (though they were not entirely sure *why*). And yet, as their stories unfolded, it became clear this was their *ideal* and not necessarily their reality. Divorce and financial straits forced some to return to the workplace; artistic passion and vocational "calling" motivated others to "compromise" their commitment to full-time motherhood. Mothers of young children *should not* work outside the home, I heard over and over, but only two women in my sample actually *never* worked. Ironically, the truly full-time mothers were by no means the most adamant about staying home; most vehement in her denunciation of working motherhood was a woman who taught ballet "purely for pleasure" while her children were four, six, and nine years old.

Hence, disheartening as it would be for me to conclude, as several insisted I should, that full-time mothering was the only means of setting society back on moral course, I would draw that conclusion—if only the evidence supported it. (After all, it would be almost a *relief* to be told, unequivocally, what we should do with our lives in order to guarantee happiness and success.) I must conclude instead that this "ideal" of full-time motherhood is precisely that: an ideal. Very rarely in history has circumstance afforded women the luxury of devoting themselves exclusively to childbearing and child rearing. Even when it has—during the '50s and '60s—women have not necessarily found themselves or their children markedly better off for it.

I came to see these women's stories in a wholly positive light, precisely because it became apparent that they were wrestling with many of the same demons plaguing us, their daughters. The gap between generations may be nowhere near as unbridgeable as we routinely imagine it. If we feel guilt because we presume our mothers never had conflicting or competing roles to balance, then perhaps our memories serve us incorrectly—or perhaps, as Stephanie Coontz suggests in *The Way We Never Were: American Families and the Nostalgia Trap*, we have allowed the media to distort our image of our own past. It is just possible that we feel guilt *because our mothers did*, ensnared by the cultural expectations of their age as well as by the expectations of *their* mothers. Perhaps there is nothing at all new about women's guilt for their shortcomings as mothers. Perhaps there are only new foils for it.

Admittedly, my sample was small. Admittedly, I am probably fundamentally biased in my perspective. Yet of the 15 grandmothers with whom I spoke, the two who struck me as truly fulfilled, positive-minded, forward-looking individuals were the part-time physician and the full-time mother of five. Looking back on their lives, neither had any regrets; looking forward to their daughters' lives, neither had any ax to grind. I find myself mildly envious of their daughters, not because I presume them to be free of inner conflict, but because I feel rather certain they are free of this peculiarly feminine legacy of inadequacy that mothers have passed on to daughters, generation after generation. They are likely to have inherited instead that confidence the rest of us still seek. As full-time or part-time mothers, they will be good enough.

Victims of Circumstance or Masters of Destiny?

One of the assumptions we seem to cherish about our mothers' generation is that women didn't make any real choices for themselves because they didn't have any. You went to school to date, you went to college to get an "M.R.S.," you had babies immediately, you stayed home while they were young however poor you were, and if you were in a bad marriage, you stuck it out because, financially speaking, you *had no choice.* "That's pretty much the way it was," Barbara Lee, 69, agrees. "Your husband decided what house you were going to live in, what kind of car you would drive. Women's opinions weren't important." Indeed, not one of Barbara's peers insisted otherwise.

But it is one thing to note a trend and another to conclude that its sheer predominance precluded individual choice. Says Margaret Austin, 80 (with grandchildren three and five and *great*-grandchildren nine months and three), "Women all the way back could have done whatever they wanted to do and been accepted. And they have done what they wanted to do"—marrying and raising children.

I discounted Margaret's observation at first, because there seems such a wealth of evidence to the contrary. I had decided, in fact, that her privileged background (she danced with the Philadelphia Ballet) had a lot to do with her perspective. But there was no dismissing Betty Winston*, who, despite a disadvantaged youth, an abusive first marriage, and a period of single motherhood, is of a mind that circumstance may have exploited her but that ultimately—by working—she seized control of her destiny.

Betty, 54, is a mother of seven: a girl and two boys by her first husband—a paranoid schizophrenic whom she divorced when the oldest was 12—and four more boys, the youngest of whom is 13, by her current husband. Betty is concerned about her first set of children, particularly her daughter, who is the mother of a three-year-old; she feels Jenny was negatively influenced by her ill father. "She was afraid of him," recalls Betty. "To this day she is a very fearful person; it bothers me that she doesn't have confidence in herself, in her gut reaction to things, and I know that's from her early exposure. That's a shame, because she's a very intelligent, creative, concerned person. I wish I'd been ready to get myself out of that situation earlier, but I wasn't."

Her first marriage, she says, was born of her own insecurity. "I always felt I got involved with this person because I was unlovable," she explains. "It took me a while to figure this out, but because he was the one person who told me how terrible I was, how unattractive I was, how overweight I was—all these things no one else saw—I thought he saw the real me and everybody else was lying to me." The reason she had such a poor self-image, says Betty, is that her parents had put her in "the first day care ever, after the war," out of financial necessity, and it was such a miserable experience ("each day was like a lifetime") that the only explanation she could come up with for being there was that her parents did not love her. Now, of course, she realizes this was far from the truth. But it set the stage for her attraction to a man who treated her as if she were as worthless as she believed herself to be.

Betty's tale of woe wouldn't be all that remarkable—victimhood being almost the female legacy—but for the fact that she *did* extricate herself not only from a bad marriage but from the ensuing string of disasters divorcees commonly experience, disasters that serve only to reinforce negative self-image and passive resignation to "fate."

"I didn't feel I had any choices," she says of that difficult transition, "but in fact I did." Knitting and crocheting for a living while watching her kids, Betty managed to earn enough money that she felt she could afford to leave her husband. After the divorce she did accept Aid to Families with Dependent Children for three years because she received no child support from her ex-husband. But when she remarried, she made sure she retained her earning power. "I like having the control of being a wage earner," she says. "It's not so much a question of money but of self-esteem. My [current] husband makes much more money than I could ever make, but the power in the relationship switches back and forth."

Thus Betty applauds her daughter's professional involvement

and the fact that she kept her own name and has her own bank account. "It's very important that one has one's own life, whatever that may be," she says. "Not that you've got to be a working mother to have that, but you can't get it by being somebody's wife or mother or daughter. It has to come from you. You need to be your own person."

Having learned to be her own person, Betty today enjoys the benefits of partnership. "I have more inner resources, more time, more emotional freedom," she observes, "because I don't always have to be outthinking or outmaneuvering someone else. My husband works with me, and I can see the difference in our children: They'll be able to reach closer to their potential than my first three."

Professionally, Betty notes, her daughter is very talented, but what holds her back is her fearfulness. "It's hard to live your life to its fullest potential with any kind of fear," she says. "Jenny's ambivalent about working because a lot of things are changing, not the least of which is she's about to have her second child. I've tried to tell her, things never stay the same—life *is* change. But change is for the *good*."

Expectations: Then and Now

The corollary to my original thesis that women didn't have much choice in the '50s and early '60s—because they were *expected* to be wives and full-time mothers—is that societal expectations for our mothers were far more constraining than what we "liberated" women feel today. Even when we don't feel so liberated, we take perverse comfort in the fact that our mothers had it worse. In our minds' eye are all those frustrated housewives, six children clutching at their skirt, hair in curlers and handkerchief in hand, sobbing over a sinkful of dirty dishes. Thank God, we say to ourselves when we cannot summon even the dregs of energy at 5:30 P.M., *thank God* we don't have to wear girdles, fix three-course luncheons for the Junior League, wear makeup and a dress for our hubbies, and have dinner waiting on the table the minute they come home.

Even if we were born in the '60s, we still see Mom enslaved to society's expectation of her as Homemaker, Doting Wife, and Dedicated Mother. Such expectations, we are convinced, drove more than a few of these women to despair: Linda Bodini (introduced in chapter five) swore she would not grow up to be "powerless and dull" like her mother; Nancy Belser (of chapter seven) remembers thinking, of her mother's life, "That wasn't a lot of fun, cleaning dishes and doing laundry"; and Nina Decker (of chapter four) determined she would not repeat her mother's "servile" relationship with her husband.

Connie Lezenby (introduced in chapter one) recalls her mother being very "depressed" at home until she went back to school. "Mothers were really shut down," she insists. "My mother was a child prodigy, a genius; she wanted to be a doctor, but her parents said no way. They saw their job as getting her married and taken care of, and her being a doctor would have gotten in the way of that plan. She was robbed of what she wanted to be, and boy is she angry. She pretends she isn't, that her expectations were fulfilled. But all that energy got channeled into running our lives, pushing us to be perfect, and that wasn't healthy for any of us. I can remember thinking, at a very young age, 'I need to do something to avoid this depression.'"

Rita La Rocca, 65, who had five daughters in seven years, paints the picture a little differently. Lots of children were, of course, expected, she says: "There was no such thing as birth control if you were Catholic—even if you weren't." Mothers stayed home, naturally; no woman in Rita's family worked, ever. The mothers on her block all had broods of seven or nine children: "Everyone was doing it!" she says. "Those were the Kennedy years. Large families were in. Your life was carved out according to your upbringing, your religion—I had no question about what was expected of me."

Neither does Rita have any regrets. "My greatest pleasure is looking at all those pictures in my living room, of five weddings and six grandchildren," she says. "All I ever wanted was to see each of my girls with a family of her own. I had no great ambitions; I was raised in parochial schools, in an unsophisticated way, and I guess I'm parochial still. But I took great pleasure in raising them. I got what I wanted."

Rita is all for women working: Two of her three daughters with young children are working mothers, and Rita insisted that all five be educated "in case they ever needed to fend for themselves." But she doesn't feel they are any luckier for it; on the contrary, their lives seem harder to her. "They're still doing two jobs, no matter what they say: When they come home, they're doing everything they would have had to do if they stayed home, and they have the extra job of the children. It's the nature of the beast, given their biological tradition." The ideal, Rita believes, is to postpone work until the kids are in school, at the very least. She doesn't buy into the theory that most women have to work. What she sees instead is too many women working in response to materialistic expectations. "I'm not criticizing younger people, but they have to work to maintain the two vehicles, the pool, the stereo, the car phone, and on and on," she notes.

Among Rita's peers there is a disturbing consensus that women today labor under much harsher expectations than they ever did: the material standard they must work to uphold, and the traditional standard they must meet in addition to professional expectations. "My sister puts in a full day on the job, and her husband still screams at her if dinner's not on the table when he comes home," says Cammie Carlton*, 53. "The other day I saw him lose his cool because there wasn't a can of Mountain Dew in the house. I don't see how working makes a woman's life any easier."

Donna Costello*, a radiologist in her mid-60s, has worked by choice at least part time all of her married life, except for the five or six months she spent at home after the birth of her daughter. But even Donna feels women contend with punishing expectations today. "Women feel the need to prove something nowadays," she observes. "I just wanted to do my job, make my contribution; I wasn't out to conquer the world. I guess women have been excluded from so many things for so long they feel they have to prove they can do it. But things are much rougher for women now because they have no protection. Years ago men were expected to protect them, do things for them. The freedom women have is better, but now they're expected to take care of themselves."

The Trade-offs of Full-Time Motherhood

If there was ever boredom, frustration, or a sense of entrapment in the job of caring for young children, these women have either blocked it out, forgotten it, or, as they insist, never experienced it. Motherhood was an overwhelmingly positive experience, as my interviewees recall it.

For one thing, it was highly social. Rita remembers with great fondness the families in her neighborhood and the fun they used to have. The kids all went to the same school; the adults all attended the same church. They'd gather at one another's homes on weekends after the children had been put to bed and then take turns darting across the street to check up on everybody's kids. "The children were each other's playmates, and we raised them almost communally," Rita explains. "We had a lot of support [as mothers] in those days."

Annette Barnes*, 62, recalls being a military wife "dumped in Virginia with two teenagers and two toddlers" while her husband was away at sea, sometimes for months at a stretch—but she was never lonely, as other military wives were similarly situated and made a great effort to form their own community, even off-base. And Lynne Harper, 55, remembers, during the lean years when she was raising her kids, going out to eat maybe once a *year*, but never feeling cooped up and miserable. "I loved being home," says Lynne, who worked part-time factory and administrative jobs to make ends meet when her oldest was 10. "A lot of women today think it was some kind of prison sentence, but I really enjoyed my kids."

Rita so enjoyed her children that it truly pains her to see three of her grandchildren in day care. Not that she perceives any maladjustment or suffering in the kids: It's her *daughters* she feels are losing out, missing what she feels are the best years of motherhood. "Those are the years I'd never have traded," she says. "In my heart I feel the mothers are going to pay the price long-term—not so much the kids."

But as Barbara Lee and Bertha Stewart*, 64, will attest, women of their generation who stayed home pay another kind of price, long-term. Two years ago, Barbara's husband of nearly 50 years died of Alzheimer's. It wasn't a happy marriage; to this day Barbara has misgivings about the relationship. "I'm not proud of the fact that I didn't get along better with the children's father," she says. "But in those days, women with children didn't divorce. Financially, it was a nonoption." She was particularly disappointed in the father her husband proved to be. "He was never one to enjoy his kids, like these fathers I see today, playing basketball with their sons. He was too busy correcting them," she explains, noting that he used to whip her older son.

But it was her role to wait on him, bring him dinner, starch his shirts, and do everything around the house. And, of course, she took almost exclusive care of her two sons and daughter, even taking the boys fishing because her husband "hated that sort of thing." It was his role to do everything else—everything financial, that is. Up until his last year, says Barbara, he was still writing all the checks. "He'd never let me do anything. I'd ask him to tell me things, explain things to me, but he never would."

And then one day "he went from being a man in charge to a man who couldn't remember where he lived." Suddenly, says Barbara, "everything was dumped on me. I was a widow with a house, a yard, a car, and a lot of bills. Every time I turn around, it seems, there's something else. I want to say, 'I can't do this.'" Friends, she says, have been helpful but don't seem to understand her depression. In fact, she senses their exasperation. "'What more do you want?' they say. 'You can come and go as you please! What's your problem?'

"You'd think I'd be enjoying my freedom," she adds, "but I'm not, because I don't know how to cope. You women today are lucky: You're so much better prepared, working. You have a career; if I had my druthers, I would have gone to college and trained for some kind of career, because then I could have chosen to work part time while the kids were young and then, later, had it to fall back on. I loved what I did, working in the school district's guidance office. I used to think I wasn't smart enough to hold a job, but then when I went to work I found that wasn't true. People respected me. And I was very pleased with myself.

"I don't think I longed for a career when I was raising little children," she reflects, "but I wish now I had a career I was going back to."

Barbara feels there's a good and a bad side to both staying at home and working. She felt proud of the work she did but felt, too, the pull of wishing she could do more with her children. But she believes women today are "so in tune, so aware, so wonderful" that they know when it's important to be at the swim meet or dance recital.

The curious thing about Barbara is that she has always been "a champion of women." Even as a child she can recall asking her mother why she and Barbara's aunts were all working in the kitchen while the men listened to the radio. But then, says

Barbara, she herself "went ahead and did all the waiting-on too." It was the times, she guesses. Or maybe she just didn't really know her husband when she married him. She is pleased to see that her daughter, though married to "a very opinionated Germanic man," speaks for herself. She is also very attached to her oldest son's ex-wife, Linda, "a real barracuda in the business world." She's delighted to see the role young men assume as fathers, although she admits good fathers have always been around. Her own sons "are for women," she says, because she raised them to be.

But Barbara fears her five-year-old granddaughter's spirit is already broken, because as a society, she says, we are still harsher on daughters—excusing the sons because "boys will be boys." And she fears that women are still not handling "the essential problems"; not taking charge of what's going on in the world. "More women would like to grow up to be Madonna than a U.S. senator," she observes. "What is going to become of us?"

Half a century of an unhappy marriage and arguably *any* woman would emerge remorseful and depressed. Education, privilege, and a good marriage, on the other hand, might ensure a healthier outlook. But Bertha Stewart, with daughters 36 and 33, finds herself suddenly in a position where she has no responsibilities, where she can do whatever she wants for herself—and she doesn't know what that is. "I never thought I'd be in this position," she admits. "You think it happens to other people, that it won't happen to you, but here I am looking back more than I am looking ahead. It's true that most of my life is behind me, but I figure I've got 20 good years left, and there's no point in being alive if I don't do something constructive with them."

Being a full-time grandmother to her one-year-old granddaughter is not enough. "She's not my child," says Bertha. "If I'm needed, fine, but I don't want to be a grandmother who can't get out of her daughter's life." Going off to "elephant country" (Florida) to play golf isn't it, either: "That would be like saying

I'm dead." Taking courses or doing something with her hands isn't enough. And although she holds a graduate degree in adolescent psychology, going back to teaching holds no appeal whatsoever: "I don't want to cope with the kinds of kids out there today."

It is Bertha's great regret that she never went back to the workplace after her children were grown. There were always excuses; she was "never one to want for problems, for responsibilities, for things to be involved in" as a wife and mother. But if she could give advice to her older daughter, it would be to "remember that when Cassandra is grown, you will still have a life ahead of you, so make sure you're prepared for it." Take courses now, pursue what interests you, Bertha would like to tell her daughter, "because I'm a perfect example of what happens if you don't."

The difficulty, Bertha elaborates, lies in the nature of mothering. A child should be the center of the universe, she believes, and the mother should sacrifice for the child. But then, as the child grows, the mother should withdraw to the periphery and gradually return to being the center of her own life. It's not an easy transition, Bertha admits, because in making the child the center of the mother's universe, the mother loses a sense of herself. "It's difficult for me to conceive of a woman doing a good job as a mother *and* maintaining her own identity," she says. A tremendous number of mothers, she believes, maintain their professional identity at irreparable cost to their children. (Bertha blames the women's movement for this "unnatural" maternal behavior.)

"But I'm aware that the transition has to be made," she continues. "I realize I have to have an identity of my own. I'd say to both my daughters, 'You're no good to anyone until you're a whole person yourself. You can't solve problems or make a happy relationship unless you have fulfilled yourself, and no one—not even your children—can do that for you.'"

The Unacknowledged Benefits of Working

Donna Costello, the radiologist, is Bertha's sister—a fact I feel compelled to point out because no two siblings could be more polar in terms of their views and outlooks on motherhood. Donna, like Bertha, completed college because their mother, "a woman way ahead of her time," insisted that both girls be prepared to support themselves or their families if they had to. But Donna, who liked school and "didn't want to go out and work," elected to go on to medical school. Her father, "an old-fashioned man," thought she should go to Women's Medical College, but Donna opted to go to Syracuse instead, reasoning that it was a man's world she'd be practicing in. After a residency in Valhalla, New York, she worked at the renowned Lahey Clinic in Boston. She didn't marry until nine months before the end of her residency, figuring that if she got pregnant right away she could still finish her training.

Five years and many painful tests later, she conceived for the first and last time. When her daughter was born, she had no thought of going back to work. But five months later, a former colleague of hers begged her to return, going so far as to plead with Donna's mother. "And my mother convinced me," Donna recalls. "She said, 'Don't be a fool like me—I stayed home seven years! You have a duty to your profession!'"

Donna went back three days a week, only after she had secured "a very good person" to look after Jane. "I felt I spent all that time taking a man's spot in medical school, and I shouldn't waste it, really. It was an obligation—and I loved it. I felt very good, not torn. I had such a wonderful woman taking care of my daughter; my husband was actually jealous that Jane would prefer her to us. And I had a very supportive husband; I couldn't have done it without him. I felt very happy that I could work and still have children; I think it made our marriage stronger. And today I feel fulfilled as a physician *and* as a mother."

The only other woman to have a career as opposed to a job (all my interviewees worked out of a need for income at some point in their lives, save for Bertha and Rita) was Margaret Austin, the great-grandmother who believes women have always done as they pleased. Certainly she is proud of her own choices to quit the stage, marry, and rear three children. And yet the first thing she told me about those years when her children were four, six, and nine was that she ran a ballet school and that she "loved every single minute of it." Was she at all conflicted? "Not a bit," she declares flatly. "I never thought a second about it."

Yet she is begrudging in her support of working mothers—it's acceptable "only if they have to work to supplement the family income," she believes. Was that why she taught? For money? "Absolutely not," she says. "I did it because I loved it, because I loved children, and because it was an art that was mine." So why the caveat for working mothers today? "Women these days want to have a career," she explains. "I didn't feel that way; I never pursued the teaching. It just materialized naturally. And it never conflicted with my family's schedule—I saw to *that*." Margaret taught only part time, after school hours and on Saturday mornings. Her daughter, she says, "was right there next to me," while her two sons were "off in the field" with their father. "Working didn't affect my family at all," she reiterates. "I was there for meals, for all the things a mother should be."

Margaret feels she did a good job with her children but credits her husband for passing on "wonderful values." He was "right there beside them in every activity," she recalls, while she was teaching. "I didn't go to swim meets, but he did—every one. He had a love for sports as I had for dancing." As a result, she adds, her sons are "real men": one is a Marine Corp colonel, the other an officer in a corporation. Her daughter, she notes proudly, is "an excellent teacher."

Margaret is not at all sure, however, about the choices her grandchildren are making. One, the daughter of the Marine, is a commercial airline pilot married to a Navy pilot; their children have a wonderful nanny, according to Margaret, "but it's a situation that worries both grandmothers a lot." Feminism, to Margaret, is a bad word: "I don't like it one bit," she asserts. She loved being home, whereas today's women "aren't willing to sacrifice" the material rewards afforded by two incomes. The problem in too many families today, as she sees it, is that women "don't really need to work." (She hastens to clarify that, while she didn't either, her work was an art; had it been typing, she wouldn't have done it.) Family values have failed—not in *her* family, she says, but in the broad sense—"and it has a great deal to do with women working.

"Mothers are disinterested, mostly, in what their children are doing," she concludes. "They have other interests."

Child Care: The Real Crisis

If there's one other ground on which Margaret justifies the pursuit of her "other interest," it's the fact that she could call on her mother and husband to baby-sit. If her mom hadn't been available, she would never have run the school, Margaret insists.

Mothers and family members were indeed a built-in safety net for previous generations. It is hardly surprising to learn that our mothers' greatest reservation about women working today is the dearth of decent child care; every one of my peers is equally concerned. Only Betty Winston, of all people—Betty, whose experience of early day care was so scarring—maintains that the situation has improved, that parents have much greater options now. "There'll always be bad day care," she observes. "Part of parenting is picking and choosing."

And Rita, the only mother who seems never to have had to rely on any surrogate, is ironically the most open-minded about the effects of nonmaternal care. To be sure, it makes her sad that her grandchildren's young lives are so regulated so early; when she visits the center where her two- and four-year-old grandkids spend their days and sees all the high chairs lined up for lunch, it reminds her of what she sees when she visits the local nursing home. "It seems so institutional," says Rita, "and they've got so much of that ahead of them in their little lives." But she feels the quality of care her grandchildren receive couldn't be better. "It's not just baby-sitting," she marvels. "It's safe, it's educational, and we're friends with all the caregivers. We have yet to see, of course, any grown day-care children, but I haven't seen any evidence of harm to my grandchildren. My oldest granddaughter, who just 'graduated' from day care, is a very happy little girl."

Many caregivers—ideally members of an extended family—can have a positive effect on children, maintains Annette Barnes, whose parents, uncles, aunts, and relatives from three older generations helped raise her first two children when single motherhood forced her to work full time. "Single moms nowadays have it a lot harder, lacking the great support system I had in my family," Annette observes. Her role with her kids was "more like an older sister who could do fun things with them" than a mother whose primary job was to discipline.

But in light of the problems her second child manifested in adolescence and early adulthood, Annette is not entirely certain that grandparents constitute ideal child care. Her father, unlike her mother, never asked for her opinion on how to raise her kids. "He had very strong ideas on how children should be reared, and while it was very helpful for the oldest boy, I do not think he was a positive influence on my daughter. He thought boys were smarter, that boys could do more; he was much more attuned to my son. Michelle was treated like a nice little girl, a cute child—she was treated like I was. There was always a subtle put-down as far as girls were concerned in my family; I could see, growing up, that my grades were not as important as my brother's. I could see it with Michelle, too, but there wasn't a lot I could do about it. And I feel sure it had something to do with her unhappiness later on."

Annette holds out hope that Michelle may yet overcome the influence of her grandfather and the displacement she felt when Annette remarried and had two more children. For years mother and daughter have been distant—quite literally, as Michelle married an Italian and lives in Italy with her two children. Annette wishes they might be closer geographically but finds, when Michelle does write, that communication is much better now that she has two young kids of her own. "Motherhood is the bridge," says Annette. "I think she's beginning to understand why it wasn't always easy for me [first as a single mother and then as a military wife with two toddlers sapping her attention from the two adolescents] as it isn't for her [as an American married to an old-world-style husband, living in a patriarchal culture, consumed with caring for two preschoolers]."

In some ways, Annette regards her working years as a single parent negatively, in light of her father's detrimental influence on Michelle and the subsequent gulf that developed between Annette and this child. And yet Annette—a "professional volunteer" who tutors reading, teaches fitness to the elderly, assists in her youngest daughter's third-grade classroom, and works in a hospital gift shop—is a staunch supporter of working women. "I'd feel very badly if I had to give any of it up," she says of her workweek. "It gives me a lot of balance and good, close friends.

"If the country gets any day-care system really working so that women can have that choice [to work], knowing their children are safe," Annette concludes, "then I think working is an enormously positive influence. I see most young mothers, even if they're working, spending a lot of time with their kids; I think they do so much more with their children nowadays. Very definitely you can be a good mother and be working. Sometimes I think it might be better—particularly part time, with a terrific caretaker."

Marriage, Divorce, and the American Family

A third of the grandmothers I spoke to suffered through divorce firsthand; more than half saw their children go through family breakup and remarriage; two have grandchildren born out of wedlock, and three have daughters in their 30s who have never married. (Only Rita seems to have sailed through with nary a marital storm on the horizon.) Marriage has never been easy, it would appear. Only now, observes Cammie Carlton (who has married and divorced three times), it's easier to undo.

Rather discouragingly, even those grandmothers who champion women's rights seem to feel that women's emancipation has a lot to do with the current divorce rate. Lynne Harper, for instance, would seem an ardent feminist: She fumes that when her husband left his job at a friend's electroplating firm because "they couldn't afford him" she was considered the ideal replacement because it was expected that a woman would do just as good a job but would cost half as much. ("His income was too low," she recalls, "but mine didn't count.")

She was so angered and upset by the abuses documented by Betty Friedan that she couldn't finish reading her book. She loved being home but feels there are a lot of women who "ought not spend a lot of time with their kids" because they're terrible mothers, and there are women she knows who stayed home and whose children don't seem to be any more successful for it. She laments that half the population must be "sacrificed" to raise children; she feels her own talent and ability have never been fully tapped, although at the age of 55 she went back to school to be certified in cytotechnology so that she could work as a hospital technician—a job she enjoyed very much until eye problems forced her to quit.

But ask Lynne what's wrong with society and she will pinpoint the collapse of the family as the catalyst for rampant crime, loosened morals, and an absence of taboos. And yes, the emancipation of women probably has a lot to do with it because "now that they can earn an income, they're less willing to work things out. There's no stigma in divorce anymore."

For her own offspring, Lynne feels nothing but pride. "They're decent, moral people," she says. "They're not mean, they don't cheat, they don't lie, and they've never asked us for anything—they all put themselves through school and got themselves started." The fact that her oldest daughter, at 32, decided to have a baby on her own because marriage seemed out of the question doesn't clash with Lynne's sensibilities because her daughter "has sacrificed everything" to become a mother and because she's financially able to support herself and afford top-notch care for her child. "I still believe in, and hope for, a two-parent family," says Lynne, "but we support her decision and I'm very proud of her ability to survive." Lynne's middle daughter is now separated from her Japanese husband and has moved back to Seattle with her two children to try to support herself selling real estate, but she's having a rough time of it and has leaned on her parents for help. Lynne supports her decisions, too: "The children weren't making it in Japan," she observes. "They were too headstrong, too terribly misfit in that culture. I think they're better off here."

Interestingly, Lynne doesn't even view her grandchildren as emblematic of the societal breakdown that so concerns her. "They'll be the responsible ones," she explains. "But there won't be enough of them. It's the hordes of kids who aren't getting any parenting whatsoever that makes me fear for my poor little grandchildren. What are we going to do with *those* kids?"

Cammie Carlton, another early feminist ("I was probably the first one out of the gate," she notes), doesn't believe men, marriage, or the family have changed one bit for all the talk of revolution, liberation, and the "new man." "Just as many women are abused today, and women do the same amount of work," she says, although she admits she doesn't know any modern couples. The only good news: Marriages are no worse, nor are families any more fractured, than they've ever been. "Everybody's just more open about their unhappiness today," Cammie observes. "My aunt and uncle have been married almost 65 years, but not because they're particularly in love with each other; I believe they hate each other's guts. It's just that they've been together so long they wouldn't know any other way."

Most ironically, given Cammie's unhappiness in her three marriages over nearly 30 years, she is distressed that her daughter, Liz, at 29, is not married and seems to resist the idea (although when one of the boyfriends Liz rejected got married and had a baby, she cried, according to Cammie, for three days). "I just don't feel a daughter is settled—that my job is done—until she's married and has children," says Cammie. "I'm not saying it's right, but it's something innate to motherhood. All mothers feel this way."

Yes, Cammie will concede, her own divorces have probably hurt Liz. More than anything, Cammie blames Liz's father, who was good with child-support payments (until he remarried) but never took an interest in the kids and to this day doesn't know them; he sent Liz a basket of fruit for her twenty-ninth birthday. But her son, Cammie says, seemed to have weathered his mother's experience with men altogether differently. Like his mother, he "ran off and got married young" but is today, ten years later, still married and the father of a gifted son and twin daughters.

What Cammie makes of this disparity in outcomes (because while she is proud of both her children, she insists Liz is unhappy) is that she communicated two different, even antithetical, messages. Her son picked up on the fact that she grew up believing, as her mother did before her, that her happiness and identity depended on having a man in her life; her daughter, in contrast, picked up on her intense unhappiness with men and focused on the ample evidence that men couldn't be trusted. Which is why Cammie feels women's lib has changed nothing: The foundation begins at home.

"Feminism didn't give me any foundation, just banners and headlines," she recalls. "What daughters get they get from their mothers, who got it from their mothers. There's no overestimating the mother-daughter bond, and my mother just didn't know any better than to raise me to get married. I don't know what I've raised Liz to do. She seems very independent, like I always wanted to be, but she's not, really. Like I wasn't."

Not all my progressively minded interviewees sounded such a bleak note on marriage. Donna, who observes that her work as a radiologist made her marriage stronger, feels she enjoyed a thoroughly modern marriage *because of who she was*. She likes to tell the story of her engagement, when her fiance came to her parents' house and her mother explained to him that "Donna hasn't been trained as a regular wife." "I know that," Donna recalls her husband-to-be replying. "But if I could have Donna as my wife, I'd be willing to forgo all that."

Donna laughs and says, "I've been reminding him of that all his life.

"The germ of a good relationship is not tied up in homemaking, in being a good maid," she explains. "I married him for companionship, for his sense of humor. And I wanted a child. But most importantly, I married him for his character: That's everything in a man. Someone who won't lie or cheat, who will be upfront about everything. I needed cooperation too, and he was always willing to cooperate, especially where it concerned Jane. As for the housework, neither one of us enjoyed that, so we had help, but I can remember telling him once, 'Don't make me choose between you and the maid!'"

The "new" man, according to Donna, has been around a long time. It's just that one needed to be a "new" woman to find him.

Looking Backward

What would these women have done differently, if they could do it all again?

"Nothing," declares Margaret. "Everything," sighs Cammie. And in these two remarks, I perceive consensus among our mothers' (and grandmothers') peers, because what Margaret and Cammie are both saying is that the experience of marriage and children determined their sense of fulfillment. Happily married women with happily married children (Margaret, Donna, and Rita, certainly) have no regrets because their ambitions—to be married and raise children—were realized at little emotional cost. The widowed, divorced, remarried, or currently dissatisfied women (those who believe they failed their children, or themselves, in some way) look back both ruefully and fatalistically: They'd like to have done things differently, but they can't see how they might have done so.

Annette Barnes would have liked to have gone to college. Then she might not have married so young, might not have become a single mother so soon, might not have felt compelled to remarry, might not have married a military man, and might not have subjected her older daughter to all the attendant duress. She sees what a difference college has made in her younger daughter Karen's life: Karen has a wonderful job, says Annette, and by waiting to get married got a wonderful husband, whereas her older daughter, Michelle, didn't go to college, occasionally teaches English as a second language, and is now married to her third husband.

Lynne Harper wishes she had been more available to her middle daughter when her daughter needed her. Her first daughter was just two when her second was born, and a year and a half later Lynne was pregnant with her son. Because this second daughter was "independent from day one," and because Lynne was busy with the other two, she didn't get the attention or even the parental oversight she should have, Lynne feels. "When I look back on the things I allowed her to do, I just can't believe it," she says. "I mean, letting her walk to nursery school by herself at age three!" And then, when her middle daughter was in junior high school, financial circumstances drove Lynne back to work and blinded her to the kind of friends her middle child was making. That's when her troubles started, says Lynne; but she believes it was her unavailability during her daughter's early childhood that predisposed her to problems later on.

Betty Winston regrets that the father of her second four children wasn't the father of the first three, and that she didn't get out of the first marriage sooner. She says the older children are a little resentful of her youngest, a gifted child, in particular: "They wish they could all be the special one," she says. "And I wish I could have given them what I'm able to give now." Bertha, on the other hand, feels she may have given her daughters too *much*. "Every wish was granted, and they still expect that," she notes. "They never asked for anything that wasn't good, so I didn't see the point in denying them. But as I see it now, they have no sense of responsibility, no sense of limitation, no self-control."

Not all these women want to revisit the past to re-parent their children. Bertha regrets she did not return to a profession she might now be enjoying; Cammie and Barbara, at financial crossroads in their single lives, wish desperately they had a career to return to. "I'd like to have settled down to one job so I wouldn't be desperate at 53," opines Cammie. Says Barbara, "I wish I had gone to college and gotten a wonderful job. I've never been an assertive person, and now I don't know how to cope. I'm just scared."

Our Mothers, Our Daughters

There seems no limit to our curiosity concerning our own mothers. Their motivations, their passions, their marriages, their attitudes toward us, and their attitudes toward themselves constitute a mystery we never tire of trying to solve, certain that in so doing we will have the answers we so avidly seek. Now that we are mothers ourselves, whatever our relationship—distant or close, resentful or grateful, as parent and child or as equals and friends—we acknowledge that there *is* a bond, flexible but inviolable, constraining, perhaps, but infinitely supportive. The primal bond we spent our adolescence trying to ignore or deny has reasserted itself with a vengeance.

We can no longer "not care" what our mothers think, because it is our nature, as mothers, *to care.* To be a mother *in any generation* is to be "relational," to define ourselves according to the role we play in other people's lives. Such is the root of our frustration, because we cannot control those people, even when they are our own flesh and blood; we are defined, and judged, by who they are, and yet it is not our role to be them, to live through them, to deny them the right to be themselves irrespective of us. (Without this irresolvable conflict between mother and child, would the modern science of psychoanalysis even exist?)

The mother-daughter bond is so strong, some of my interviewees believe, that it precludes any societal influences or trends. That would imply that women are doomed, or graced, depending entirely on what kind of mother they had. Not "the times," not socioeconomic circumstances, not even singular twists of fate could be blamed, or credited, for how the daughters turned out. The degree to which the mother was a "whole" person would be the degree to which the daughter individuated enough to marry happily and raise children who in turn could stand on their own. The example a mother sets, more than the beliefs she espouses, would then dictate her daughter's fate.

Dependent women in unhappy or broken marriages *do* communicate to their daughters, not surprisingly, the desire to marry and reproduce without the model to do so successfully—one vicious cycle of the many my peers have identified in this book.

Yet I believe that is a gross and misleading generalization, because daughters escape the vicious legacies as often as they fail to adopt the positive ones. I do not care to suggest that the mother-daughter bond is trivial: If it were, my generation would surely have less difficulty in charting a new course for themselves, confident at least that they had the approval of previous generations. We might derive substantial comfort, however, in recognizing that the mother-daughter link can only go so far—can only predict or determine *to a point* our own experience. I say comfort not because I assume our mother's influence or experience to have been a negative one but because I am anticipating the day when we blame ourselves for having "failed" *our* daughters in some life-altering way or, just as inevitably, to the day when our daughters blame us for their shortcomings. If we choose instead to derive comfort from believing we are predestined by our mothers to act a certain way, then we can only deserve our self-recrimination, or the recrimination of our daughters, a generation hence.

Diane Ehrensaft has pointed out that mothers perceive their children as extensions of themselves. But whereas eventually they must distance themselves from their sons in recognition of sexual boundaries, there is no such incentive to construct boundaries between themselves and their daughters. Given the conflict that is corroding our self-esteem, gnawing at our conscience, and ultimately reflecting negatively on our children, I think it behooves us to construct such boundaries with our daughters as well as our sons, allowing them to live their lives as we would like to be allowed by our mothers to live ours: differently.

The advice more than one grandmother wanted to give her daughters was just that: Be whole, be your own person. Bertha

Stewart may not have succeeded, but she is trying not to let that fact impinge on her daughters any more than it already has. If we, as a generation of conflicted mothers, accomplish little else toward our daughters' happiness, let it be the resolution of our conflict, so that no matter what their choices, we might not engender in them the sense of inadequacy our mothers may have inadvertently engendered in us.

Changing Expectations for Our Daughters

Are we getting any happier? Studies linking women's emotional well-being to the multiplicity of their roles would indicate the current generation of jugglers is the happiest yet. For more than a decade, researchers have examined women's occupational resources, marital responsibilities, and parental obligations to determine their bearing on levels of self-esteem, depression, and pleasure, and they have found, repeatedly, that women who combine marriage with work and parenthood report higher levels of satisfaction with their lives than do single or childless women or unemployed married women with children.

A now-classic study of 238 women ages 35 to 55 published in 1985 revealed that of those never married, married, married with children, and divorced, life satisfaction was greatest among the employed married mothers, leading the researchers to conclude that "the more roles a woman occupied, the happier she tended to feel with each particular role."[1] Another survey of 816 dual-career couples, 40 percent of them with children, concluded that working mothers were happiest because their marriages tended to be more egalitarian—meaning husband and wife shared decision-making and responsibility for children and housework.[2] These results were echoed in Ethel Roskies's

1992 study of professional women (doctors, lawyers, engineers, and accountants). The psychological health—self-esteem, life satisfaction, and depression being the indices used—of married women with children was far greater than that of their unmarried and childless peers.[3]

The benefits of "juggling" (a term I consider misleading, but which I recognize to mean "being multiroled") far outweigh the day-to-day stresses of managing work and family, argues Faye Crosby, a recognized expert on the phenomenon and the author of *Juggling*. Not only do jugglers feel happier about themselves than do other women, she writes, but they feel better about their marriage, their home life, and their children. Perhaps most importantly, jugglers are happier because they perceive that their children benefit—by having a more involved father, more intimate acquaintance with the working world, more contact with other children and adults, a more egalitarian view of men and women, and more self-confidence and initiative.[4]

But Crosby and those who concur that having many roles expands women's opportunity for fulfillment also concur that the *quality* of the roles matters. "Woe to the woman who has a bad marriage and a miserable job," Crosby notes.[5]

A 1992 survey of 3,000 women supports this observation, showing that women who work but do not enjoy it or accord it any value tend to be far less satisfied because they tend to be playing the more traditional role in marriage—the less equal one, that is. Women who work outside the home but have old-fashioned marriages in which the husband makes all the financial decisions report "a less satisfying sex life," find it difficult to talk about sex with their husbands, and even kiss them less each day; argue more about money; and "feel less intimate since having children."[6] Marital satisfaction, researchers have long noted, is an important factor in women's psychological well-being, and the more equal a woman's marital relationship, the more satisfied she tends to describe herself as being.[7]

Yet interestingly, equality in marriage is *not* measured by money but by how women *perceive* their job. "The extent to which mothers asserted the importance of their own careers relative to their spouses' was the best predictor of equality levels," found those who studied the dual-career couples. Mothers achieved equality "primarily through a *psychological belief* in and assertion of their own deserving"[8] (italics mine).

Hence a woman who *feels* trapped in her job, not liberated from domesticity; depleted by her work commitment, not enriched; and guilty about her example as a mother, not proud, unquestionably influences her children negatively. Working mothers are fond of noting that while a happy mother might not guarantee a happy child, certainly an *unhappy* mother (in their case, a mother who communicates verbally or nonverbally that she does not enjoy being home all day with her offspring) ensures an unhappy child. Full-time mothers who feel obliged to defend their choice to be home might well point out that a mother who works and *resents every minute of it* is exerting just as negative an impact as the unfulfilled full-time mother.

Indeed, according to Anita Shreve, author of *Remaking Motherhood*, the *attitude* of the working mother may be "the single most important" factor in shaping the child's perceptions. "If a mother is oppressed in the home by her husband or by her economic situation, and in the workplace by the nature of her job or by her supervisors, the ideas that she will convey to her child about the value of working—*and the effects of that mother's employment on her child*—will be considerably different from the mother who is happy and comfortable in her home life, who is proud of her accomplishments in the workplace and who is pleased with the way she is combining the two," writes Shreve. *"It is not the working itself that has such a powerful effect on the child, but what the mother conveys to that child about her own satisfaction or dissatisfaction with her life as a working mother"*[9] (author's italics).

Only *meaningful* work, or work the mother enjoys, can set in motion the juggernaut of benefits so many experts attribute to the act of juggling: A woman who feels good about herself feels worthy enough to demand an equal marriage (which reinforces feelings of well-being), in which androgynous role models give children, arguably, double the range of adult options (both male and female) to choose from, which in turn enhances the possibility that those children will pursue that which is most likely to offer them fulfillment, which consequently assures them of a happier marriage and happier children and so on, generation after generation.

Daughters stand to gain the most from a positive working-mother role model, according to Shreve, particularly in terms of self-esteem, autonomy, and a feeling of mastery. "At-home mothers . . . may unconsciously allow their children to become overly dependent on them because these mothers see their primary role as 'mother' and may need to be needed," she observes (Bertha Stewart, of the previous chapter, admits as much), and such mothers produce in their daughters ambivalent attachment and frequently an inability to separate from their mothers.[10]

Certainly many, if not all, of the role models I've identified in this book feel the impact of their choice on their daughters is one of the strongest arguments for their work-family compromise. "I've thought very deeply about it," says Connie Lezenby (introduced in chapter one). "It's a generational thing: Daughters who are not allowed to be who they are, but only what society's rigid roles dictate, grow up to be mothers with a very deep fear of inadequacy, which they then pass on to their daughters, who consequently don't have the courage to break out of that role.

"I'm relieved to see my oldest daughter, at 14, is grappling as I am at 38 with this issue of who she is and who she wants to become," Connie continues. "She's firmly convinced she's not a feminist, but she has a vision for her life, and while she may or may not have children, she's determined that she have that choice. If she does have children, she says, she's going to stay home with them. And that doesn't make me mad or make me feel guilty: I'm grateful she can think for herself. I'm grateful I can hear what she has to say without having to have her be me. I understand my choices and why I made them, but for a long time I was too dependent on what other people thought and what they thought I should do. She'll be better equipped than I was, because she listens to herself; she trusts her own voice. And as a mother of a daughter, nothing could give me a greater sense of satisfaction than seeing that."

Sons, too, benefit from a healthy example of multiroled motherhood, though the benefits are harder to see and quantify because sons tend to emulate their fathers, who already enjoy autonomy and a sense of competence. Shreve points out the wider range of opportunity they will enjoy, unhampered by sexual stereotype; she believes that because the husbands of "happy jugglers" tend to be more involved, nurturing, physically affectionate fathers, the sons stand a greater chance of growing up to be emotionally uninhibited. My own role models have made the observation that their sons will be more sensitized to the needs of women and less likely to devalue the feminine contribution. But a point not often made is that sons of contented working mothers grow up to see their own work as a source of pleasure. "It's nice to think that Julian will see working not as a grind but something creative, something that can make other people happy," says Jan Neiman, the photographer from my introduction.

One might indeed argue that it is the sons, more than the daughters, whom we should want our example of working motherhood to influence long-term. If men, as Susan Faludi intimates, are perpetrators of the backlash and stonewallers to change, then it is our male offspring we should take care, as mothers, to affect positively. It is our duty to womankind to ensure that we don't raise yet another generation of oppressive men. (Faludi never once dares mention that the men she finds most abhorrent do not come from another galaxy but are raised by women, probably because it would be bad politics to "blame the victim.")

But let us not infer that we need to raise our sons one way, our daughters another. The course of action we must take as mothers is quite simple, really: We must trust our instincts, trust ourselves to do what is right *for us* and our families.

A straightforward enough mandate, surely. And yet most mothers, contemplating the stakes of child rearing, imagine motherhood to be a vocation they must study up on, lest they make a mistake and "fail." So, like Carolyn Marth, the mother of a three-year-old, herself the daughter of adoptive parents, they pore over all the child-rearing books, survey all the women at the park, grill the pediatricians, call up their friends, and try to make sense of a mishmash of advice from total strangers before throwing up their hands in frustration and heeding their gut instinct. Carolyn recalls being in torment over conflicting information on breast-feeding, discipline, sleep habits, and even how to play with her daughter, Eliza, until she realized she was relying too much on what other people were telling her and their assumptions about her child. "If I'd just listened to Eliza's cues and my instincts," she says today, "I'd have been *fine.*"

But it is by no means easy to heed those instincts. We are surrounded by naysayers and guilt-sowers, men and women with expectations we cannot possibly hope to meet and frustrated ambitions we cannot hope to fulfill. We are exposed daily to idealized images and false icons, political ideologies and cultural "trends" whose conflicting messages can paralyze those who would attempt to decode them. If we are to tune in to what our children, and our consciences, are quietly telling us, then we must tune out this static. We must listen closely to what our guilt over working may be saying, as it might well be telling us we are tipping the scales too much in favor of our jobs. We must candidly assess our strengths *and* weaknesses as parents so that we might accurately weigh the role surrogate care should play and choose for our children the arrangement that complements our strengths and covers our weaknesses. And we must similarly scrutinize ourselves in order to determine what we can contribute—and what we cannot, or would rather not, contribute—to our partnerships, the better to determine our role as a *team* of parents.

Above all, we must *just say no* to the carrot of perfection. Jack of all trades, master of none—that's us, *and we're proud of it,* because the alternative is to be jack of one trade and *still* master of none (in that perfection is never actually achieved, only pursued to the exclusion of more realistic—and more rewarding— goals). No one is a Perfect Mother. As even the full-time moms will concede, She's one of the Undead, a role model that must be destroyed before She sucks the lifeblood from all who would try to emulate Her. The overwhelmingly good news we should instead be focusing on is how many of us are *good enough,* precisely because the only thing we are perfect at is compromise. Compromise, denigrated as a tactic of the weak, is our strength. Compromise, a kind of damnation eschewed by feminist and antifeminist zealots, is our salvation. Because only through compromise will we achieve balance. And only with true balance will we know fulfillment.

Notes

Preface

1. Neil Howe and William Strauss, "The New Generation Gap," *The Atlantic Monthly,* Dec. 1992, pp. 67-89.

2. D. W. Winnicott, *Playing and Reality* (New York: Routledge, 1989), p. 10.

Introduction

1. U.S. Bureau of Labor Statistics, "Current Population Survey March 1992" (Washington, D.C.: unpublished data, U.S. Department of Labor).

2. Amy Dacyczyn, "The Two-Income Whiners," *New York Times,* 17 Feb. 1993, pp. A17, A19.

Chapter One

1. Sylvia Ann Hewlett, *A Lesser Life: The Myth of Women's Liberation in America* (New York: Warner Books, 1986), pp. 12-13.

2. Hewlett, pp. 49-50.

3. Hewlett, p. 334.

4. Sylvia Ann Hewlett, "The Feminization of the Work Force," *National Perspectives Quarterly,* Winter 1990, p. 13.

5. Hewlett, *A Lesser Life*, p. 185.

6. Susan Faludi, *Backlash: The Undeclared War Against American Women* (New York: Crown Books, 1991), p. 317.

7. Faludi, p. 316.

8. Hewlett, *A Lesser Life*, p. 24.

9. As quoted by Carol Pogash in "The Brains Behind 'Backlash,'" *Working Woman*, April 1992, p. 104.

10. Telephone interview with Ethel Roskies, 22 Jan. 1993.

11. As quoted in an interview with Susan Faludi, *Backlash*, p. 253.

12. Results of exit poll of 15,241 voters conducted by Voter Research & Surveys, as reported in *Newsweek*, Special Election Issue, Nov./Dec. 1992, p. 10.

13. Hewlett, *A Lesser Life*, p. 381.

14. *Ibid.*

15. Hewlett, p. 341.

16. Hewlett, "The Feminization of the Work Force," pp. 13-15.

17. Faludi, p. 456.

18. As quoted by Susan Faludi, *Backlash*, p. 254.

19. Charles Sykes, *A Nation of Victims: The Decay of the American Character* (New York: St. Martin's Press, 1992).

20. Nadine Joseph, "Mommy Myths," *Redbook*, Oct. 1992, pp. 130-133, 142.

21. Sylvia Ann Hewlett, *When the Bough Breaks: The Cost of Neglecting Our Children* (New York: Basic Books, 1991).

22. Keith Bryant and Cathleen Zick, "Are We Investing Less in the Next Generation?: Historical Trends in Time Spent Caring for Children," a paper presented at the 1993 American Statistical Association Winter Conference, Fort Lauderdale, FL, 3-5 Jan. 1992.

23. Faludi, p. xxiii.

24. Faludi, p. 57.

Chapter Two

1. Shakti Gawain, *Creative Visualization* (New York: Bantam Books, 1982), pp. 50-51.

2. Gloria Steinem, *Revolution from Within* (Boston: Little, Brown and Co., 1992), p. 322.

3. Steinem, pp. 124-125.

4. Gawain, p. 51.

5. Alex McNeil, *Total Television: A Comprehensive Guide to Programming from 1948 to the Present,* Third Ed. (New York: Penguin Books, 1991), p. 296.

6. McNeil, p. 86.

7. Amy Stevens, "Personal-Injury Lawsuits by Students Are Endangering University Budgets," *Wall Street Journal,* 18 Nov. 1992, pp. B1, B13.

8. Wade Lambert and Junda Woo, "Suit Over AIDS Victim's Death Allowed," *Wall Street Journal,* 18 Nov. 1992, p. B13.

9. Cathy Young, "Victimhood's Strange Bedfellows," *Wall Street Journal,* 3 Sept. 1992, p. A10.

10. Leslie Spencer, "The Tort Tax," *Forbes,* 17 Feb. 1992, p. 41.

11. Spencer, p. 40.

Chapter Three

1. As quoted by Anne Turgesen, "Growing Role for Mothers: Nurturing Each Other," *Philadelphia Inquirer,* 25 Nov. 1992, pp. D1, D3.

2. *Ibid.*

3. Jay Belsky, "Infant Day Care: A Continuing Cause for Concern," a paper presented at the International Conference on Infant Studies, Washington, D.C., April 1986.

4. Jay Belsky, "Developmental Risks Associated with Infant Day Care: Attachment Insecurity, Noncompliance, and Aggression?" *Psychosocial Issues in Day Care,* Ed. Shahla S. Chehrazi (Washington, D.C.: American Psychiatric Press, Inc., 1990), pp. 37-62.

5. Michael Lamb, Kathleen Sternberg, and Margarita Prodromidis, "Nonmaternal Care and the Security of Infant-Mother Attachment: A Reanalysis of the Data," *Infant Behavior and Development* 15, 1992, p. 80.

6. As quoted by Terry Minsky, "Advice and Comfort for the Working Mother," *Esquire,* June 1984, p. 157.

7. As quoted by Diane Eyer, "Infant Bonding: A Bogus Notion," *Wall Street Journal,* 24 Nov. 1992, p. A14.

8. Penelope Leach, "Are We Shortchanging Our Kids?" *Parenting,* April 1991, pp. 86-93.

9. Leach, p. 90.

10. Brie Quinby, "You Can Go Home Again," *Child,* Sept. 1991, p. 85.

11. David Elkind, *The Hurried Child: Growing Up Too Fast Too Soon* (Reading, MA: Addison-Wesley Publishing Co., 1981), pp. 120-121.

12. Elkind, pp. 124-127.

13. Elkind, pp. 36-38.

14. Elkind, p. 129.

15. Elkind, pp. 37-38.

Chapter Four

1. Newsbrief, "Bag the Guilt," *Wall Street Journal,* 13 Oct. 1992, p. A1.

2. Keith Bryant and Cathleen Zick, "Are We Investing Less in the Next Generation?: Historical Trends in Time Spent Caring for Children," a paper presented at the 1993 American Statistical Association Winter Conference, Fort Lauderdale, FL, 3-5 Jan. 1992.

3. Bryant and Zick, p. 18.

4. *Ibid.*

5. Barbara Berg, *The Crisis of the Working Mother: Resolving the Conflict Between Family and Work* (New York: Summit Books, 1986), p. 41.

6. Berg, p. 37.

7. Berg, p. 41

8. Berg, pp. 59-60.

9. Berg, p. 62.

10. Colette Dowling, *Perfect Women: Hidden Fears of Inadequacy and the Drive to Perform* (New York: Summit Books, 1988), pp. 21-38.

11. Dowling, p. 38.

12. Dowling, p. 43.

13. Dowling, p. 44.

14. Dowling, p. 62.

15. Dowling, p. 240.

16. Deborah Fallows, *A Mother's Work* (New York: Houghton Mifflin, 1985), pp. 24-42.

17. As quoted by Susan Faludi, *Backlash*, p. 247.

18. Faludi, pp. 296-300.

19. Judith Posner, *The Feminine Mistake: Women, Work, and Identity* (New York: Warner Books, Inc., 1992).

20. Posner, p. 50.

21. Posner, p. 48.

22. Carol Tavris, *The Mismeasure of Woman* (New York: Simon and Schuster, 1992).

23. As quoted by Meredith Wadman, "Often Belittled by Their Male Colleagues, Women Doctors Also Find Pay Disparity," *Wall Street Journal*, 25 Nov. 1992, pp. B1, B6.

24. Roger Rosenblatt, "Season of Crowds," MacNeil/Lehrer NewsHour, 28 Nov. 1989, as quoted by Felice Schwartz, *Breaking With Tradition: Women and Work, The New Facts of Life* (New York: Warner Books, Inc., 1992), pp. 273-274.

Chapter Five

1. Hayes, Palmer, and Zaslow, *Who Cares for America's Children?* (Washington, D.C.: National Academy Press, 1990), pp. 147-158. It should be noted that for children under five, the proportions shift somewhat: Only 18 percent are in group or center care; 32 percent in family day-care homes; 11 percent in their own homes, cared for by nonrelatives; and the remaining 39 percent in their own homes, cared for by a parent or relative.

2. Hayes et al., p. 148

3. Hayes et al., p. 157.

4. Jerry Adler, "The Good Father," *Redbook,* June 1993, pp. 80-82.

5. Adler, p. 82.

6. As reported by Diane Crispel in "People Patterns," *Wall Street Journal,* 12 May 1993, p. B1.

7. Fredelle Maynard, *The Child Care Crisis: The Real Costs of Day Care for You—and Your Child* (Ontario: Viking/Penguin Books Canada Ltd., 1985), p. xv.

8. Maynard, p. 25.

9. Maynard, p. 115.

10. Maynard, pp. 118-119.

11. Maynard, p. 136.

12. Maynard, pp. 166-167.

13. Maynard, p. 249.

14. Maynard, p. 191.

15. Maynard, pp. 197-202.

16. Sylvia Ann Hewlett, *When the Bough Breaks,* pp. 242-258.

17. Hewlett, pp. 280-281.

18. Telephone interview with Felice Schwartz, 3 March 1993.

19. As quoted by Sylvia Ann Hewlett in "The Feminization of the Work Force," *New Perspectives Quarterly,* Winter 1990, p. 14.

20. Schwartz interview, 3 March 1993.

21. Schwartz, *Breaking With Tradition: Women and Work, The New Facts of Life* (New York: Warner Books, Inc., 1992), pp. 127-148.

22. Schwartz, pp. 235-257.

23. Schwartz interview, March 3, 1993.

24. As quoted by Marilyn Berline Snell in "Careerus Interruptus," an interview with Felice Schwartz, *New Perspectives Quarterly,* Winter 1990, p. 16.

25. Schwartz, *Breaking With Tradition,* p. 272.

26. As reported by Barbara Presley Noble in "Women Pay More for Success," *New York Times,* 4 July 1993, p. F25.

27. *Ibid.*

28. Schwartz, p. 282

29. Schwartz, pp. 304-307.

30. Schwartz interview, 3 March 1993.

31. Hayes et al., *Who Cares for America's Children?,* p. 195.

Chapter Seven

1. Barbara DaFoe Whitehead, "Dan Quayle Was Right," *The Atlantic Monthly,* April 1993, p. 50.

2. The Editors, "745 Boylston Street," *The Atlantic Monthly*, April 1993, p. 4.

3. Whitehead, p. 50.

4. Whitehead, p. 60.

5. Gerald Seib, "Americans Feel Families and Values Are Eroding But They Disagree Over the Causes and Solutions," *Wall Street Journal*, 11 June 1993, p. A12.

6. As reported by Sue Shellenbarger, "Work and Family: Odds and Ends," *Wall Street Journal*, 11 June 1993, p. B1.

7. Arlie Hochschild, *The Second Shift* (New York: Viking Penguin, Inc., 1989), p. 211.

8. Hochschild, p. 215.

9. Hochschild, p. 213.

10. Hochschild, p. 254.

11. U.S. Department of Labor, Report 841, "Employment in Perspective: Women in the Labor Force" (Washington, D.C.: Bureau of Labor Statistics, Fourth Quarter, 1992), p. 1.

12. Hochschild, pp. 200-201.

13. As quoted by Anita Shreve, *Remaking Motherhood: How Working Mothers Are Shaping Our Children's Future* (New York: Viking Penguin, Inc. 1987), p. 174.

14. As quoted by Debra Kent, "Sex and Housework," *Working Mother*, Sept. 1992, p. 20.

15. Joseph Pleck, "Are 'Family-Supportive' Employer Policies Relevant to Men?," a paper prepared for Jane Hood (Ed.), *Work, Family, and Masculinities* (Newbury Park, CA: Sage Publications, fall 1993), p. 4. Pleck notes that the 34 percent figure is derived from data collected in 1985.

16. Letty Cottin Pogrebin, *Family Politics* (New York: McGraw-Hill Book Co., 1983), pp. 144-145.

17. Shreve, p. 175.

18. Shreve, pp. 188-189.

19. Hochschild, pp. 195-199, 258-259.

20. Telephone interview with Joseph Pleck, 18 June 1993.

21. Pogrebin, p. 125.

22. Shirley Sloan Fader, "Is One-Paycheck Thinking Spoiling Your Two-Paycheck Life?" *Working Mother,* Nov. 1992, p. 74.

23. Fader, pp. 74-76.

24. Fader, pp. 76-77.

25. Fader, p. 77

26. Diane Ehrensaft, *Parenting Together* (New York: The Free Press, 1987), pp. 57-75.

27. Ehrensaft, p. 94.

28. Ehrensaft, p. 129.

29. As quoted by Ehrensaft, p. 95.

30. Shreve, p. 189.

31. Shreve, p. 177.

32. Harriet Webster, "Part-Time Togetherness," *American Health,* Oct. 1991, p. 36.

Epilogue

1. Grace Baruch and Rosalind Barnett, "Role Quality and Psychological Well-Being," as published in Faye Crosby (Ed.), *Spouse, Parent, Worker* (New Haven: Yale University Press, 1987), p. 68.

2. Janice Steil and Beth Turetsky, "Marital Influence Levels and Symptomatology," *Spouse, Parent, Worker,* pp. 74-88.

3. Ethel Roskies and Sylvie Carrier, "Marriage and Children for Professional Women: Asset or Liability?," a paper presented at the APA/NIOSH Conference "Stress in the 90's," Washington, 19-22 Nov. 1992.

4. Faye Crosby, "I'm OK, They're OK," *Working Mother,* March 1992, pp. 43-47.

5. Crosby, p. 45.

6. Carin Rubenstein, "The Joys of a 50/50 Marriage," *Working Mother,* April 1992, pp. 59-63.

7. Steil and Turetsky, p. 87.

8. *Ibid.*

9. Shreve, *Remaking Motherhood,* pp. 64-65.

10. Shreve, p. 82.

Bibliography

"745 Boylston Street." Editorial. *The Atlantic Monthly,* April 1993, p. 4.

Adler, Jerry. "The Good Father." *Redbook,* June 1993, pp. 79-83, 131.

"Bag the Guilt." Newsbrief. *Wall Street Journal,* 13 Oct. 1992, p. A1.

Belsky, Jay. "Infant Day Care: A Continuing Cause for Concern." Proc. of an International Conference on Infant Studies. Washington, D.C.: April 1986.

——————. "Developmental Risks Associated with Infant Day Care: Attachment Insecurity, Noncompliance, and Aggression?" In *Psychosocial Issues in Day Care.* Ed. Shahla S. Chehrazi. Washington, D.C.: American Psychiatric Press, Inc., 1990, pp. 37- 62.

Berg, Barbara. *Crisis of the Working Mother: Resolving the Conflict Between Family and Work.* New York: Summit Books, 1986.

Bryant, Keith, and Cathleen Zick. "Are We Investing Less in the Next Generation?: Historical Trends in Time Spent Caring for Children." Proc. of a Conference of the American Statistical Association. Fort Lauderdale, FL, 3-5 Jan. 1992.

Crispel, Diane. "People Patterns." *Wall Street Journal,* 12 May 1993, p. B1.

Crosby, Faye (Ed.). *Spouse, Parent, Worker: On Gender and Multiple Roles.* New Haven: Yale University Press, 1987.

——————. "I'm OK, They're OK." *Working Mother,* March 1992, pp. 43-47.

Dacyczyn, Amy. "The Two-Income Whiners." *New York Times,* 17 Feb 1993, pp. A17, A19.

Dowling, Colette. *Perfect Women: Hidden Fears of Inadequacy and the Drive to Perform.* New York: Summit Books, 1988.

Ehrensaft, Diane. *Parenting Together: Men and Women Sharing the Care of Their Children.* New York: The Free Press, 1987.

Elkind, David. *The Hurried Child: Growing Up Too Fast Too Soon.* New York: Addison-Wesley, 1991.

Eyer, Diane. "Infant Bonding: A Bogus Notion." *Wall Street Journal,* 24 Nov. 1992, p. A14.

Fader, Shirley Sloan. "Is One-Paycheck Thinking Spoiling Your Two-Paycheck Life?" *Working Mother,* Nov. 1992, pp. 73-77.

Fallows, Deborah. *A Mother's Work.* New York: Houghton Mifflin, 1985.

Faludi, Susan. *Backlash: The Undeclared War Against American Women.* New York: Crown Books, 1991.

Gawain, Shakti. *Creative Visualization.* New York: Bantam Books, 1982.

Hayes, Cheryl, John Palmer, Martha Zaslow, eds. *Who Cares for America's Children?* Washington, D.C.: National Academy Press, 1990.

Hewlett, Sylvia Ann. *A Lesser Life: The Myth of Women's Liberation in America.* New York: Warner Books, 1986.

——————. "The Feminization of the Work Force." *New Perspectives Quarterly,* Winter 1990, pp. 13-15.

——————. *When the Bough Breaks: The Cost of Neglecting Our Children.* New York: Basic Books, 1991.

Hochschild, Arlie. *The Second Shift.* New York: Viking Penguin, 1989.

Howe, Neil, and William Strauss. "The New Generation Gap." *The Atlantic Monthly,* Dec. 1992, pp. 67-89.

Joseph, Nadine. "Mommy Myths." *Redbook,* Oct. 1992, pp. 130-133, 142.

Kent, Debra. "Sex and Housework." *Working Mother,* Sept. 1992, pp. 18-24.

Lamb, Michael, Kathleen Sternberg, and Margarita Prodromidis. "Nonmaternal Care and the Security of Infant-Mother Attachment: A Reanalysis of the Data." *Infant Behavior and Development* 15, 1992, pp. 71-83.

Leach, Penelope. "Are We Shortchanging Our Kids?" *Parenting,* April 1991, pp. 86-93.

Maynard, Fredelle. *The Child Care Crisis: The Real Costs of Day Care for You—and Your Child.* Ontario: Viking/Penguin Books Canada Ltd., 1985.

McNeil, Alex. *Total Television,* Third Ed. New York: Penguin Books, 1991.

Minsky, Terry. "Advice and Comfort for the Working Mother." *Esquire,* June 1984, p. 157.

Noble, Barbara Presley. "Women Pay More for Success." *New York Times,* 4 July 1993, p. 25.

Pleck, Joseph. "Are 'Family-Supportive' Employer Policies Relevant to Men?" A paper prepared for Jane Hood (Ed.), *Work, Family, and Masculinities.* Newbury Park, CA: Sage Publications, 1993.

—————. Telephone interview. 18 June 1993.

Pogash, Carol. "The Brains Behind 'Backlash.'" *Working Woman,* April 1992, pp. 64-67, 104.

Pogrebin, Letty Cottin. *Family Politics.* New York: McGraw Hill, 1983.

Posner, Judith. *The Feminine Mistake: Women, Work, and Identity.* New York: Warner Books, 1992.

Quinby, Brie. "You Can Go Home Again." *Child,* Sept. 1991, pp. 84-85, 104-107.

Rosenblatt, Roger. "Season of Crowds." *MacNeil/Lehrer NewsHour,* 28 Nov. 1989. In *Breaking With Tradition: Women and Work, The New Facts of Life.* Felice Schwartz. New York: Warner Books, 1992.

Roskies, Ethel. Telephone interview. 22 Jan. 1993.

—————. "Marriage and Children for Professional Women: Asset or Liability?" Proc. of the "Stress in the 90's" conference of the APA/NIOSH. Washington, D.C., 19-22 Nov. 1992.

Rubenstein, Carin. "The Joys of a 50/50 Marriage." *Working Mother*, April 1992, pp. 59-63.

Schwartz, Felice. Telephone interview. 3 March 1993.

—————. "Careerus Interruptus." An interview with *New Perspectives Quarterly*, Winter 1990, pp. 16-19.

—————. *Breaking With Tradition: Women and Work, The New Facts of Life*. New York: Warner Books, 1992.

Seib, Gerald. "Americans Feel Families and Values Are Eroding But They Disagree Over the Causes and Solutions." *Wall Street Journal*, 11 June 1993, p. A12.

Shellenbarger, Sue. "Work and Family: Odds & Ends." *Wall Street Journal*, 11 June 1993, p. B1.

Shreve, Anita. *Remaking Motherhood: How Working Mothers Are Shaping Our Children's Future*. New York: Viking Penguin, 1987.

Spencer, Leslie. "The Tort Tax." *Forbes*, 17 Feb. 1992, pp. 40-42.

Steincm, Gloria. *Revolution from Within: A Book of Self-Esteem*. Boston: Little, Brown and Co., 1992.

Stevens, Amy. "Personal-Injury Lawsuits by Students Are Endangering University Budgets." *Wall Street Journal*, 18 Nov. 1992, pp. B1, B13.

Sykes, Charles. *A Nation of Victims: The Decay of the American Character*. New York: St. Martin's Press, 1992.

Tavris, Carol. *The Mismeasure of Woman*. New York: Simon and Schuster, 1992.

Turgesen, Anne. "Growing Role for Mothers: Nurturing Each Other." *Philadelphia Inquirer*, 25 Nov. 1992, p. D1, D3.

U.S. Bureau of the Census. "Labor Force Participation Rates for Wives, Husbands, Present, by Age of Own Youngest Child: 1975 to 1991." No. 621, *Statistical Abstract of the United States 1992*, 112th Ed. Lanham, MD: Bernan Press, 1992.

Voter Research & Surveys. Exit poll results. *Newsweek,* Special Election Issue, Nov./Dec. 1992, p. 10.

Wadman, Meredith. "Often Belittled by Their Male Colleagues, Women Doctors Also Find Pay Disparity." *Wall Street Journal,* 25 Nov. 1992, pp. B1, B6.

Whitehead, Barbara DaFoe. "Dan Quayle Was Right." *The Atlantic Monthly,* April 1993, pp. 47-84.

Winnicott, D. W. *Playing and Reality.* New York: Routledge, 1989.

Young, Cathy. "Victimhood's Strange Bedfellows." *Wall Street Journal,* 3 Sept. 1992, p. A10.

Index

Note: Names followed by asterisks indicate pseudonyms.